MW01379937

What's Really Happening

THE BRW (BUSINESS·REVIEW·WEEKLY) LIBRARY

What's Really Happening

AUSTRALIA'S BUSINESS WORLD

Robert Gottliebsen

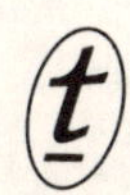

THE TEXT PUBLISHING COMPANY
MELBOURNE AUSTRALIA

The Text Publishing Company Pty Ltd
220 Clarendon Street
East Melbourne Victoria 3002
Australia

Copyright © BRW Publications, 1992

All rights reserved. Without limiting the rights under copyright above, no part of this publication shall be reproduced, stored in or introduced into a retrieval system, or transmitted in any form or by any means (electronic, mechanical, photocopying, recording or otherwise), without the prior written permission of both the copyright owner and the publisher of this book.

First published 1992

Typeset by Guntar Graphics Pty Ltd

Printed by Australian Print Group, Maryborough

National Library of Australia
Cataloguing-in-Publication data:
Gottliebsen, Robert.
What's really happening: Australia's business world.

ISBN 1 86372 020 0.

[1]. Business—Australia. 2. Australia—Economic conditions—1990- . I. Title: Business review weekly. (Series: Business review weekly library).

330.994

Contents

What's Really Happening is based on articles I wrote in *BRW* between June 1991 and September 1992. It would not have been possible but for the work of my personal assistant Colleen Cowley.

Preface

I really have one of the best jobs in the world. Few people have the opportunity to write an opening commentary in their country's most widely-read business publication; a similar one in the only Asian publication devoted to Australia and New Zealand; appear on television each night across the nation and on radio in three states on most mornings. But with those commitments, of course, comes great responsibility.

When in 1980 I brought together the team that started *Business Review Weekly* magazine, we were very much the underdogs. I had started the Chanticleer column in the *Financial Review* some six years earlier and, during the 1970s, won a Walkley and Perkin award for journalism. But the launch of *BRW* was a much bigger task, because to succeed it had to change the business reading habits of the nation and beat the Kerry Packer-owned rival, which had the benefit of being launched six months earlier. We had two advantages: the powerful Fairfax company and its management of 1980 was right behind us and the people who joined at the start, and who were to come later, were among the most talented people ever assembled to develop a new publication.

When *BRW* started we all realised we had to find a much wider audience than that covered by existing business publications. We included a special accountancy section and from day one every *BRW* has included what we now call our 'Up and Comers' segment. When we first started writing about small and medium business, people said we would never be able to find enough businesses to keep it up. We have never been short of enterprises to write about, although many didn't make it through the recession. I believe Australia's future lies with the development of small and medium business and I have been a strong critic of our ignorant politicians, arrogant public servants and foolish bankers who all too often think that Australia starts and ends with the likes of BHP. My father was a basket maker and in the good times, when the factory could not cope, we assembled the cane hoop kits on the dining room table. We are going to see a significant change in small and medium business in the decade ahead and if I write another book in ten years' time, the last sentence in this one will be the beginning of the next.

The end result is that with *BRW* chief executive, Stuart Simson (an original), in 1992 I head a business publication group that, according to Morgan research, reaches about half a million people through *BRW* magazine, *Personal Investment*, *Australian Property News* and *BRW International*.

Every *BRW* since that first issue in April 1981 has started with my 'Comment', so I get the opportunity to help a large number of business and investment people and express views on a wide number of topics. I also get the opportunity to choose subjects I want to write about at length and this book is based on recent articles and 'Comment's. As *BRW* editorial director, I join with *BRW* editor David Uren in the planning of the major articles in the magazine.

All this involves talking to a wide range of people from chief executives of large companies to small business men and women. I am on an aircraft most weeks and ideas come from many places, both in Australia and overseas.

As chairman of the BRW board I am involved in the business strategies of BRW Publications which has remained part of the John Fairfax group. Thanks to our readers and advertisers, we have enjoyed great success.

I always believe that journalists should be able to communicate ideas in both print and electronic media and my radio and television appearances were of great assistance in developing *BRW* magazine. As so often happens in business, such exercises often taken on a life of their own and become important activities in their own right. The *BRW* report now appears on radio stations 3AW, 2GB and 4BH and has been part of their breakfast programs for more than a decade.

On television I did not believe bald men had any long-term future, so when the ABC asked me to present business on their evening news as part of a new format called The National, I didn't think it would last long. But in the end it went for four years even though it was very different from the traditional ABC presentations. To my amazement my television career didn't end with the ABC and I have survived the changes at Channel Ten to present a business segment in the Late News with one of Australia's great news presenters Anne Fulwood. That Ten Network program has become one of the most successful news presentations in the country. And, of course, in my spare time I like to meet *BRW* readers, viewers and listeners as I make the odd speech.

I believe we must educate our young people and it is a privilege to be vice chairman of my old school, Penleigh and Essendon Grammar, and I was delighted one of its student's topped Victoria in 1991. I am also chairman of the Board of Advice of Monash University's David Syme Faculty of Business. Monash University's Vice Chancellor, Professor Mal Logan, has recognised the work at Syme and is centralising the University's business and economics program, which will emerge as a powerful force in Australian business education.

None of this would be possible without Barbara, the most wonderful wife of twenty-five years.

CHAPTER 1

A Vision for the Future

THE BLUEPRINT

EVERYWHERE I go around Australia the most common question asked by business people is: is the recovery under way and how far will it go? The simple answer is yes in most areas, apart from employment. Barring an unexpected world catastrophe, we have well and truly reached the bottom. Companies such as Burns Philp and Nine Network have shown in their results that small rises in turnover convert to big lifts in profits and this will be repeated by many of the companies that have tackled their costs and moved towards being internationally competitive.

But if recovery is substantial, it will be followed almost certainly by another enforced downturn because our overseas debt level does not allow us the luxury of rapid growth in consumer demand satisfied by imports. Clearly, something more fundamental is required for us to return to long-term prosperity; on this front there is much to be excited about in Australia. But with each potentially exciting development comes a concern that needs to be overcome. I want to set out some of the developments I find exciting and the concerns that go with them.

Excitement

For the first time in our history we are throwing off our 'island' mentality. Enterprises are required to work to international standards or they are being encouraged to either shut down or phase out.

Technological advances enable Australians to communicate with, and be part of, world business developments in a way not possible a decade ago. So, Australian architects and engineers can design for Asia and other regions. People based in Australia are now heading significant overseas operations.

Here at *BRW*, we edit *BRW International*, transmit the data by telephone and then print in Hong Kong a monthly business magazine about Australia for Asians and other overseas readers. This would not have been economic five years ago. The opportunities are boundless and it is possible for businesses to enjoy the advantages of being located in Australia without being bound to operate within our shores.

Concern

After two centuries of isolation, Australians may not be up to dealing with the change. We see the problems being faced by eastern Germany and the former Soviet Union after a much shorter period of isolation. Although our business system has been capitalist-based, our managers and union leaders have engaged in fantasies that were only possible in a remote location. Our educators do not understand that they must train people to compete with the rest of the world.

Excitement

We have inflation down to a level we never thought possible; as a result, when we make a decision, we do not have to keep adjusting it for changes in the value of money. At the same time, the value of our cash savings is protected and the public purse is not lined through the taxation of inflationary gains. We are at last tackling high-cost government business enterprises. Telecommunications charges will be slashed and, with the new Compass and the Australian Airlines/Qantas merger, there is a good chance of achieving much lower air-transport charges.

Concern

Syntec research shows that private-sector inflation dropped to 2.4% in the year to 31 March 1992 but public-sector prices rose by an annual rate of 9.5%. Significant areas of public administration seem to have no interest in lowering charges to world levels and even the former Liberal Premier of NSW, Nick Greiner, lifted prices after the Premiers' Conference in May 1992, proving that the disease is on both sides of politics.

The waterfront is a national disgrace and Canberra, which is a giant middle-management bureaucracy, has remained relatively untouched by the massive cost-pruning in the private sector. If governments can't provide low-cost, world-class service, companies will have no choice but to close down their Australian operations and go overseas. New investment will be greatly curtailed.

Excitement

By the year 2000 we will have a Swiss-style large-company structure. Most of our top fifty enterprises will be bigger overseas than they are in Australia (groups such as BHP, AMP, National Australia Bank,

Brambles, TNT, Mayne Nickless, CSR, Boral, Amcor, Pacific Dunlop, News Corp). This will give Australians an opportunity, undreamed of ten years ago, to operate on the world stage.

Concern

Government tax policy will move to curb overseas expansion, resulting in our large companies cutting the cord with Australia. Already, dividend imputation, which was a great innovation by the Government, has the side-effect of working in this direction.

Excitement

There is great potential in pursuing things we are good at. Our advantages include abundant resources, the ability to grow and process food, more arable land per person than any other country, a workforce with basic skills and innovative talents, a high-quality government research and development base, and proximity to the Asia-Pacific region.

For the past ten years we have banned most new resource projects on environmental or Aboriginal cultural grounds, leaving enormous potential for us to create wealth and employment in the 1990s if a more flexible approach is taken.

Our agricultural areas have scope to develop once we understand that Asians and possibly Europeans look to us as an important source of clean processed food. Once we start thinking along these lines, aiming at the export markets, the potential is almost unlimited.

There is great scope also for expansion in tourism and in service sectors such as medicine, education, architecture, design and engineering. We are now training our young people to even higher levels of skill.

At the same time—leaving aside the present low level of economic activity—there has not been such a favourable business environment for decades. The fall in property prices has lowered rents and it is possible to lock in a fixed rental at low levels until the turn of the century. This provides a wonderful base for business in the non-property area.

Interest rates have come down a long way, even though they are still higher than smaller and medium businesses would like, while technology is enabling the same tasks to be done at a fraction of the previous cost. Wages are stable and the workforce is committed to low inflation. We are seeing work-practice changes we could only have dreamed of five years ago, particularly now that more enterprises are negotiating deals with their workforces. Accordingly, the value of good businesses is rising sharply.

Concern

Many good businesses were lost in the recession—businesses we really needed to create wealth. They may never be replaced. And some efficient businesses are being wiped out because of unfair practices in other countries or high government charges in Australia. The property slump may have delivered low rents but it has destroyed a large amount of our capital, including good basic businesses that invested in property. Banks have little expertise in judging small and medium-sized privately-owned businesses and there are not enough capital sources to develop these businesses beyond a limited size. And we have not found ways to reward our teachers. The consequence is that the skill base available to pass on to the next generation and to export has been reduced.

Excitement

The profit potential being opened up for Australian companies in this business climate is huge. Businesses that can cope with present levels of economic activity and have adjusted their costs will make a fortune on even a minor upturn in the economy. This has been recognised by the sharemarket. As the decade proceeds, our profit- and wealth-creating powerhouse, including our ability to export, will lift our employment capacity beyond anything we have seen for a long time.

Concern

The community, including the daily press and electronic media, has little understanding of the link between wealth and employment, so the country will continue with policies that, in their naivety, almost make it appear that the community wants high unemployment. People still do not link the banning of billions of dollars worth of resource projects by governments with the fact that their children and grandchildren can't get jobs.

We need to recognise that tens of thousands of people who have missed out on jobs have been sacrificed to appease environmental extremists, anti-uranium protesters, Aboriginal activists and other interests. Sometimes new developments have been blocked for good reasons. But each time a project is denied permission to proceed, another opportunity is missed to put people to work.

Similarly, employers cannot afford to employ people to work outside 'normal' hours when they must pay them up to triple time. Setting the starting wage for young people at high levels has further restricted the number of jobs available. No tax deduction is available for home help, which means that such work is either paid for in cash or is simply not done.

These work rules directly affect people with lower skills but they also greatly restrict investment that would also employ more highly-skilled people. The Federal Government may have realised Australia's enormous tourist potential but investment capital is going to Asia because of our labour add-ons.

Excitement

The Labor Government rather than the conservatives began the changes that opened up the possibility of a world-class Australia prepared to tackle the steady decline in its standards of living. Better still, despite the problems, Paul Keating has continued to drive for international competitiveness.

Concern

Because in the 1980s the community did not understand the repercussions of the changes Labor was bringing about, great pressure is building up to go back to the past, as indicated by the result of the Wills by-election. Such pressure groups do not realise that, rightly or wrongly, we have gone too far to turn round. Worse still, we have borrowed to the hilt and can no longer afford the luxurious work practices and stunts that characterised the past thirty years. Nevertheless, no Australian government will be immune from such pressure.

Excitement

Australia has a stable government, with both political parties in agreement on the basic direction in which we should head. Few countries in Asia can offer businesses this advantage.

Concern

The Labor Government cannot finish off what it started, particularly in areas such as the waterfront, the transport systems and overall work-practice reform. The Liberals are likely to deliver on these fronts but they have an array of unpopular policies that may cost them the election and the chance to finish off what Labor started.

I think we will grasp the opportunities and overcome the concerns. There is no country on earth that is richer in natural advantages. We only have to get it three-quarters right to deliver a prosperous, growing economy. But if Australia can't throw off the shackles of the past, the alternative is chilling: there is no other way to stabilise our debt.

THROWING OFF THE SHACKLES

ALTHOUGH Australia has had more natural advantages than most other countries, those advantages have generally been squandered. Now we are embarking on a course of fundamental change to upgrade standards of performance and capitalise on our potential. It will not be an easy task. Many Australian managers will not be able to meet the higher standards that will be required. For example, too many are afraid of making decisions on industrial relations and technology, both of which, along with marketing, will be key factors in achieving profitability in a time of relatively low growth and rapid change.

In addition, the fact that such a large proportion of Australia's population is not trained to match world standards means that we will have high unemployment for a long time. This is especially true because so many of the organisational changes the country needs involve performing tasks with fewer people. Pressure will mount to reverse the reform process in order to preserve jobs. It would be a great pity if the understandable sympathy for the unemployed halted the modernisation of Australia.

It is important that all our political leaders develop innovative but useful ways of generating employment without blowing out the budget deficits. There is a clear need to foster growth in service industries, including restaurants and tourism-related activities.

Australian manufacturing needs attention. If the sharp reduction in tariffs develops work practices in Australia that are up to international standards, then it will actually attract investment—as we saw recently when Toyota announced its decision to build a new plant in Victoria. But complete elimination of tariffs is only possible if everything goes right in the next decade.

If Australia is to generate jobs in the private sector, it is very important in the long term to have efficient governments and a world-competitive depreciation rate in order to encourage companies to invest in modern equipment. Unfortunately, depreciation is not understood in Canberra. The OECD in its latest survey places Australia among those countries with the lowest inflation levels and the highest real interest rates. This emphasises the scope we have for further reducing interest rates provided world rate relativities continue in line with the OECD survey. Treasury boffins will argue that doing this too rapidly would over-stimulate the economy, but the message I am getting from the business community is that the risk of such an outcome is very low. We need to be world-class in capital-related areas, as well as in labour practices.

SILENCE AT THE TOP

SOME TIME ago I was dining with a group of 150 junior engineering executives and engineering students. Among the people at our table was an engineer employed by a company whose workers and managers had embraced the concept of world-best practices, and which was installing plant to match. The engineer was bursting with pride and excitement.

Also at our table was another young executive engineer working for the local arm of an international company. It has reasonable work practices by Australian standards, but its plant is not up to world-class levels and its unions do not understand the new rules. We discussed the parent company's future decision on whether to stay on in Australia. The young engineer agreed that it might do better to close down if its workers, management and capital (the plant) could not attain international standards. If that happens, I hope the people who lose their jobs will be able to explain the consequences of their folly to others.

The dinner was on a Saturday evening and the young engineers had been at seminars all day. I expected to be given a harsh reception for any remarks in my speech that strayed from humour or delayed traditional weekend pursuits. Instead, the question period ran over time and for an hour afterwards a large number of people crowded around comparing views on Australia's future direction. If the country is allowed to become a management, technology and work-practices backwater, then most of the engineers who were at that dinner will pursue their careers overseas. (Our long-term prosperity will be linked to our engineers' ability to ensure that every task we undertake is up to world standards.)

Potentially, Australia is a marvellous place in which to develop technology, whether related to engineering, computer software, biotechnology, medicine, building design or other areas. The revolution in world communication systems has ended our isolation. Our young people, as well as the rest of the population, are crying out for direction, partly because our leaders are not explaining the overall purpose of the moves being made to change Australia's style. All too often every move is analysed only from a short-term employment aspect.

No one explains, for example, that our savings must rise to pay for the overspending of past years, and to provide the capital needed to rebuild our business and infrastructure. And no one explains that pay restraint in an accord only delivers prosperity if it is associated with world-class work practices and initiatives to introduce and utilise the latest technology to the maximum advantage. It is absolutely essential that our teachers understand the importance of similar excellence in education, both for their students and for those in the workplace who need to be retrained.

Australia's dream

The four situations explained below appear isolated and unconnected. But they involve the key pillars of our country: capital, labour, commodities and government. They are typical of a series of events occurring as the nation stirs towards making the greatest set of changes seen since federation.

- A drama unfolds in the AMP Society's Sydney offices, producing a change of leadership and direction that will leave few Australians unaffected by the middle of the decade. In effect, the board decided its survival depended on being equal to the best in the world.
- In Tokyo, a deputation of Australian union officials is explaining to the Toyota board just what can be delivered on the labour front to make an Australian motor plant operate at international standards.
- It is a cold Sunday evening in Ballarat and the best of Australia's dairy farmers are together for a historic meeting to look change in the face. They do not find it easy, but they know that if they do not adapt they could be wiped out.
- Four Commonwealth career public servants call in advisers to help their fight against others who want to 'consolidate' their section to increase their own power and the cost to the community. The four know work should be contracted out to improve service and cut costs. As the discussion proceeds they realise they could tender personally.

Australia has become a nation of contradictions; new and old practices are running side by side as we come to terms with the fact that commodities can no longer underwrite our way of living.

For a long time Australia refused to accept the new reality and went to borrowing, to the point where our creditors now control our currency and money markets. We have only to look at South America to see what could happen next. Indeed, in some states the education system is preparing children for a much lower standard of living by taking out the competitive spirit and trying to lower standards to a common denominator. Those who believe we have a chance to reverse the process and regain prosperity are not getting the message through to the young. They are understandably depressed at the prospect of a whole generation spending long periods queuing for the dole.

It is encouraging that the major political parties are in fundamental agreement over the direction to take to restore economic health—despite their difference of opinion over method and pace of change.

Both parties are nervous about what pace of change Australians will tolerate. Unfortunately, with time running out, there may be no choice but to implement the changes quickly. These days it is fashionable to blame Paul Keating, Bob Hawke and the unions for our problems. It would be just as accurate to blame former Prime Minister Malcolm Fraser and business. We have all played a role. Indeed, the much-maligned Hawke Government can claim credit at least for much of the change in mood.

With hindsight, our mistakes are now so obvious. We had a nation richly endowed with commodity wealth and a political system that was the envy of other countries, particularly those in the Asia-Pacific basin. But the technology boom caught us out. For the most part we ignored the vast improvements in processing and transporting goods and services, plus the new management systems that arose.

Our managers and unions blamed each other over work practices, equipment, investment policy, management systems and quality of service. In practice, both sides were to blame as Australia's standard of business slipped behind our rivals. As we fell back we debated the symptoms instead of the cause. For example, both sides in the tariff debate are partly right. There is not much value in protecting bad work practices, unions and managers—either in private or government enterprises—although it is worth protecting world-class enterprises from blatant dumping.

Manufacturers can correctly claim that the tariff game is grossly unfair. They are forced to pay trumped-up charges to finance government waste and over-regulation, and Australian unions have rorts enshrined in law which, along with management games, are destroying the transport and other service systems. All these difficulties are lumped on top of a genuine problem of scale—the greatest hurdle in reaching world-best practice in many areas. And while exports may overcome the limitations of the market, Australian manufacturers face tariffs and other obstacles in selling to other countries.

However, tariffs are declining as a world protection medium. What the Hawke Government did, knowingly or in ignorance, was to reduce the tariffs and create the carnage that will force us into world-best practice in labour, government costs and management.

Like the recession, it is a brutal and inefficient way to achieve change. But, given the politics of the union movement and the Public Service, and the reluctance of manufacturers to modernise, it may have been the only way to do it. Although traditional free traders will be shocked, once we have cleaned the system of rorts a strong case will be made for some form of efficient protection against dumping which is tied to attainment of world-best practice.

Another process that sent all the wrong signals was the accord arrangements, where the backroom deals simply did not work. The workers exercised 'wage restraint' by effectively cutting their remuneration, thinking they were doing the 'right thing'. At the same time their overseas counterparts in modern countries were often lifting their pay rates and increasing their holidays. The overseas workers woke up to the fact that in manufacturing and services it is not always pay that is the issue, but the way time is used to harness new technology.

Investors saw little sense in investing in technology in Australia, not only because of unions but because of government charges and depreciation rates. So investors went into property and many lost heavily. We now have much less money to do what needs to be done, which is one reason community savings must rise and why we might need to rely more on overseas capital.

There are signs that the community is starting to understand how to get it right. In its new plant north of Sydney, Master Foods (part of the Mars group) will embrace world-best practice: workers will be responsible for repairs and operation of the plant, engendering pride and total care. Clear career paths will give workers incentive to perform and the company's profits are set to soar. In Melbourne, the Daimaru store brings a new dimension to shopping, on both sides of the counter. Its new pay deal offers the chance to rid waste that has been costly to enterprises and workers. On the other hand the recession affected Daimaru's turnover and as a result they did not gain the expected rewards.

If the commercial ideas behind both operations work, then their workers and enterprises will be richly rewarded. It's a big if, but we need success stories to inspire others. If we fail to adopt world-class operating practices, managers and workers will be standing in dole queues blaming each other. Yet few realise they are in the same boat.

The Opposition spokesman on industrial relations, John Howard, is 'a passionate believer' in employment contracts on an enterprise basis. He says if these were offered there would be an exodus from the present system of industry awards, particularly in service industries and non-traditional manufacturing. 'The biggest single change is you have to give people the legal right to conclude agreements without the interposition of an employee organisation, which you just simply cannot do under the law of Australia at present', Howard says. What does he say of the future of unions? 'If I were a union leader I would meet the challenge. What I would try to do is, sort of, out-Howard Howard'.

Howard says that to retain their members and their legitimacy, unions must demonstrate that they have the ability to deliver a much bigger cake to an enterprise and a bigger slice of that cake to their members. Howard is dubious as to whether unions can fulfil this role, which is akin to being a management consultant.

Paul Keating has declared this 'the recession we had to have'. That's not true, of course. With proper leadership the process of change could have begun years ago. The recession has wrecked enough good businesses to damage Australia's industrial infrastructure, and has lifted unemployment to the point that restructuring, although no less vital, becomes socially dangerous. The terms 'microeconomic reform' or 'restructuring' are euphemisms for using less labour to do the same task. They cause great social strains and lead many people to believe that Australia is a country without hope—damned if it makes the changes and slaughtered if it does not.

What Paul Keating was telling us was that only with a big pool of unemployed workers will managers, young people, unions, management and educationists start thinking about their mistakes and how to learn from them. Now he is no longer Treasurer he says he believes that without some form of extra employment the revolution will cause too much pain. But a big rise in government spending to create jobs would rekindle inflation and create a new round of uncertainty. An alternative way to boost employment is to offer attractive infrastructure securities to superannuation funds to get new projects off the ground.

THE CATCH-UP PROCESS

THE BEST way to visualise what Australia might look like later in the decade is to look at the way some of our leading enterprises and institutions are revolutionising their activities as they try to catch up with the rest of the world. We must assume their trailblazing will be followed by others and be co-ordinated.

Nowhere is the catch-up process more important to both small and large business than in Australia's biggest capital provider, the AMP Society. Like many other life offices, the AMP in past decades allowed its administration, production and marketing costs to balloon. It watched banks emerging as better generators of product and taking market share. The AMP had a young turk, Ian Salmon, in its management ranks. Salmon had made a name for himself in the 1970s when, as the society's Victorian manager, he took on and beat Builders Laborers Federation chief Norm Gallagher in a dispute over the society's Collins Place project in Melbourne. In the mid-1980s the board decided against a revolution and passed him over in favour of Ian Stanwell as new managing director.

Salmon took over the top job from Stanwell late in 1990, with the brief of overhauling the AMP. The task he faces is much tougher than anything that has gone before. To be effective, the overhaul will need to bring costs down by 25–50% and expand output dramatically. The MLC has already beaten the AMP in reducing administration charges; other life offices will go out of business unless they do the same thing. Asked what the AMP will be like by the middle of the decade, Salmon says, 'We'll be much leaner and healthier . . . running the business on what we intend to be best international standards . . . We will therefore be expanding, perhaps modestly, into other territories. We will want to behave like a world-class operator in what we do.

What criteria will the AMP adopt for future investments?

> We will seek businesses that are most competitive in the industry. We try to avoid businesses that are not . . . We will be looking for businesses that are free of government support. We look for good structures within an industry, low-cost structures, the right sort of technology, whatever is required according to the type of business, whether it is manufacturing or mining or whatever.
>
> We will want companies that have got good management and management systems that are appropriate to their business: a board and a management team that's focusing on creating wealth for the shareholders as well as maintaining the ongoing health of the enterprise and not concentrating on the health of the enterprise at the expense of the shareholder.

Given that many of Australia's large companies are not up to the AMP's criteria for companies of the future, smaller enterprises will get a chance to come through—although one of the great dangers facing Australia is that capital will only be available to big companies because superannuation fund trustees are too conservative. The culture change coming at the AMP reduces that risk and, assuming Salmon does not lose his nerve, will emerge as a key event of the decade.

The AMP's largest single corporate investment is in BHP, where managing director John Prescott has staked his reputation on making the Big Australian equal to the world at everything it does. He and Salmon have the same philosophy. Because he is prepared to do it at BHP, Prescott will require the same initiative of his small and large suppliers, and is now urging his customers to change their practices.

'If we are to compare our steel companies with what's done in Japan, there are some things we can't match the Japanese on', he says.

> Now what does that mean, we give up? What it should mean is that you recognise that you have to find some other means to be competitive, something to offset the disadvantage. And the more you are prepared to commit

> yourself to finding means to offset the disadvantages, the more you develop a flair and an innovative, entrepreneurial pattern of behaviour that allows you to go one up rather than just equal.
>
> It involves a change of approach, a different, outlooking way of thinking that's perhaps not as common as we would like it to be. These comparisons are not just with our past performance; they're comparisons of the very best performances in the world and how you logically translate those to tangible benefits, not only for your own firm, but for the country. Australia could be a very exciting country. [This approach] could have a very significant impact on our trade position.

If Prescott fails to deliver, or the nation fails to grasp the opportunity for change, BHP may be foreign-based within ten years. Alan Jackson became the darling of the institutions when he introduced his own brand of world-best practice at BTR Nylex—reducing costs by contracting out many functions previously performed by staff and changing other management procedures. BTR, BHP and many other groups will be put to the test by Philip Brass at Petersville. Suppliers including BTR (glass), Amcor and Pratt Group (packaging) will be required to perform at world-best levels. And so the chain goes on.

What if BHP tinplate is too expensive because the plant is not up to scratch or work and management practices are outdated? 'We are prepared to stand up and be counted', Prescott says.

If BHP, BTR and Amcor fail to meet world standards on price and quality there will be a huge outcry—no one will attack the delinquent boards and managements harder than their large shareholder AMP. The only permissible excuse will be if goods are being dumped in Australia substantially below world market prices.

At CSR, Ian Burgess put a stiff broom through head office operations and is now studying every aspect of the group for areas where the group is behind the world's best. Early indications are that most of CSR's operations are better than world standard but middle management in branches and divisions has not yet attained the standards of Japan where one of the secrets of successful enterprise is to have most of the emphasis on operations rather than middle managers.

But the greatest revolution in moving to world-best practice will occur in the service area. The AMP and MLC leads will not only extend to other life offices but must come to banks, particularly given the Westpac joint venture with AMP.

Cost-cutting is likely to be dramatic in the public sector. Nick Greiner understood that his greatest task was to substantially reduce the cost of government. Lower government charges to business will attract a lot more employment-creating businesses to the state.

Queensland Premier Wayne Goss was handed a brilliant balance sheet by his predecessors and is already using it to attract industry.

In Victoria the former Premier Joan Kirner eventually understood that the only way out of Victoria's problems was to make her Government more efficient. But because of her Government's entrenched union connections it was slow to execute the changes required. Business will go to where the cost of government is lowest. Jeff Kennett faces the daunting task of enabling Victoria to catch up. To achieve that, in view of the size of the state debt, Victoria's Government must be made the most efficient in the country.

Another state under pressure, Tasmania, has been active in reorganisation and is a pioneer in cutting the cost of education. The crises in South Australia and Western Australia are forcing them to do likewise.

The area in which there is still the most waste is the Commonwealth. Pressure will mount for federal change as the states demonstrate how service and quality can be improved. The Federal Public Service has made a start by separating government business enterprises and making other changes, particularly in defence.

David Block was chairman of the efficiency scrutiny unit and administrative reform units that advised the Prime Minister and Cabinet between 1986 and 1988. On the overall performance of private and government activities, he says

> We have a long way to go to achieve best competitive international practice. If we face the reality of our woeful performance, poor productivity and lack of competitiveness, there is clear evidence that we can improve dramatically. The numbers are utterly dramatic—effective micro-economic reform could add 3–4% to the real annual growth. There is some evidence of change but we continue to seek solutions by blaming others and are unwilling to alter our own behaviour—our optimism can only be based on our own efforts. It is much too early to accept that we have made the changes. The jury is out; we can but hope and pray! Who will save us if we refuse to save ourselves?

Block believes about $10 billion a year could be saved in the public sector by ending unnecessary programs and rorts.

> I'm a great fan of work done by the best of the Public Service but the results are spotty and one of the problems is the people who do worst, such as departments that ignore effective management, always get bailed out, whereas those who are efficient really cut their own throats. So, in other words, there's a kind of perverse incentive that if you manage badly you get bailed out, if you manage well nobody says thank you. Nevertheless, I am very proud of the recent achievements . . . if we had not made the changes in

> 1987, certainly government expenditures could well be a couple of a billion dollars a year higher at least.

Block points out that targeting benefits correctly can save a lot more than by cutting running costs.

REFORMER LOOKS BEYOND PROTECTION

PROTECTIONISTS and high-cost manufacturers have been the usual targets of the Industry Commission. But its new chief Bill Scales believes that debate has been settled. Now the body's targets are more likely to be the vested interests that are keeping Australia's waterfront charges among the highest in the world, and other obstacles to the internationalisation of business by governments, managers and unions. It is significant that the commission is moving to Melbourne, the city hardest hit by such artificial barriers to growth.

'Australia doesn't have any option; it has to do everything right. We are a small nation a long way from major markets, and that means getting everything right in the industrial sector, everything right in the government sector, everything right in the tertiary sector', Scales says. He believes Australia is not getting it right, and there is no better illustration than the waterfront.

> There has been significant labour productivity improvement on the waterfront generally over the past two years, but what we are not seeing yet are the dividends from that reform.
>
> People on the waterfront are saying that the only dividends you will get will be in quality and delivery, not in price. That is not acceptable. We have to see that dividend right across the range of government services.

Scales' remarks, made as the Industry Commission is conducting an inquiry into port authorities, contrast with the Hawke Government's effusive praise for the reform process. Scales believes the Government's efforts on behalf of change are not matching those of manufacturers. The breadth of his views has, so far, been obscured by the media's concentration on whether a breakdown in protection policies will result from his appointment and the move to Melbourne.

Scales believes this may be partly attributable to the unfortunate focus in Victoria on the textile, clothing and footwear industry, which is being seen in political circles as a watershed. 'It's a shame in a way, because there has been a sectoral plan for that industry now for three years and it really does have very, very high levels of assistance. Even by the year 2000 it is going to have very high levels of assistance.'

Scales says the continued identification of Victoria's problems with the textile, clothing and footwear industry gives the wrong impression to the rest of the country. 'Victoria has as many strengths as any other state; it has as many free-traders as any other part of the country and as many high-tech companies.'

His agenda for the Industry Commission does not involve going backwards over textiles, but dealing with basic questions such as opportunities for Australia and its businesses when the recession ends. He is interested in whether Australia has the commitment and discipline required in the government sector, the union movement and the business community for participation in the international economy.

Scales says that overseas there are doubts. During recent trips to New York and Japan he was questioned on this. 'I spent some time with Nomura Securities in Japan, and they would say to me, "But Mr Scales, are you really convinced that your managers are capable of doing those things?" ' On Toyota's decision to build a new plant in Melbourne he comments, 'It's a gamble on their own organisation . . . It's also a gamble about Australia'.

Before taking the Industry Commission post, Scales was chairman and chief executive of the Automotive Industry Authority. 'I think the biggest problem I found was not lack of management skills but lack of leadership. I always found it very difficult to get senior executives of companies to think more broadly than the existing paradigm and to begin actually to create their own environment.'

Scales was frustrated by executives' reluctance to assess where they wanted to be in five and ten years' time and how to get there. He would have liked to see more readiness to accept that they might have operations located in the US, Europe or perhaps Malaysia in addition to good and flexible operations in Australia.

Scales believes companies need to think broadly about their future so they can begin to influence their own environments. Small and medium-sized businesses need to appreciate that they will never have big enough markets in Australia to achieve world-best practice individually. They need to recognise their limitations and aim for strategic co-operation.

> You have to say, 'I'm not big enough, but if I combine with my unions and my workforce, if I combine with some other suppliers around the area, I can, (even though we've got different objectives), co-operate in a way that will allow me to get where I want to be'.

Scales believes that sort of co-operation extends to governments and that companies must ask how they can use the existing infrastructure, looking for long-term contracts with governments and other companies.

Another basic problem that Scales pinpoints is the attitude of businesses towards change in the labour market. 'I don't think business people have yet understood the extent of the flexibility within our labour market.' He notes that when he talks to senior ACTU officials, such as president Martin Ferguson, and to leaders of individual unions, they say that if a company has a long-term vision and can explain to union members how they will benefit, then they will do their utmost to clear labour restrictions from its path. They are ready to extend working hours, remove demarcations and reduce the number of unions. 'I am surprised that many more business people are not taking advantage of what I can see as a great preparedness within the union movement to actually shed past practices', he says.

Scales believes that middle management has a difficult adjustment to make. In the past, they have mainly been supervisors of labour. Now, he says, new production techniques mean that 'they are actually expected to be . . . trainers'.

Is it the Industrial Commission's task to address all these concerns? 'Well, if it did, it would be a new role for the commission', he says, adding that it is a bit early to say.

> I think what it can do under the new industry development references that the Treasurer is putting to us is to begin to get the various parties together in a way that will help them identify what the impediments are and encourage the various parties to remove many of those impediments. I don't think it would be appropriate for the commission to try to tell businesses how they ought to run their own business.

Should the commission just talk to business, rather than issue reports? 'I am personally going to do that. People across a range of industries have said to me, "Would you be prepared, as chairman of the commission, to come into our factory and at least tell it like it is to our middle managers and to our workforce, so we can think through the issues in some sort of logical way?" '

Scales says he believes strongly that once a policy is in place, it should be adhered to for some time so people can make long-term decisions.

> I didn't agree with the Kodak decision [the Government agreed to assistance for the company so it would stay in Australia]. I don't believe sufficient analysis was done. I think it sent completely the wrong signals

> about what the Government's intentions were with regard to industry development measures.

He believes Australia's relatively low productivity threatens to turn it into a low-wage country and notes that South Korea, by contrast, is increasing wages substantially because it has been able to achieve big increases in productivity.

What does he hope to achieve during his five-year term? 'At the end of five years, I would hope that this organisation could be giving government policy advice that is far-reaching . . . that acutely identifies in a practical way the impediments that are stopping this country from growing.'

TAKING ADVANTAGE OF CHANGE

WHAT MIGHT Australia look like when we have actually reformed our society and begun to take advantage of the changes we have started? If we do it properly there would be no country on earth where there was more opportunity to prosper. Our combination of natural advantages, geography, and a modern management and workforce style would be unique. In the short term, as we move through our society eliminating situations where two or three do the job of one, the social problems created by the retrenchments will be severe unless at the same time we are creating new avenues of employment and preparing those now in schools, tertiary colleges and apprenticeships to adapt to the new environment.

It is not easy to tell an apprentice electrician, or fitter, that his or her future lies with multi-skilling (except where very high levels of sophistication are involved). It is even harder to tell children in schools that Australian strikers export their jobs (and those of the managers they strike against) to Asia when their own teachers strike at the drop of a hat and few have any concept of the entirely different environment their pupils are headed into.

Like everyone else, those teachers that cannot adapt to the 1990s will need to look for a new vocation. Teachers are often frustrated by the sheer waste in the huge teaching bureaucracies, which are squandering the money that should be paid to retain and attract the best talent available to prepare our young people for a different way of life.

Education standards equal to the world's best are required along with flexibility in hours. Some of the most dedicated professionals in Australia are teachers, yet they have allowed themselves to be led by people who have destroyed their reputation and self-esteem; what has happened to teachers is an illustration of what has happened to the nation. When teachers regain esteem, the nation is back on the road to success.

If we handle it right, education can be a great growth area for jobs as we retrain our workforce and export our training skills to Asia. We are having an influx of fee-paying Asian students to Australia. Understandably, the countries now sending us students will want to develop their own institutions. Some Australian tertiary colleges have opened campuses in Asia, including Curtin University of Western Australia, the David Syme Business School of Monash University, Victoria, the Royal Melbourne Institute of Technology, and the University of Sydney. In the future many Australians will do a year of their course in Asia as we come to grips with our geography.

Educational facilities and nearness to Asia are high on our list of advantages to be exploited. Resources, tourism, agriculture-related processing, engineering, high technology, the 'savings industry' and selected areas of services and manufacturing represent some of our best hopes to get out of the problems we face. But in each case we need a different approach, and the spirit of change beginning to sweep the economy needs to embrace the growth areas. The fight to stop change will be bitter as the reactionaries dig in.

Normally, new resource developments cushion Australian recessions, but the Hawke Government's effective black-banning of new resource projects prevented that. Now that the Government is trying to foster development, some of the projects will be resurrected, but secondary processing of minerals will only be viable if unions are prepared to embrace flexible work practices with guarantees not to strike and if clear environmental standards are established. We have developed an international reputation of not wanting development and the world capital community is happy to go elsewhere.

Asia and other regions buy most of our agriculture exports in bulk. Fixing the agriculture problem is harder than mineral resources because, whereas in mining the answer is in reversing our own stupidity, in agriculture we are caught up in an international price war. But the price war merely highlights flaws in the way we organise agriculture. These days the profits in agriculture are made by processing materials and developing brands. In future years more huge food-based conglomerates will emerge.

Rather than developing efficient world-best processing plants and/or brands here and abroad, our farmers have set up, or have allowed to be set up, a series of boards, and co-operatives that emphasise immediate rewards. This was what the dairy farmers were facing up to in Ballarat, but the same situation applies to a range of commodities, and growers in those areas have not even begun to address the problem. We still have a chance to recover in food because we are seen in Asia, and around the world, as a clean, healthy place to process and brand foodstuffs—particularly dairy products, but also grains and other agricultural commodities.

One person who has shown how to link farming with brands is Doug Shears, head of the ICM group, which has sold its Uncle Tobys operation to Goodman Fielder Wattie. He says agriculture, as our largest employer of labour, is vulnerable because the world food industry is going to be dominated by a few large companies. Despite its importance, Australia has only the one major food processing company—Goodman Fielder Wattie—with Petersville having the opportunity to grow in to 'something worthwhile for Australia' since being taken over by Pacific Dunlop.

Shears says

> We've got to urgently establish Australian-owned corporations out of the myriad producer groups that exist, using both public and private capital. For example, in fruit we should see the coming together of the SPCs and Ardmonas, Letonas and Golden Circles into one major national organisation, which would then rationalise and compete very strongly on the domestic market with its brands and maybe even become a significant exporter. We should do the same in dairy and in other major commodity areas, including grains and wool. They've got to be multi-billion-dollar industries. They won't be worthwhile if they don't have a revenue base of at least $1 billion.

In addition, Shears believes that biotechnology will have a marked effect on Australia in many areas, particularly as we are at the leading edge of the technology. It is quite possible that during the next year or two the price of many commodities will rise. It will be a disaster for all Australians if we allow that price increase to cause us to forget change. Indeed, we must use any increased revenue from better prices to provide some of the investment capital required.

Meanwhile, in tourism we are actually seeing the wonderful advantages that come from deregulating the airlines, as enterprises ranging from Cairns hotels to Melbourne theatres come alive because people can afford to reach them. How much greater will the boom in employment and prospects be once Australia adopts an open-door airline policy to world airlines, and the third runway is built at Sydney? An avalanche of job-creating tourists will arrive. It is only a matter of time before the penny drops in Canberra. The Liberals are punting that the government jobs lost by necessary reforms will be taken up by tourism and other service areas.

But, of course, Australia wants more than just tourism to satisfy the ambitions of its people. We sometimes underestimate our advantages in other areas. The world's largest pharmaceutical company, Merck Sharpe & Dohme, sent one of its important executives to a BIE-*BRW* Manufacturing Outlook Conference to deliver the message that if Australia is prepared to pay world prices for pharmaceutical drugs and modernise its regulations, Merck will develop Australia into a world centre for the development of biotechnical products. The Government responded and pharmaceuticals are becoming a major area of export growth.

Apple Computer told the same conference that although Australia was rich in software talent looking for work, Japan was desperately short of this talent. The two were not coming together but the potential was there. Our telecommunications standards are among the world's best and we have a real chance to develop in this area. In architecture we are beginning to design hotels and commercial buildings around the world because we have the right technology and talents. While most world chemical makers are writing off Australia, Du Pont converted Fibremakers' nylon plant to world-best practice and it can therefore integrate into its Asian operation. In many ways the new Toyota plant at Altona in Melbourne is a continuation of the Fibremakers development. Toyota would not have reversed a long-established policy of not locating 'greenfield' operations on a new site in Australia but for a union undertaking.

There has never been change in Australia on this scale before. If it works, we will develop a hub of high-tech research and production operations in technology and telecommunications; our architects, engineers and accountants will play a big role in the region; Japanese are falling in love with the art of Ken Done; Australian food, wine and beer brands will be recognised and sought after by Asians (Penfold's David Combe is showing the way ahead); Asian middle classes will come to Australia in droves to visit our wineries and farmers as well as other tourist attractions. We have the opportunity to be a leading mineral and paper pulp processor using the latest technology and world-best environment practice.

Small business has a vital and increasing role in such a vision. It is apparent that large congregations of labour are usually inefficient so we will see them broken up if the tasks can be performed better by small contract groups. As this change sweeps through the service sector, including banks, life offices, the Public Service, retailers, tourism, and other areas, it will create enormous opportunities for those with initiative. We are likely to see clusters of small companies develop that have the advantages of large enterprises and the flexibility of small ones. The recent uniting of Tasmanian food companies for export purposes is a good example.

The sharply reduced cost of government will enable a combination of lower taxes, lower charges and better social services for those who really need help. It would help cement low inflation—and in turn low inflation will cause Australians to put less emphasis on investment of their savings in their home and more on productive job-creating schemes. The home will always remain an insurance against inflation and, of course, lots of money will be made by clever renovation and cheap purchases.

If we keep inflation low, interest costs and the cost of job-creating capital will fall. At the same time, we must develop a pool of savings outside the home to pay for our previous borrowing binge. The Labor Government introduced compulsory superannuation—the Liberals might do it differently but the good news is that both parties understand the need to lift savings.

The modernisation of Australian equipment to provide world-best practice in services and manufacturing will require the availability of large amounts of capital, which is where the superannuation money is important, provided trustees are prepared to take a long view. We will also need this money to finance many infrastructure projects such as roads and power stations, which will be forced to provide a return. The Sydney Harbour tunnel is a model project.

Of course, although there is a vision, we have really only made a token effort to get there and the way we are going about change ensures it will be a nasty experience which might induce us to retreat. Whether we get our house in order or let it decay, another major debate will emerge later in the decade—our land to population ratio. There is no way we will be able to maintain our low population policy in the next century, given what is happening around us.

Acts Worth Following

IN ESSENCE, if you are a chief executive of a large or medium-sized corporation, the pressure is on to match the world's best or give the game away. Those chief executives still offering excuses for why they can't move to world-best practice are in danger of having to explain to their directors why they are the wrong person for the job. The task is not easy but the strategies of three Australian CEOs, Telecom's Frank Blount, Pacific Dunlop's Philip Brass and Du Pont's Richard Warburton are providing role models for modern chief executives to examine and possibly follow. New Zealand industry is also producing many role models. Lindsay Pyne at the Bank of New Zealand has taken customer service to a new dimension in a service industry and it will be fascinating to see BNZ's new owner, the National Australia Bank, take some of Pyne's lessons back to Australia.

Moving your company on to a world-competitive basis involves looking at every single activity, trying to discover whether someone else in the world has found a better way, and making sure the operation is focused on total customer service. The Labor Government set up the environment for this change but took a long while to understand the implications for employment and unions. Warburton and Brass have the runs on the board in the manufacturing sector, but Blount still has to prove himself in the Australian services sector. History will not judge him kindly if he fails.

BLOUNT SPELLS IT OUT

ONE CAN only speculate about whether the Government fully understood what it was doing when it deregulated telecommunications. In essence, it gave Telecom's competitor access to the most profitable part of Telecom's operation on a marginally costed basis. The unions believe Telecom will eventually retrench 15 000 workers and that the early reductions were merely opening moves. By any standard that is a huge cut to be forced by a government concerned about unemployment. I should emphasise that Telecom's new head, Frank Blount, will not be drawn on numbers, particularly given the high cost of retrenchment. But clearly, something dramatic needs to happen to Telecom's costs or revenue sources. In the US, cuts of 30% were not uncommon. Telecom had 77 000 staff when Blount joined the group.

Blount now has the task of going through almost every operation of the enterprise, redesigning it, then discovering the labour requirement to undertake the modified task. If he goes ahead with this, it will create a union conflict of unprecedented proportions.

Blount's approach is disarmingly simple, which may be the key to success. He is aiming to put all the relevant people in a particular operation into a conference room or 'war room'. 'We're going to start with butcher's paper all the way around the wall', Blount says.

> We're going to say: 'You are not leaving this room until we diagram and get agreement on how we're doing it'. And then we're going to stand back and say: 'Is that right?'
>
> If we get agreement on that, then the next step is to take another whole clean sheet of butcher's paper and we're going to tape it on the wall below. Then we're going to bring in suppliers and we are going to take this process all the way back to the suppliers.

Given the size of the Telecom operation, Blount is going to need a lot of butcher's paper. His suppliers include Ericsson, Alcatel, Siemens and NEC. But the task he and some of his suppliers are attempting is what Warburton did at Du Pont and what Brass is now doing at Petersville. Blount's task is far more difficult because of the long history of government monopoly and the many unions involved. There will be a lot of 'I told you so' if he fails, and not much left of the national telecommunications carrier.

WARBURTON'S ACHIEVEMENT

THERE IS A tendency among American executives to regard Australia as a great place to visit but a dangerous place in which to invest. This is because of union attitudes and what they perceive as the cowboy spirit of Crocodile Dundee. But the managing director of Du Pont (Australia), Richard Warburton, 50, managed to persuade the hierarchy of his parent in the US to go against its judgement and buy the old Fibremakers nylon plant in Melbourne. Warburton believed the plant represented a once-in-a-lifetime opportunity to show his peers at Du Pont and all other US companies that there was more to Australia than Crocodile Dundee.

In many ways what Warburton has done at Du Pont has shown Australian manufacturers what can be done with good management. Warburton won the *BRW*/Alcatel 1991 manufacturing award for his achievement.

Du Pont took over ICI's European nylon operation, which means it has between 40% and 50% of the world nylon market. The gap in its network is Asia and its plans are for Australia to play a vital part in the push into Asia against Japanese nylon groups. The capacity of the old Fibremakers plant is expected to be doubled.

I cannot recall any big international chemical company using Australia as a base for an important strategic push into Asia, as distinct from exporting surplus capacity. Australian manufacturers who complain about work practices will need to study what Du Pont has done. Its success may inspire other big world chemical groups to adopt a similar strategy.

By any yardstick, the Fibremakers exercise was a long shot. ICI had failed to make the business work and the Liberman family, which bought it from ICI, had not done much better. The Warburton plan required a $150-million decision by Du Pont to buy Fibremakers and invest in new equipment, aided by a once-only government payment of $36 million arising from the end of a bounty scheme. The previous owners had found difficulty gaining a return even with the aid of a big bounty, and the new owners would not have the bounty protection. The Libermans had installed some modern equipment, although bad work practices nullified much of the advantage.

Warburton knew the only way to succeed was to convince employees and unions to work on the basis of world-best practice. Du Pont had two trump cards in its hand: it knew exactly how the plant and work practices had to be changed, and it was the supplier of the raw material.

Warburton started by shutting down the entire plant for two weeks while he and other Du Pont executives met all employees, in small groups, to discuss the changes. Full pay was maintained during the two weeks, helping to generate goodwill and to strengthen the new-start outlook. Du Pont brought twenty-four of its US employees, accompanied by their families, to work alongside Australians at almost every level of the operation. An international standard approach to safety was introduced and executive perks, including a special dining room and allotted car-parking spaces, were discontinued. The ten unions on site agreed to participate in a joint single-bargaining unit, although as the new workplace evolved, management and workers solved most of their own problems. Retrenchments were required, but a long period of notice was given, and job security was guaranteed to those remaining.

The plant is supplying only the local nylon market at present. Although turnover is below original estimates, cost reductions and quality have been achieved much more quickly and the plant moved into the black in 1991 ahead of budget, although in 1992 severe price competition affected returns. The turning around of the company has been noted in Du Pont board papers as a model for a new project. Du Pont executives are examining some of the Australian processes to assess their suitability for use in other plants. The company has plans to double the size of the Australian plant and to integrate it with Asian nylon operations.

The success Warburton achieved in converting the old Fibremakers plant to current world-best practice is expected to encourage many other American companies to invest in Australia. Warburton has accepted an appointment as chairman of the steering committee for the Australian international best-practice study, which will assist other Australian managers to move towards world-best practice and to overcome obstacles often created by second-rate management.

DUNLOP'S CHALLENGE

PHILIP BRASS has had a record of success at Pacific Dunlop but he put everything on the line when he paid $800 million for the food processor Petersville. The outlay would only make sense if Petersville's Australian plants were to move to world-best practice. Those that failed were closed down and the products they made produced in other Australian plants or overseas.

Australians have always seen food processing as a potential export business. Unfortunately, although we succeed with bulk commodities, we have fallen behind in many other areas, including fruit and vegetables. A different approach is required by growers so that their costs and yields are brought into line with overseas levels; they must also provide additional varieties that the market requires.

Australia can be promoted as a clean food processing region in export markets, but it is hard to justify cases against dumping when there is so much room for improvement on farms and in processing plants' work practices. The Petersville closures may shock the Government and unions. In particular, they signal the end of marketing boards and other organisations that set prices high enough to keep inefficient farmers alive, while giving efficient local and New Zealand farmers a bonanza. Petersville is putting out a challenge to all other food processors to move to world-best practice or shut down. We know that the Heinz plant at Dandenong is considering its long-term future, particularly after its Watties NZ takeover. Although improvements have been made there, more money must be spent and big changes made to work practices to justify modernisation.

The other large food processor in Australia, Unilever, will doubtless look at its options during the next five years. The consensus is that Australian workers are not costly compared with the rest of the world, but their work practices and on-costs depress the economics of modern high-technology plants so that they can't compete. If the unions persist with their present attitude, growers cannot adapt. Australia's transport and packaging costs will remain high and most of Australia's food-processing will move to New Zealand.

Suppliers of sugar, cardboard boxes, steel cans and plastic packaging face contractions unless they reduce their own costs. If sugar tariffs are not reduced, even more processing plants will be threatened. Everyone is in the same boat.

Philip Brass's leap of faith

Institutional managers and stockbrokers from around Australia filed into the University of Melbourne Graduate School of Management to attend Pacific Dunlop's day-long seminar on one of its five business groups. Philip Brass knew he had a lot of doubters in the audience who believed he should never have bought Petersville. But he and his food group chief, Grant Latta, had an incredible story to tell: by 1993–94 the food group's profit before interest and tax would rise by almost $60 million to about $90 million, and the final wash-up would leave Pacific Dunlop's purchase price equalling an effective after-tax price/earnings ratio of just eight, a ridiculously low figure given that Brass painted the prospect of even better results in the years ahead.

To achieve that profitability Brass has to virtually rebuild Petersville from scratch and rewrite the food industry rule book, not just for growers and employees, but also for suppliers such as BHP, Amcor and ICI, and retailers such as Coles and Woolworths. Very few of the institutional managers at the Melbourne seminar had seen management looking to virtually redesign the way a company does business and at the same time revamp large segments of a basic Australian industry. In the process, it became apparent that most of Pacific Dunlop's traditional activities had limited growth prospects.

Food provides the 'blue sky' for the company at a time when its results for the year to 30 June 1992 were depressed again. Not only is Pacific Dunlop being affected by the difficult Australian economic circumstances, but also it had an expensive product change-over problem with the Nucleus medical group, which has since been overcome, and the new Ansell rubber-glove plant in Sri Lanka ran into unexpected difficulties.

There were few people at the seminar who were not impressed by Pacific Dunlop's courage in making such a bold forecast and all agreed that if it could achieve its aims, the company and Australia's food industry would be transformed.

In a nutshell, Brass told institutions that there was an enormous opportunity in food, that Australia had not taken advantage of its closeness to Asia as a source of clean processed products because of the attitude of everyone in the food industry: the multinational companies that dominate 70% of food processing, the plant managers, the unions, the growers, the suppliers of packaging and the operators on the waterfront. Brass and Latta believe they can virtually transform every aspect of Petersville because business conditions in Australia offer a once-in-a-lifetime opportunity. And if they can't, they will replace Australian industry with New Zealand or Asian activities.

They clearly believe many of their international opponents in Australia have been incompetent and they were scathing in their criticisms. Brass said that all too often the managers of these international companies saw their appointment as a stepping stone so, to avoid confrontation, had made concessions to unions and growers that made the Australian businesses uneconomic for the long term. The companies, Brass and Latta said, had not invested in local research and development and essentially had been run as 'brand-minding' branch offices of world food groups. What made the Petersville opportunity so exciting was that its brands were either first or second in almost every segment of the market. Also, retailers were now much more open to working with food suppliers to mutual advantage, rather than simply looking for the lowest price.

The task that Pacific Dunlop is attempting has few parallels in Australia and some institutions represented at the seminar are obviously nervous about whether it can be done, especially as the groups being challenged to reform range from the largest companies in Australia to the smallest farmers and, of course, employees. Most of the doubting institutions have big shareholdings in BHP, Amcor and ICI.

Latta, using a series of graphic slides at the seminar, made it very clear that each supplier company would have to be tackled eventually. That strategy will ruffle a few feathers inside Pacific Dunlop because chairman John Gough sits on the board of BHP and Amcor. But these companies are also anxious to shed the old ways and they will use

Pacific Dunlop's pressure to clear the blockages, some of which are governmental. In the case of BHP, Pacific Dunlop says the cost of tinplate means the price of cans is 39% higher than in Italy, whose food processors are some of Edgell's main competitors. Pacific Dunlop found that other food canners were irate about the cost of tinplate and the fact that it was sometimes sold to New Zealand below Australian prices.

Pacific Dunlop is taking advantage of the anger and assembling some of the biggest food canners in Australia into one buying collective, with plans to require can makers to call tenders for tinplate from two overseas countries and BHP. Such a collective is without precedent in the Australian food industry and it will lead to the largest tinplate buying exercise attempted. The Trade Practices Commission is aware of the arrangement and if it proceeds will probably require to be in the room when the tender takes place to make sure the rival food groups are doing nothing but making sure they can compete with imports. If BHP cannot compete with the imports, it will lose the tender and its Wollongong tinplate plant may become uneconomic. Pacific Dunlop is also looking at alternative packaging to cans. Whether it is able to use the same techniques to reduce the price of film and board remains to be seen.

A variation of the BHP approach is being applied to the workforce and growers. Latta showed the seminar the labour on-costs that made Edgell uneconomic to export. One remarkable graph showed that if Edgell operated a third shift, production costs would actually rise because of labour penalty rates.

Many growers, particularly in Tasmania, have been hostile to the changes Pacific Dunlop is proposing. They complain that Pacific Dunlop's quoted yields and costs from the states of Washington and Idaho are selective. Pacific Dunlop says it used these figures to try to convince farmers that they had to change because these are the areas from which the United States sends the exports that dominate the Asian potato market. Also, other areas of the US are not competing on world markets and are merely regional suppliers.

Pacific Dunlop is prepared to negotiate only with the 20% of farmers in Tasmania who it considers to be efficient, encouraging them to use the moisture measurement techniques adopted in the US, to pool their machinery and to run their businesses on a much larger scale. Some financial help may be needed to do this but above all it will require abolition of the outmoded marketing boards, something the Western Australian Government eventually did in October 1992.

But the changes required to enable Australia to export food go much further than BHP, employees and growers. Latta told the institutions that they should not believe any politician who claimed there has been progress on the waterfront; the changes made have not benefited exporters. Pacific Dunlop, of course, is not the only company being ravaged by the shambles of Australia's ports.

The Pacific Dunlop strategy is to tackle the Petersville reorganisation on two fronts. First, change the basic business using conventional techniques. Second, and simultaneously, attack the harder issues of penalty rates, union rules, grower practices and supplier price cuts to enable the group to match importers and export. The profit projections put by Brass and Latta do not take account of this second and more controversial stage. Instead, the company has focused on the existing parameters. It engaged in a vigorous price war in the closing stages of the old ownership as it tried to maintain market share. In some cases it became overstocked as imports hit the market.

The great problem for all food suppliers is the enormous concentration of retail buying power. The biggest customer of Pacific Dunlop's food operation is Woolworths, at about $124 million of business a year. Not far behind are the independents, such as Davids Holdings, QIW, Composite and Foodland. These independent groups are likely to be working much closer together in the future, which is one reason Davids Holdings is making its moves, including the bid for QIW.

Third on the customer list is Coles Myer with purchases worth about 25% less than the combined total of the independents. It is a dangerous position for Coles to be in and is the result of the mistakes of the past few years. Further back is Franklins, although its power is increased by a concentration of business in New South Wales and the fact that the range of brands it stocks is more limited than the other supermarkets.

Pacific Dunlop faces the difficult task of trying to claw back margins given to retailers in the past two years. In some cases it will be by trying to insist on more services in exchange for concessions. The group plans to use the entire Pacific Dunlop base, not just food, in these negotiations. This clawing back is an important part of Latta's profit projections, and talks with the retailers are likely to be as intense as those between the company and suppliers of raw material.

This is probably what institutions are most nervous about, because if the old management of Petersville found it necessary to give away margin to keep market share, then it will not be easy to reverse. Pacific Dunlop is well aware of the importance of market share under present business conditions. However, the company may be helped by a new attitude emerging among retailers based on the possibility of making more money by forming alliances with suppliers rather than taking out the last cent in margins.

The great boom of retailing in the 1980s was generic products but many retailers have realised that margins on these products are low and so they are now not getting maximum yield on every shelf. Pacific Dunlop also hopes to gain some margin advantages with retailers through product innovation. In particular, it has isolated microwaveable food as a huge growth area for the future. In most areas of food processing Australia tends to follow other countries, but if Pacific Dunlop wins on the development of microwaveable food through its Quick Shot brands, it will be a world-market leader and will have achieved a technology that might well be applicable to Asia.

Pacific Dunlop's food operation is now in four divisions: Edgell–Birds Eye, Peters, Herbert Adams Bakeries and Socomin. The group is looking closely at how to take advantage of the unique distribution arrangements of the four operations. This may help in winning a much bigger share of the food service market, such as supplying caterers, restaurants and fast-food operators. Each of the divisions is looking at lowering costs and introducing new products, and each is being managed by people who were hired before Pacific Dunlop took over the reins late in 1991.

The Edgell–Birds Eye revamp is perhaps the biggest of the four and is being managed by Barry Gilbert, who joined Petersville during the takeover process and previously was with Heinz and Murray Goulburn. Stan Steele, who heads Herbert Adams, has been with the bakery two years and before that was a long-serving Edgell executive. Phil Harrison joined Peters in the 1980s from Carlton & United Breweries' Queensland operation. Socomin's Mike Harper came from Britain to join Petersville early in 1991.

The food operation is now earning at the rate of $50 million a year before tax and interest—a 66% increase on the 1991–92 profit rate. The quick turnaround by Latta was possible partly because his predecessor, Bob Cumberlidge, had brought the team of executives together and hired the Pappas Carter consultancy (now part of the Boston Consulting Group), which had an action plan ready for Latta to work on. There was also a store of ideas and new products within the group that had remained dormant while previous owner Adelaide Steamship struggled to survive.

For example, the Socomin operation essentially involves making or marketing products for international food groups such as Twinings. Originally, Pacific Dunlop was going to sell Socomin but decided to keep it when it was realised just how much potential it had to introduce Asian food products into Australia and how much knowledge there was to be gained by working with international groups.

All four food divisions operate on a five-point plan: reducing costs;

better management of assets, including working capital and property (some brands have been closed); development of new products; invigorating brands; and overseas strategies where appropriate.

The food operation has been classified the Pacific Brands food group, recognising the advantage of sometimes combining food with the great strengths of Pacific Dunlop's operations in its clothing and footwear brands. Total Pacific Dunlop advertising spending will exceed $40 million annually, putting it among the top five consumer advertising spenders in Australia. Within that total, advertising expenditure in the food operation will be increased to $25 million and food product advertising will be more entertaining.

To achieve a price/earnings ratio of eight in 1993–94, Brass will rely first on Latta's promise to deliver in that year earnings before interest and tax of 9.6% on sales of just more than $900 million—about $90 million. That is a big task, because in 1991–92 the food operation's earnings before interest and tax will be 3.6% on sales of just less than $900 million.

In effect, Latta has to lift profit by $58 million in two years without taking into account any gains from new-product plans, changes in dealings with growers, greater use of plant through ending shift allowances, a breakthrough in tinplate pricing, and an export drive or a switch to overseas production. These gains require future agreements from other parties.

In fact, sales fell fractionally in 1991–92 because some operations were closed. The biggest single contribution to the profit rise will be doing the same tasks with fewer people. At 30 June 1991, before the takeover, Petersville had a staff of 5449. When rationalisation has been completed there will be 3830 staff, a reduction of almost 30% in two years. That includes an 85% cut in head-office staff and savings in other overheads that alone will be worth $11 million. Few companies have been rationalised to that extent. Clawing back margins will also be important in achieving the profit rise.

Pacific Dunlop effectively paid $1 billion for Petersville, made up of $400 million for the equity, the $500 million debt that was inherited and $100 million in reorganisation costs. In all, about $400 million will be raised through asset sales, including the forestry operation in Tasmania, the US commercial office supply and retail group AAM Inc, Adelaide Steamship group shares and other operations. Another $100 million is being released from stock reductions and property sales.

There is a tax benefit from the reorganisation costs, which leaves debt for the group at $60 million without allowing for any further capital expenditure required in Australia, New Zealand and Asia.

Imputing an 8% interest charge on the debt and a normal tax rate, Latta is promising about $50 million after tax for the year to 30 June 1994—a price/earnings ratio of eight on a capital cost of $400 million. Pacific Dunlop earned $216 million in 1990–91 but its interim profit was lower, so the food group is set to be one of its big profit centres.

The big prize, however, is to have the food operation contributing closer to $100 million later in the 1990s. To achieve that, the group must become a big player in the Asian food market. Australia now exports food worth about $11 billion in a world-trade food market worth $350 billion. But 90% of Australia's food exports are not processed. The food market in Australia totals $23 billion, of which Petersville's target markets are worth $3.4 billion. It has sales of $870 million, of which only $6.7 million are exports, so it won't be easy to change the culture.

Petersville gained early encouragement when growers, employees and the Western Australian Government agreed to the changes required to make the group's WA plant economic. The company decided to shut plants at Cowra in New South Wales and at Bairnsdale in Victoria either because they could not be made economic or because switching their capacity was necessary to give other plants a chance to survive.

The Ulverstone potato plant in Tasmania was also facing the axe but the ACTU helped to negotiate an umbrella agreement for Pacific Brands that includes much more flexible hours of work, enabling more to be done in peak processing times without shift allowances. Provided this agreement is ratified in the workplace and satisfactory agreements with growers are obtained, the company will invest $26 million to make the plant economic for the local market. Ulverstone is perhaps fortunate that it can survive on the local market alone. If employees there agree to forgo all shift allowances the company will invest a further $16 million to upgrade the plant for export production. It will then be ready to attack the potato markets in Asia and its use of potatoes will jump dramatically.

The Bathurst plant in New South Wales cannot be economic in the long term without exports and there is a good chance that the $50 million Pacific Dunlop has earmarked to spend there will go to Asia or New Zealand; feasibility plans for operations in both countries have been drawn up.

The company says that if Bathurst is to retain vegetable processing, employees have to abandon shift allowances so that exports are viable; the ACTU umbrella agreement is not enough to save processing in the area. The ACTU helped the attempt to overcome the many people in Bathurst who preferred the plant to be shut or, let it gradually decay before being shut in a few years, rather than giving up shift allowances, changing the practices of growers, and having $50 million of new investment pumped into the town.

Pacific Dunlop's strategies and decisions are being made against a background of increasing strength in global brands and world food groups that are forming joint ventures either to penetrate new areas or swap brands in their home markets. The company hopes to form strategic alliances with several global food makers, both to improve its technology in the local market and assist in exports. For example, it is having discussions with Conagra in the US with a view to operating in Asia, and with Japanese trading house Mitsui to set up fish operations in Australia for the Asian market.

The bakery division is having discussions with Rich's in the US on technology that will enable the company to manufacture finished pies and pasties to be distributed frozen and thawed out on site. They have a shelf life of three to six days, which means that instead of fresh pies being delivered daily, they can be distributed once or twice a week. Other Rich's technology enables frozen cakes and other bakery products to be sent virtually as raw material from the factory to bakery shops in supermarkets, fast-food or other outlets, where they can be baked on demand and decorated on site.

Other alliances are being formed with Fleury Michon in France and Northern Foods in Britain to take advantage of the latest technology in chilled meals.

In many ways, the dream of Australia becoming an internationally-based business community rests on initiatives such as those Pacific Dunlop is taking. The scale of the task shows how far many companies, particularly food companies and their suppliers, had fallen behind. With Unilever already considering the shut down of manufacturing in Australia in five years, and Heinz on a knife edge, if Pacific Dunlop does not achieve the necessary breakthroughs there will not be much left of food processing in Australia in a few years.

LINDSAY PYNE'S CAMPAIGN

WHEN the Bank of New Zealand realised in 1989 that it had big problems, its board took a step that none of the major banks in Australia have had the courage to do: it recruited a new chief executive from outside its own ranks. The man who was appointed, Lindsay Pyne, had previously reorganised the New Zealand Post Office Savings Bank into a low-cost bank, calling it Postbank, and had supervised its sale to the ANZ Banking Group. Pyne's brief after the Bank of New Zealand head-hunted him was to uncover the problems, deal with them and return the bank to profitability. His approach to the BNZ problems differs markedly to the approach of many of the Australian banks to their problems. It was a strange coincidence that the hardest hit of the Australian banks, Westpac, revealed its losses in the same week as the BNZ announced a remarkable recovery. If the BNZ makes the sort of progress that Pyne has planned, its techniques could well become a template for banks on the other side of the Tasman—provided that the BNZ culture is not eliminated by the National Australia Bank, its new owner.

The problems of the BNZ have been well documented, but Pyne's radical solutions are only just becoming known outside the bank. By about May 1989, and working in conjunction with the consultancy firm Booz Allen, Pyne had a good idea of the sources and the extent of the bank's losses. A rescue package of $NZ600 million ($440 million) was negotiated, including a direct injection from the merchant bank Fay, Richwhite. At the time, the Australian economy was still prosperous and only a general provision was made for possible Australian losses. Eighteen months later, and soon after the election of the Bolger Government in New Zealand, the full extent of the Australian disasters became apparent. The new Government and Fay, Richwhite were forced to assist in another rescue.

Serious as they were, the Australian problems provided an opportunity for the BNZ to copy a technique pioneered by Mellon Bank in the US—the formation of a separate company to take most of the bad loans. Pyne had already isolated the bad loans and passed them over to a special management team, so the transfer to the new company, Adbro Investments, went smoothly. In all, problem loans totalling about $2.8 billion were transferred to Adbro. In BNZ's books the problem loans were replaced by a single asset—an advance of $1.1 billion to Adbro. The Government funded $420 million of the loans and Fay, Richwhite $50 million. Under the arrangement, BNZ lost its tax deduction on the $2.8 billion of loans and is repaying the $420 million plus 15% interest by tax payments. The Fay, Richwhite $50 million is repayable in cash at the end of five years, and carries a rate of 14%. Unlike most rescue operations, it has proved remarkably profitable for the rescuers. The Government has already collected more than $150 million in tax revenue, and shares in BNZ rose to the point where Fay, Richwhite, which had been facing a huge paper loss, almost broke even in the sale to the NAB.

But the really dramatic transformation has been in the operation of the bank itself. When Pyne began assessing the bank's affairs, he found it was financing the excessively high proportion of about 60% of the New Zealand business community (the figure is now between 40%

and 50%) and that it had no effective credit control system. Its costs were bloated and he considered it had little understanding of the need to provide service. Pyne immediately introduced the Citibank credit policies. He believes that in future, as bank products become increasingly similar to each other and margins are squeezed, the essence of successful banking will be tight control of costs and excellence in service.

To cut costs, Pyne reduced the number of regional centres from seven to three and flattened the whole management structure. Its expenses base was reduced from $800 million to $600 million. But the present structure still includes the cost of collecting the outstanding loans, and when this requirement ends the total reduction in costs is expected to be well over 30%. None of the big Australian banks have attempted such an enormous cost-cutting exercise in such a short time. In effect, the BNZ was rebuilt from scratch, an operation that is usually possible only when someone is brought in from outside.

While the cost-reduction program was being applied, Pyne set out on one of the most extensive world benchmarking exercises yet attempted by a bank. He wanted to determine world-best techniques for training and development, competency, assessment systems, rewards, the performance measurement of management, internal communications and other areas of reform. Although he examined some banks, he concentrated on international non-bank companies, including All State Insurance, Apple Computer, Whirlpool, Motorola, Xerox, Federal Express, Corning, Du Pont and General Electric. Participants in the BNZ benchmark exercise received a copy of the conclusions for their own use. BNZ's part in the exercise gave it the opportunity to introduce world-standard techniques in a wide range of applications.

Pyne also turned his attention to an internal restructuring, creating three separate banking arms, each with its own recruiting policies. In consumer banking he recruited young people prepared to be marketers, operating in much the same way as McDonald's and other consumer retail organisations. For his business banking sector, he brought in many of the branch managers who had long experiencein banking for smaller and medium-sized businesses. Where the business banking section required branches, it paid rent to the consumer banking section. The third arm was a special bank for 100 top organisations and businesses, strengthened by a considerable degree of outside recruitment.

With the help of an independent research group, an extensive survey was carried out into the banking needs of all the accountholders in the top-100 corporate section, most of the 6000 or so business customers, and many of the private customers. The result of the survey let the bank establish strategies and criteria for executive performance within the three arms of the bank. Staff members were also extensively consulted for views on how to improve the bank. Every six months, staff in the top corporate banking sector are evaluated by a survey of each of the 100 customers. A similar survey is done every year of the medium-sized business customers. Executives who are rated badly by their clients are given special consultation and helped, but if they fail to attract votes in the next survey, they are asked to move on. The same process is now extending into consumer banking, and account-holders are being polled. Pyne believes that a high level of motivation is being developed that will build a successful future for the bank, provided the new owners follow the pattern.

The bank has learnt much from its losses, but in particular it has absorbed a stronger realisation that capital is precious and needs continuing protection. A careful risk-evaluation process has been introduced as the bank strives to prevent a repeat of past mistakes. The last balance sheet prior to the takeover showed a rise in government securities because the bank was unable to find sufficient low-risk business at the returns it regarded as acceptable. Pyne believes the business will return as the New Zealand economy improves and as the market begins to recognise the commitment to service that the bank has made.

Perhaps the greatest visible change is the opening of three redesigned BNZ branches operating as pilot merchandising centres. Many younger staff are in the area of the bank used by customers—on the other side of the counter to the tellers. They help customers with a variety of investments. Just as a McDonald's counter operator asks whether a customer would like an additional product, bank tellers are also being trained to sell additional products and to suggest better ways for clients to handle their money. Career paths are being designed for tellers and other merchandisers so that it is not necessary to go to administration to get rewards. The same technique is being used in rural areas, changing the long-established pattern in which bank officers could rarely get pay rewards in country postings.

It remains to be seen whether the revamped bank can emerge as one of the most profitable in the region under the NAB or whether the scars of what has happened and the present insistence on good margins will stunt growth in an environment that is very different from that of the 1980s. The bank's share of the New Zealand consumer market is well below its corporate share, so its consumer experiment is important to its future growth.

Nevertheless, the bank's performance in its last independent year, to 31 March 1992, left its supporters satisfied that it is well on track. Group profit rose 27.7% to $NZ171 million, which represented 8.7

cents a share. The bank's assets totalled $NZ19.8 billion, but in terms of risk rating they fell from $NZ15.4 billion to $NZ13.6 billion. The scars of the past have left their mark, with the result that its asset backing in the last independent accounts was only 44 cents a share. The return on average assets, however, rose from 0.7% to 0.87%.

The figures leave the bank with considerable room for improvement, but the bold restructuring carried out by the bank in the face of a widespread financial crisis enabled the BNZ share price, prior to the takeover, to exceed asset backing by a greater amount than any of the major Australian banks. Accordingly, the BNZ's two major shareholders, the New Zealand Government and Fay, Richwhite reckoned the premium was attractive enough to sell and the cash-rich NAB was prepared to pay the price.

BRW'S RICH LIST

IF IT HAS done nothing else, ten years' publication of the BRW rich list has dispelled the view that wealth in Australia is hereditary. For generations, Australians believed that family fortunes were handed down from one generation to the next, and that unless you were lucky or robbed a bank you could not hope to generate new fortunes to match the old.

But when the first list came out in 1983, there for all to see were names of migrants such as Antico, Adler, Abeles, Brender, Graf, Joss, Lustig, Lowy and Triguboff. When these men came to Australia, they saw it as a land of promise and they set about taking advantage of the opportunities available. There are now sixty-seven migrants in the *Rich 200*.

In the past ten years there has been remarkable growth in the total wealth recorded in the list. Back in 1983 the total wealth was only $4.6 billion. That first list was smaller than today's, but when a comparable ranking was assembled a year later, total wealth was $7 billion. Nine years after that, in 1992, the rich are estimated to be worth $25 billion—more than a threefold increase. In 1983 only one group, the Murdoch family, was worth more than $200 million and only eight had more than $100 million. Today, twenty-four individuals or families are worth more than $200 million and fifty-two are worth more than $100 million.

The other thing the rich list has highlighted is that it is almost as hard to hang on to wealth as it was to achieve it in the first place. That list in 1983 included people such as Warren Anderson, David Cookes, Keith Williams, George Herscu, Tristan Antico, Alister Norwood, Jim

King, Abe Goldberg, Kevin Parry, Sid Londish and the Grace family. No one could have guessed that they, along with many others, would make business mistakes in the 1980s that would result in their being dropped from the 1992 list.

We estimate that about 250 individuals and fifty families have appeared on the list for a time and then disappeared from it. Only eighty individuals and twenty-two families have appeared every year since 1984.

Many think that rich people keep their fortunes in cash. But most wealth is in businesses, property and other investments that can rise and fall in value. During the 1960s and 1970s, money could be borrowed at low real interest rates. One of the great money-making schemes was to develop a cash-generating business and borrow heavily, using the money to develop property and invest in shares in growing companies. The business serviced the debt.

With financial deregulation came unlimited credit; many greatly increased their borrowing and boosted their paper wealth enormously. But at the end of the 1980s this money-making machine was sent into reverse by much higher interest rates and falls in asset values, particularly property and lesser-quality shares. Many fortunes were wiped out and banks lost a lot of money. As interest rates fall and share prices rise, new wealth is being generated from the changing cycle.

People who make fortunes usually dream of passing that wealth down to their children and their descendants. But sons and daughters and their offspring rarely show the same business skills as the originators of the wealth. And those not involved in the business like to get their hands on the inheritance to use for their own purposes—a bigger house, perhaps.

So the family money is spread, and thus it disappears from the list. During the past ten years some of the great family names of previous generations have dropped off; the Grimwades, Baillieus, Carpenters and Gadsdens have all succumbed to this process.

But there is an interesting exception to this trend. One of Australia's great families, the Darlings, whose money and experience played a big role in BHP's development, disappeared from the list, like so many of the other families. But then the family produced an outstanding son, Michael, who has restored its name to the list.

Three families have resisted the trend: the Myer, Smorgon and Murdoch clans. The Myers have had a difficult decade as the late Ken Myer and Bails Myer, the sons of the family fortune's founder, Sidney, went different ways and the next generation ran into some financial disasters. During the past twenty years the family has tried to diversify away from the Myer retail business, but has not always been successful; meanwhile, the base holding of Coles Myer shares has performed remarkably well. This experience is in stark contrast to that of Sydney's Grace family, which took its cash out of the retailing business and lost most of it.

The Smorgon family went to extraordinary lengths to keep all its members in the business, but in the end found this was affecting profitability; the policy has been modified. This will place extra strains on the family in the 1990s, but there are plenty of examples to show them what to beware of.

Although the base of the $2.3-billion Murdoch fortune was established by the late Sir Keith Murdoch, Rupert Murdoch is the person who greatly extended it. The great challenge for the family will be to manage the fortune into the next generation. The Murdochs have enjoyed a remarkable rise, and every 1-cent increase in News Corporation's share price adds $1 million to the family's wealth. But in 1990 the Murdoch family had a nasty scare: it suffered the indignity of seeing Rupert go personally to each of his bankers asking for more time to pay his debts. In 1991 News Corporation's share price fell below $4; many observers thought it would never recover, but Rupert has come back with a vengeance and the shares have been trading at more than $24 in 1992.

Richard Pratt went through a similarly difficult experience in his paper-board business, and he also came out on top. Pratt found himself in a price war with Amcor and Smorgon at the same time as his cash was being drained by an ill-judged diversification into financial services and other areas. He bought out part of the Smorgon operation, and then withdrew from his mistakes as best he could. The tough times forced Pratt, like Murdoch, to concentrate on his core businesses and his wealth is now on the rise again.

The late Robert Holmes à Court, who built up a $1.4-billion fortune at his peak, was also in danger of falling off the list at one point in 1988. The Holmes à Court empire is now managed by his widow, Janet, who has been forced to concentrate its activities and sell assets. The Holmes à Court wealth, calculated at $350 million in 1992, might have declined further but for some 'help' from Alan Bond. In 1988, in an attempt to get access to cash, Bond (with WA's SGIC) offered a remarkable sum for Holmes à Court's Bell Group shares.

Many would say that Murdoch, Pratt, Holmes à Court and others who survived difficult situations were just lucky. But most of those who achieve wealth almost inevitably have to fight through difficult times to hold on to it; it requires great skill to get through.

Australia's richest man, Kerry Packer, faced a different sort of fight: he had to overcome a heart attack suffered on the polo field. Like Holmes à Court, he was grateful for 'help' from Bond and his financiers, who bought the Nine network at a price that was well above its worth. But Bond's big purchase alone was not enough to lift Packer's wealth from $100 million to $2.7 billion in ten years; it required a remarkable talent for making money. At the base of Kerry Packer's performance is the fact that he can probably run a television station better than anyone else in Australia.

As *BRW*'s first rich list was published in 1983, Packer had just completed buying the public shareholding in his company at what turned out to be a very low price. Then he had the flexibility to sell his Nine network to Bond. When he was taking it back in 1990, Packer remarked: 'You only get one Bond in your life, and I've had mine'. As it turned out, he met two. Young Warwick Fairfax and the man he chose to mastermind his finances, Laurie Connell, were just as generous to Australia's richest man. Before the completion of Warwick's takeover of his family's publishing group, they sold Packer the Fairfax non-business magazines without any understanding of their worth to the Packer empire. When Packer incorporated them into his operation, the purchase price was, in effect, at a price/earnings ratio of between one and two times.

But Packer did not always get it right during the 1980s. For example, in 1986 he bought the 2UE radio operation from the Lamb family at too high a price. It then passed into the Bond machine and returned to the Lambs for a fraction of the price Packer had paid them.

Looking back ten years, the two great businesses to be in during the decade were the media and big suburban shopping centres. The media reached their peak value in the mid-1980s and a string of media owners appeared on the list, only to be wiped out in the slump that followed. But the long-term owners such as Packer and Murdoch now head both the individual and family lists. The huge amounts of money to be made in this sector have often attracted property people seeking to diversify. As the Lowys, the Heines and Leon Fink have discovered, this can be disastrous.

The boom in large suburban shopping centres was responsible for enormous rises in the wealth of Frank Lowy, John Gandel, Maurice Alter and, indirectly, Solomon Lew, the Myer family and Marc Besen. Until 1985 Besen and Gandel jointly owned the Sussan clothing store chain. Gandel sold his shares to Besen and put his money into suburban shopping centres. In 1984, $40 million separated the two men's wealth. Now the difference is $290 million. Gandel is worth $550 million and Besen $260 million.

Solomon Lew started the decade well down the ladder with a textile and clothing business and a newly acquired parcel of Myer shares; the success of the Coles Myer merger lifted that wealth ten-fold.

Two groups that made brief but spectacular appearances on the list during the decade were the technology kings and the sharemarket players. Of the first group, only Ralph Sarich remains (in stark contrast to the situation in the US, where some of the great enduring fortunes have come from new technology). Ron Brierley is the only survivor among the share players.

Alan Bond was worth $25 million when he appeared on the 1983 list, and reached a peak of $400 million just before the sharemarket crash in 1987. In effect, that was the base equity behind an $8-billion empire. By 1990 he had disappeared from the list and there was no equity. The 1992 list displays three trends that may prove very important in the decade ahead. The first is the remarkable rise of Lindsay Fox. The Fox formula during the 1980s was to undertake transport activities that large companies found difficult because they could not manage unions. Now he is applying that technique to governments, which are delighted with the savings Fox offers them, even though there is still a good margin for Fox. The technique Fox uses in transport could be applied to a wide range of other services.

The second trend illustrates how the wealth of dominant shareholders in smaller public companies has risen. The list includes Ian Howard-Smith (Queensland Metals), Walter Johnson (Futuris), Alan Burns (Altrack), Brian Sherman and Laurence Freedman (Equitilink). The third trend, the success of Australian artists and entertainers on the international scene, stands in contrast to our failures in technology.

Where the wealthy made their money
(% of individual fortunes)

Industry	1983	1987	1992
rural	8	6	13
investment	14	16	13
property	31	37	32
media	5	6	5
retail	10	8	11
financial services	7	6	2
resources	7	5	3
manufacturing	8	9	10
inheritance	4	3	2
other	6	4	9

Source: *Business Review Weekly*, 22 May 1992

Artist Ken Done, author Colleen McCullough, actor Mel Gibson and two members of the rock group INXS have joined the list.

The American journalist Walter Lippmann wrote that those who made themselves rich took on an obligation to tend their wealth so they could pass it on to their descendants, who would then be free to follow careers in politics, philanthropy and the arts as well as commerce and industry. In this way, a civilised society would emerge. Evidence of the acceptance of this social contract can be found in the history of the development of US capitalism. However, how deeply this sense of duty has penetrated the culture of America's elite is open to debate following the events of the 1980s. Australia's wealthy have not seen this as their duty.

Learning from Other's Mistakes

HINDSIGHT is a wonderful thing. It is so easy to look at our past actions and see where we went wrong. During the 1980s enterprises and individuals made many mistakes. As we head into the 1990s it is important we recognise those mistakes and make sure they don't happen again.

WHERE BRIAN QUINN WENT WRONG

THE SAGA at Coles Myer has few parallels in Australian corporate history. The company is now in a remarkable position to take advantage of the strong foundation that was laid by Brian Quinn. At the same time, the mistakes that were made following the merger of the Coles and Myer giants, though not fatal, are still affecting the company and are a lesson for all those who might attempt a similar exercise. With the new management team, there is enormous potential in the company for future profits.

The Coles company, which engineered the merger, had a very different heritage to Myer. It was run with a 'five and ten cents' mentality, first by the Coles family and, second, by a remarkable group of expansionist executives headed by Tom North, Bevan Bradbury and Quinn, who all started with the company early in their working lives and rose to the top. By contrast, the Myer family and their business operated in an upmarket environment. For the downmarket men at Coles to take over the prestigious Myer business had seemed impossible. But in 1985 the businesses came together as Coles Myer with Coles men taking the key positions.

Bradbury became chairman; Quinn chief executive and two more Coles executives who had started at the bottom, Graeme Seabrook and

Stucki, headed almost all the operational departments. The Coles executives wanted to run the company and be seen to be running it. But achieving the 'impossible' had a strange effect on many Coles executives. The task of managing a business three times the size of Coles required different skills and, although no one realised it at the time, the Coles management team was thin. For about eighteen months after the merger, the four-person operating team at the top of Coles Myer looked strong. Then, in August 1987, Bradbury retired as chairman. He could have been replaced by deputy chairman Bails Myer, but that would have resulted in the Coles team reporting to the head of the Myer family. The Coles people were still savouring their win and that was not an option.

As a result, Quinn took over as chairman and chief executive. At the time, many other chief executives also acted as chairmen of their companies, and the dangers of the dual role did not become apparent for several years. The job of chairman at Coles Myer was particularly demanding as the holders of half the company's equity stock sat at the board table, putting up plans for capital reorganisation and other ideas that required attention.

Quinn believed that if he took on the dual role he would have to appoint either Stucki or Seabrook to take charge of the group's retail operations. In such situations, whoever is passed over for the job normally leaves. It was a decision that Quinn had to get right. He chose the popular Stucki over the more prickly Seabrook who later left the company to move to Britain where he became chief executive of Kwik Save, a discount supermarket chain owned by Dairy Farms International (part of the Jardine Matheson group). The 770-store Kwik Save chain was recently named British retailer of 1992.

In little more than a year, the Coles management team of four had been halved and there were no obvious successors to Quinn in the ranks. But that fact was obscured in 1987–88 by the sheer power of Quinn, the boom in the Australian economy and soaring Coles Myer profits. Quinn seemed to have done everything right until then, but the boom concealed his first fundamental mistake. Stucki had a good record in the food sector, but was not the person to be managing director of the retail operations of a group as diverse as Coles Myer.

After the merger Quinn, Stucki and other former Coles executives spent a lot of time studying the new Myer business and, in particular, its department stores. Morale in the Myer stores was low but some beneficial fundamental changes had already been made. However, there was still a lot to be done to unify the cultures of the two companies and give the group a corporate identity. Soon after Bradbury retired as chairman, the company moved into its plush new Melbourne headquarters—a sharp contrast to the previous environment where executives walked through a store to get to their desks. Buoyed by the early success of the merged company, Coles Myer started preparations for extension into New Zealand and elsewhere.

The 'five and ten cents' era ended in the 1980s. By then, Coles Myer dominated every segment of Australian retailing and, in particular, had its foot firmly on the neck of Woolworths which was reeling from a succession of mistakes in the previous decade. Every Coles Myer executive who walked into his or her new office believed the company was invincible. The new complex, including the lavish quarters for the board and Quinn, seemed to confirm that invincibility. At the same time, enormous corporate energy—particularly from Quinn—was spent on creating a new company.

As a result, no one really worried when the ageing Paul Simons was recalled by Woolworths. Many years earlier, Simons had been regarded as an up and coming Woolworths executive. Unhappy with the way the company was progressing, he left to co-ordinate the successful establishment of Franklins in Australia. When Simons returned to Woolworths, he set up office at the company's warehouse at Yennora with a black phone and a wall air conditioner—the antithesis of Coles Myer's style. Simons started revamping the Woolworths merchandising policy, including placing greater emphasis on fresh foods and spending money updating the company's stores to give a new approach to super market retailing. He also lowered Woolworths prices to within 1% of those at Franklins stores.

Quinn's second mistake was allowing Woolworths to recover. In earlier times North, Bradbury and Quinn, as chief executives of Coles, lived and breathed the supermarket business. But as Simons went about introducing his changes, Quinn was looking the other way and Stucki didn't recognise the trap his wily opponent was setting for Coles Myer. Simons must have been stunned by the lack of response. Not only did Coles Myer not update its stores to match Woolworths, but in some cases, even increased prices in a bid to go 'upmarket'. Stucki imported an executive from the recently-acquired New Zealand operation to head the Coles Myer food business and oppose Simons. It was not a fair match. Inevitably, market share fell.

The K mart operation had been a jewel in the Coles crown throughout the 1970s and early 1980s. It was the result of work by a brilliant Coles team that opened up a new era of discount retailing. Coles outflanked Myer and its Target operation. There was great joy at K mart after the merger of Coles and Myer—perhaps K mart's rival, Target, could be acquired and made part of a new and wider network of K mart stores.

But Quinn's pride in the Coles victory was aimed at reviving, not killing, Myer businesses. Target was given a new lease of life under the team headed by Peter Wilkinson and Brian Beattie.

In contrast, at Target, boasting good technology and a clear sense of direction, Beattie took full advantage of a situation made for discount stores. Not only were customers looking for bargains, but manufacturers, desperate to stay in business, were prepared to sell cheaply. Moreover, local manufacturers were able to supply quickly those items that are subject to fickle fashions. Beattie was clever in mixing local buying with imports and keeping stock turnover high.

K mart outlets were carpeted, signs were changed and different merchandise introduced. Corporate historians will reflect that although the Coles executives won, those in the two great Coles businesses, K mart and food stores, forgot their heritage and reasons for success and started trying to emulate the company they had acquired. The reasons for this go beyond being influenced by the atmosphere of the group's plush new headquarters. Like the food stores, K mart had been heading in the wrong direction for several years before it became apparent to Quinn and his board.

Perhaps the sense of being part of Coles prevented K mart from adopting the simple but brilliantly effective Target technology developed by former Myer managers. Technology and buying systems had become vital to modern discount stores. But K mart believed that Target technology would be unsuitable by the year 2000 and aimed at establishing a better system. But K mart fell behind during the long program to develop new systems. It was only a matter of time before these fundamental mistakes at K mart had an effect on the firm's bottom line. For some time, K mart profits were merely sluggish, but on 12 March 1992 the company announced that they had been halved during the past year—a period when well-financed discount stores should have boomed.

K mart buyers made many mistakes. They hadn't understood that the essence of retailing is to keep stock turning over quickly. In a recession, that means being able to adapt to changes in consumer demand. But K mart buyers had been returning from overseas buying missions with huge volumes of stock that had been wrong for discount stores trading in a recession. K mart established a new distribution centre at Hoppers Crossing, Melbourne, which was, in theory, a sound move. But as the mountain of stock began to leave the wharves (often delayed), the new distribution system became clogged. The centre became a warehouse and extra space had to be rented. Getting rid of the stock caused big losses. Although it was clear in 1991 that something was wrong with K mart, the full extent of the problem did not become apparent to Quinn and his board until after August that year when Quinn gave former Grace Bros executive Bob Dalziel the job of ending Coles Myer's woes.

Although Coles' operations suffered from the merger, the former Myer operations blossomed under the touch of Quinn. Not only did Target emerge brilliantly from the merger, but Quinn had picked the right people to head the Myer and Grace Bros department stores, and they improved, at a time when they should have been under pressure from the recession, with profits continuing to rise. David Jones launched a major assault on Myer in the 1980s and seemed to be a much greater threat to the merged group than Woolworths. But Myer and Grace Bros department stores managed to hold off David Jones and are now close to dominating the department store sector, much as Coles food stores surpassed Woolworths in the mid-1980s.

In 1989 Quinn started to realise that his chosen successor, Stucki, was not the person to be operations manager of the group. Often, people in positions of great power do not admit their mistakes, but Quinn faced up to the problem. He abolished the position of managing director of the retail operation and had line managers report to him, giving him almost complete control of the company. About the same time, Lew became vice-chairman, while Bails Myer continued as deputy chairman.

The executive changes in 1989 had important repercussions. Overseas expansion plans had to be set aside, partly because the company did not have the management depth. The New Zealand exercise had been successful, but Quinn had already realised the drain an overseas venture—even one as near as NZ—could have on management time. Had Myer made a major purchase in the US at the top of the market in 1986–88, the Coles Myer story might not have had a happy ending.

Stucki, who had spent twenty-five years in food retailing before his elevation, was sent back to the food division to confront Woolworths and Franklins. But by this time, Woolworths was firing. Quinn had high hopes of Stucki repeating his previous success in the food store sector, but the Coles Myer food operation had its back to the wall. Stucki devised some excellent promotional schemes, including the computers-for-schools giveaway. New shoppers attracted by the scheme discovered Coles trailed its rivals, not only on price, but on store quality, too. Stucki followed the promotions by launching a price war.

It is now clear that Quinn did not deal with the fundamental issues facing Coles Myer. Coles supermarkets required a new approach to give them the sparkle Simons had introduced to Woolworths.

But the 1989 reshuffle involved more than transferring Stucki. It signalled the end of the dominance by the 'Coles boys' of the senior positions immediately below Quinn. Peter Wilkinson, who had helped set the foundations for the spectacular rise of Target, was put in charge of Coles Myer department stores. It was an excellent appointment. Beattie, who worked under Wilkinson at Target, grabbed the opportunity provided by the recession to become an aggressive discounter and to vigorously attack his competitors, some of whom went to the wall.

Although it was important for Quinn to place Coles executives in control of the retail arms after the merger, at the time he and Bradbury had realised that the Coles team lacked someone with the finance talents of Myer's finance director, John Barner. Not only did Barner win the respect of both sides in the merger but, during its successes and failures, Coles Myer has been financially well managed by him. Most of the present financial strength of the group stems from Barner's appointment. Barner also provided great assistance to Quinn in linking the management and the board. Among the shareholders represented at the Coles Myer board table, were the Myer family, Westfield, K mart of the US and Solomon Lew and, collectively, they controlled half the equity.

Bails Myer represented the increasingly diverse interests of the Myer family, which had reaped big gains from the merger at the expense of a loss of power. Frank Lowy and his Westfield group had a long association with Myer and were potentially long-term investors until losses in the media industry forced them to take their profits and leave. K mart has never been active in the management of the company and, a little like the Myer family, has stayed in because of the rewards and the fact that their name is an important brand for the company.

Lew had a long-held dream to head the company, but in the 1980s Quinn's reign seemed likely to extend well into the 1990s. Coles and Myer had a history of executive-dominated boards and the early Coles Myer boards were similarly structured. Gradually, the composition of the board changed with the appointment of people well known to Lew, such as the ANZ Bank's Will Bailey and transport magnate Lindsay Fox.

Lew's appointment as vice-chairman in 1989 was a signal he was heading for the chairmanship. As vice-chairman, he had a much greater mandate to visit the group's various operations and talk to executives. Quinn was in an unusual position. A chairman and chief executive can normally relinquish the chief executive officer's job and remain chairman. But Quinn had not trained a successor. The man he had selected had been returned to divisional head in 1989. Perhaps Quinn saw the inevitable and didn't move quickly to promote a successor and work to remain chairman. Indeed, much of his attention was occupied by his retirement package, and at the 1991 annual meeting, Quinn's superannuation package was underwritten against any tax changes. When Quinn finally stepped down on 24 July 1992, he took with him a very substantial sum. There was no penalty in leaving early.

Quinn and Lew had come to similar conclusions in 1991 about the Coles Myer direction: the company had to overhaul K mart and Coles food stores and Quinn, in his last year as CEO was not the right person to do it. Lew became co-chairman and started running board meetings. It was proposed to institutionalise the co-chairman's role, but Quinn stepped down remaining only as chief executive for the months leading up to his retirement. Quinn's retirement was announced along with a virtually steady profit—a good achievement given the recession and the K mart disaster.

Although K mart's earnings were slashed, the chain maintained its sales base. Similarly, the damage to the Coles food stores' sales had been arrested, while the group's department stores and Target were going well. The company was in good shape with much greater potential than either Coles or Myer had boasted as separate operations.

During the opening of the new Coles Myer headquarters at Tooronga, Melbourne, in 1987, Quinn said: 'What we have done is to simply lay the foundations for the future. It's a future with no bounds.'

Early in 1991 Brian Quinn was at the zenith of his power at Coles Myer. He was chairman, chief executive and chief operating officer of the group. No other business executive in Australia had so much power. In March 1992 Quinn and the man he chose to promote in the 1980s, Russell Stucki, announced their retirements. On the following day, about 400 Coles Myer executives gave Quinn a standing ovation as he stood alongside Lew, the new chairman. Those executives were witnessing the start of a new era in Australian retailing as the Lew family took over the mantle once carried by the Coles and Myer families who gave the company its name. Lew made it clear to the executives that he was looking for growth.

The start of the Lew era

The Lew family has become the most powerful retail family Australia has had. For generations the Australian retail industry has been dominated by families—Coles, Myer, Grace, David Jones, Horderns, Waltons and so on. Even at the peak of their influence, none of the families went close to controlling an empire that absorbs about 20% of Australian retail spending.

Solomon Lew (through his family company and the listed Premier Investments) now controls an $800-million investment in Coles Myer —the biggest individually controlled investment in an Australian public company.

Lew, 47, was made managing director of his family's Voyager Solo clothing company at the age of eighteen after his father died. He greatly improved the business, but by far his best decision was to spend $32 million in 1983 buying about 10% of Myer when the shares were depressed.

He accepted the Coles cash and share exchange offer in 1985 and used the cash to buy more shares, thus becoming a major shareholder in the merged company. He joined the other big holders, the Myer family, K mart of the US and Frank Lowy's Westfield, as the so-called 'Kings of Coles Myer'. When the merger settled down it was clear that of those four shareholders, the Lew family was the most stable. When the Westfield holding came on the market, Lew's Premier Investments was able to buy it. It is likely that during the next ten years at least one of the other two holdings will come on the market. K mart executives are no long directly on the Coles Myer board and the Myer family no longer has unity of purpose as increasing numbers of descendants get a stake. Lew's Voyager Solo family company, probably Australia's biggest manufacturer and importer of garments, is the family's cash powerhouse and it has funded the exercise. Voyager Solo owns 10% of Coles Myer and the public company, Premier Investments (about 30% owned by Lew), about 6.7%.

After the merger, Lew dreamed that one day his family might inherit a position similar to Simcha (Sidney) Baevski Myer, founder of the Myer empire, and his descendants. But it didn't seem likely given Brian Quinn's domination of the company. Lew, who values his privacy, also knew that chairmanship of Coles Myer would bring constraints on his non-Coles Myer activities and more public exposure.

But as events took their unexpected turns Lew is now very much in control. The new management structure and the key appointments all have his stamp. Suddenly, the problems in K mart and food that drove him to take a more active role are now advantages. For example, at K mart and Coles food stores it is possible to repair the damage and achieve profit growth without depending on the rate of economic recovery. There is little doubt that Woolworths managing director Paul Simons, who was running rings around Coles Myer, finds the combination of Lew, Peter Wilkinson and Brian Beattie much more formidable in food.

Lew's Voyager Solo group probably supplies more clothing and other goods to Woolworths than to Coles Myer and Simons and Lew each have a respect for the other. Lew has said publicly that he wants to revamp the Sydney and Melbourne department stores along the lines of Brisbane, Adelaide and Perth, where modern department stores have proved highly successful. In March 1992 he addressed the Securities Institute under the title 'Coles Myer Potential Unlimited', mapping out the program ahead for analysts.

A key point of the Lew plan is the management structure. He will head the board as chairman and appoint a chief executive. Lew will concentrate on company policy and non-retail areas such as property, leaving Wilkinson, the chief operating officer (retail), free to concentrate on running the retail businesses. This was essentially the structure Quinn chose after Bevan Bradbury retired as Coles Myer chairman in 1987, without the combination of the posts of chairman and chief executive.

The appointment of chief executive is important for future policy rather than day-to-day retail operations. Lew and the Coles Myer board chose former Foster's managing director Peter Bartels. Coles upper management ranks are thin and a lot of responsibility is on the shoulders of people such as Wilkinson, Beattie, K mart managing director Robert Dalziel and the new managing director of department stores, Michael Howell. Nevertheless, there are some talented executives rising through the department stores and the company is confident it has the people to sustain the momentum.

The priority will be to fix problems in the Australian operations, but when they are under control Bartels will look at plans to expand overseas or Australia and have the staff recruited to implement those plans.

Although a lot of emphasis is placed on the Coles Myer problems, the company is in a strong position. Despite profit being stagnant for four years, the gearing ratio (liabilities to tangible assets) has declined to 54%. The group has an incredible 3.2 million square metres of selling space in Australia with department stores and supermarkets each holding about 28%, K mart 23%, Target 13% and specialty stores 8%. Although about 50% of this space (K mart and food stores) is not performing to expectations, the company still has a sales base of more than $15 billion.

The department stores have shown what can be done with good management. Lew is setting high sales and growth targets for the group, believing the group's $15-billion sales base can reach $25 billion over five or six years as Coles Myer starts to take advantage of its power and premium retail sites. At the same time, more of the sales revenue should be returned for the bottom line as stock turnover and market share are increased.

Those goals, the management structure and the recent appointments, are very much Lew's decisions in conjunction with the other non-executive directors on the board. The 1990s and beyond will go down as the Lew family era of Coles Myer as its new chairman tries to finally take advantage of the opportunities the 1985 merger created.

Postscript to Coles Myer

Solomon Lew's reign at Coles Myer is likely to have a big effect on Australian commercial life, not only because of the way he came to power and his passionate desire to see Coles Myer succeed, but also because of his cash-generating family company, Voyager Solo. Although most clothing groups have been cutting back on manufacturing, Lew has realised that local makers of fashion goods have a big advantage over imports. Whereas imported goods need to be ordered many months in advance and face the vagaries of Australia's wharves, flexible local operations can supply their customers at relatively short notice. Retailers using the latest technology can now closely monitor demand and order new stocks of fast-moving items. Accordingly, they enjoy much higher stock turnover and profits. Voyager Solos' customers include a myriad small boutiques as well as Woolworths and Coles Myer. Voyager Solo's manufacturing business has doubled in each of the four years to 1992. Because K mart took a different view to its chairman and opted to buy vast volumes of imported goods, K mart has suffered the consequences: big stock write-downs and low stock turnover. Target, on the other hand, calling it right has had its managing director promoted.

Lew will be very careful to stay at arms length in any dealings Voyager has with Coles Myer. But the fact that over-reliance on imports has badly burned a section of the company at a time when its chairman was taking his own business away from importing, will not be lost on the group's executives. That means it is time for local businesses to again approach K mart and other retailers that have become hooked on imports.

Local manufacturing only works if the operator is flexible and can produce top-quality goods quickly to cater for swings in demand. Like so many other businesses, manufacturing companies need to tailor their operations to the needs of their customers. Once they do, they may find surprising advantages over lower-cost imports. On the other hand, some big retailers such as Coles Myer have often levied charges on new products, and these have motivated more innovative local suppliers to sell elsewhere.

The Premier issue

Part of Solomon Lew's reign at Coles Myer is supported by the public company Premier Investments, which he founded in 1987 before the stockmarket crash. Premier did not commit its cash to the market in the months before that October debacle, and so was in a wonderful position to partner Voyager Solo in its Coles Myer exercise in 1989. Premier bought Westfield's holding in the retail chain, and took a stake in FAI Insurances. It also owns Housewares International, which is a big importer of homeware products. Its brands include Cristal D'Arques and Arcopal, and it operates in Australia and the US. The Premier group also has about $170 million in cash.

But the sharemarket has never taken to Lew's investment vehicle, partly because the interest on its borrowings has caused it to incur losses. The company's share price has been about $1.15, compared with an asset backing of about $2.

Kerry Packer had a slice of Premier Investments but sold his parcel to Lloyd Williams of Hudson Conway as part of the rationalisation of his holdings in early 1992. In the longer term, no one who is as successful as Lew likes to have his public investment vehicle at such a big discount to asset backing.

Lew's chairmanship of Coles Myer began at a time when Coles Myer's overconfidence has been tempered by its mistakes. These mistakes have not harmed its basic strength but, rather, taught every executive that size on its own is not sufficient. We now have a giant that almost thinks it is an underdog with something to prove.

The lessons Bartels brings to Coles Myer

When Peter Bartels walked into Brian Quinn's old job as CEO of Coles Myer, he brought with him a vast number of lessons from the Foster's debacle. When Elders acquired Carlton & United Breweries it discovered unique beer-making technology, and Peter Bartels set about making overseas acquisitions so it could apply that technology to greatest benefit.

It was a brilliant strategy, but Elders thought it could apply the same principle to its other Australian operations by converting them into international ventures. Unfortunately, these moves were not as well conceived and the group found itself expanding on too many fronts at once.

Just as importantly, John Elliott and his accountants mixed Elders' trading and capital profits, and believed a price/earnings ratio could be applied as if the profits had all been derived from trading. The mistake was not just confined to the Elders–Fosters group. The accounting profession around the world is intent on pushing capital profits above the line. And although this tells shareholders the change in the equity value of their businesses during any one year, if wrongly interpreted it can lead to some very poor conclusions on trading strength.

So, with hindsight, we now know that when John Elliott's Harlin bid $3 a share for Elders two years ago, the company was headed into receivership. Fortunately, because Harlin was in desperate trouble, it began selling Elders assets as quickly as possible. Had Elliott's bid not been swamped with shares, Elders might have waited a year or two before starting to sell and, on discovering its plight, might have gone the same way as the companies headed by John Spalvins, Christopher Skase and Alan Bond.

Elders had $8 billion of borrowings and many of the assets it sold then would now be unsaleable. This would have forced it to unload Foster's at a fraction of its present value—just as Spalvins was forced to sell Penfolds to SA Brewing for a song.

Bartels won his reputation at Foster's after thrashing the Bond beer operation and helping establish Foster's as a global brand. But when the Bond breweries, Castlemaine Tooheys and Swan, came under the control of Doug Myers at New Zealand's Lion Nathan it was a different story. Bartels was spending most of his time on the internal politics of Foster's as John Elliott desperately tried to keep some value in his investment.

Doug Myers couldn't believe his good fortune, especially as he paid more than $2 billion for Castlemaine Tooheys, or $500 million more than Ross Wilson at SA Brewing was prepared to offer. Using the Tooheys brand, he took the challenge up to Foster's on its home turf, Melbourne, in the process creating a national brand to rival the Foster's brands.

One aspect of the affair that could prove particularly significant is the way Carlton & United in recent years has failed to keep on the best of terms with its main customers—the publicans. Top management and the board certainly did not mean this to happen, but it is hard for companies in near monopoly situations to maintain a zeal among their troops to keep customers happy. A business rule that will be paramount in the 1990s is: identify the needs of customers and work the business around them.

In the 1950s and 1960s, possibly even farther back, Carlton & United breweries treated publicans in a way a monopoly supplier might be expected to act. Then, in the 1960s, came the Courage launch in Victoria that was backed by several leading publicans. CUB's board surprised everybody in 1967 by appointing, as general manager, Brian Breheny, a superb marketer. He began advertising CUB products on television and, in doing so, developed CUB's long-standing tie-up with the advertising agency George Patterson. More importantly, Breheny began wooing the publicans, assuaging their resentment toward CUB.

Peter Bartels knows what it is like to be on top and challenged while being side-tracked in boardroom politics. That's what makes his appointment at Coles Myer so fascinating.

THE DUMPING OF PETER ABELES

THE JUNE sun shone brilliantly on the snow-covered peaks above Aspen, Colorado, the ski town—near Rupert Murdoch's retreat—where 130 News Corp executives gathered from around the world to discuss issues affecting their company. It was the first time in three years the News Corp managing director had brought his key executives together for a conference. The delay between meetings was partly a reflection of the difficult period the company had been going through, but the crisis was over and in 1992 it was time to plan for the future.

The conference hit the headlines when the recently-appointed head of Fox Television was sacked for hiring a male stripper to illustrate his case on censorship to an audience of visiting dignitaries that included the then US Secretary of Defence Dick Cheney.

But the real drama of Aspen 1992 never hit the headlines. For the first time since Aspen conferences began, the subject of Ansett and, consequently, Rupert Murdoch's relationship with TNT managing director Sir Peter Abeles, was on the agenda for discussion among the very senior people at the conference. Murdoch had rarely allowed News Corp's 50% partnership with TNT in Ansett and associated ventures to be debated at length because, although Murdoch was joint chief executive of the company, Ansett was Abeles' territory.

The relationship would have been unworkable if it had been dragged into News Corp executive debates. Moreover, the Abeles relationship had delivered News Corp cash and profits beyond Murdoch's wildest dreams. Indeed, the strength and breadth of News Corp, as well as the jobs of many of those attending Aspen, could be indirectly attributed to that contribution from Abeles and Ansett.

But the young turks at News Corp reckoned urgent change was required at Ansett. Abeles may have delivered in the past, but at 68 he was getting too old. He had made serious mistakes in recent times that had left News Corp dangerously exposed to further big losses and the need to inject funds. In addition Abeles' great friend, Bob Hawke, had been deposed as Prime Minister, so their partner no longer had the ear of the Government.

When new PM Paul Keating wanted to maximise the value of the Government's Qantas/Australian Airlines holding, he took the extra value out of Abeles' and, consequently, News Corp's hide. Ansett was to be hit hard because, although it was allowed to fly overseas, there were restrictions on its potential air routes and competition from a very powerful Australian Airlines/Qantas combination. (Two years earlier, when Australian Airlines was to be floated separately, Qantas had offered to buy into Ansett, but the offer was rejected.) To make matters worse, Ansett was facing the current crisis greatly weakened by big losses as a result of the pilots dispute and deregulation.

The young turks wanted Abeles kicked upstairs or, at the very least, they wanted Ansett's general manager, Graeme McMahon, removed and big associated changes at the airline.

Abeles must have known that Murdoch would be under pressure to go along with his younger executives. Abeles knew he had made big mistakes and that his back was now to the wall; however, Ansett's position was better than press reports had indicated.

At 68, Abeles was around the same age as his predccessor, Sir Reginald Ansett, had been when the late Robert Holmes à Court challenged him. Reg Ansett had anointed Holmes à Court as his successor and at one time Holmes à Court sat in Ansett's office. But Ansett later changed his mind and Holmes à Court sold his stake. In December 1980 Murdoch was given the job in the belief that 'young Rupert', whom Ansett had nursed as a baby, would never link up with Reg's great enemy, Peter Abeles. But Ansett was wrong, and in a little more than a week Abeles and Murdoch were joint chief executives of the airline. Ansett, at the age of 70, was given the title of chairman, but had no power. He retired to his home at Mount Eliza, south of Melbourne, minus the helicopter that had become a familiar sight ferrying him to and from the office. He died two years later.

Abeles could well have been destined for a similar fate once the niceties were out of the way, but he would have put up a fight. If he stepped down from Ansett, there would be pressure for a similar decision at TNT. The irony would not have been lost on Abeles, especially as rumours of his ill-health were widespread in the lead-up to Aspen.

Peter Abeles had to step down as TNT managing director four months later, but at Aspen Murdoch declared to his executives that Abeles had been too good to the News Corporation group to be cast aside—at least at that time. For Abeles, back in Australia, Murdoch's stand confirmed his faith in human nature—or in Murdoch, at least. Personal loyalty used to be a linchpin of business but in today's performance-oriented world, it is becoming rare. Nevertheless, there are few greater debts than that owed by Murdoch to Abeles.

Reasons for loyalty

It all started during the 1970s, when Murdoch set out to get a television network in Australia. The Nine and Seven networks were not available and Ten was partly owned by Ansett. Not long after News Corp and TNT got control of Ansett, Abeles agreed to sell Channel Ten in Melbourne to Murdoch for a little more than $10 million. Murdoch was later to joke that he had to buy half an airline to get it.

After Murdoch had bought Ansett's Ten television interests, he was inclined to sell his half of the airline. The story goes that Murdoch phoned Abeles as Murdoch was about to leave the US for Australia, offering his Ansett stake to TNT. Abeles agreed to buy at a price, but he also told Murdoch he was foolish to sell, because the rewards would be huge. He urged Murdoch to reconsider. On the flight, Murdoch thought long and hard and when Abeles met him at Sydney airport he had changed his mind. The rewards Abeles delivered were much higher than anything he had promised in that pre-flight phone call.

Ansett alone generated profits of about $900 million in the 1980s, of which News Corp was entitled to half. Abeles' management of Ansett in the early years was superb and TAA, as Australian Airlines was then known, was not prepared for a new-style foe. Abeles, as a road transport operator and a master of the market share game, thrived in the regulated environment and the cash rolled in.

Meanwhile, Murdoch built up the Ten network and then sold it to Frank Lowy's Westfield group in February 1987 for a staggering $800 million. And who arranged the sale? None other than Peter Abeles. By selling the Ten network at that price Murdoch was easily able to pay for the Herald & Weekly Times, which gave him a strong capital base in his own country.

But the relationship between Murdoch and Abeles was not all one-way. Murdoch introduced some very profitable deals to Ansett and his support helped Abeles at a time when the transport man was under attack, particularly by the now defunct weekly newspaper, the National Times.

The strong Ansett earnings were very helpful to Murdoch, who was expanding in Britain during the early 1980s, and bonded the relationship between the two men. Then, in 1985, Abeles came up with an idea for which Murdoch would be eternally grateful: Ansett Worldwide Aviation Services (AWAS). Ansett had been involved in used-aircraft leasing in Australia almost since Abeles and Murdoch joined forces, but now AWAS would extend the group into a massive international business: leasing new aircraft.

Abeles' idea came just as Murdoch was gambling his whole empire on the belief that he could set up a fourth television network in the US. Even Murdoch's closest supporters were stunned that Murdoch, having come so far, was prepared once more to risk everything on a new venture. Murdoch's faith in Abeles' ability to deliver was now very strong, so he incorporated the News Corp share of AWAS directly into the Fox television group. That meant AWAS profits would cushion the losses of starting up the network. Of course, if Abeles got it wrong, those losses would have ballooned.

Abeles and Murdoch organised the AWAS capital structure so that although its earnings would go into Fox and TNT in the US, neither balance sheet would be affected because the Ansett company provided the necessary guarantees. AWAS was no ordinary leasing venture. It made money on straight leasing transactions, but the big profits were generated by arranging the purchase of aircraft at a low price then incorporating them into a lease contract at much higher prices. The low purchase prices were achieved by bulk buying and good negotiating in a rising international aircraft market. During that crucial time for Murdoch, AWAS made about $450 million, of which half went to Fox, reducing its losses and allowing it to achieve success faster.

That success encouraged Murdoch to take another big risk: expanding Sky TV in Britain. Once again, he is on the winning side. News Corp was in deep trouble with its bankers eighteen months ago and Abeles was able to find some extra cash in the Ansett empire to help out. Without AWAS and Ansett at crucial times, it might have been a different story for News Corp. Of course, TNT also was expanding during the 1980s and received the same assistance as News Corp, but it contributed much more in management time.

Yet during those years of plenty, Abeles was sowing the seeds that would germinate at Aspen a decade later. He was falling into a trap that all executives need to avoid: he believed he could not be beaten and he lost respect for his opponent. So, when TAA introduced business class in 1982, Abeles did not follow. Many of his executives, including marketers such as Tom Dery, are said to have opposed the decision. For some years it seemed as though Abeles was right.

Abeles' great friend, Bob Hawke, became Prime Minister in 1983. Curiously, Abeles spoke to Hawke less frequently after he became Prime Minister, but the conversations were more significant because Abeles was one of the people Hawke used as a sounding board. Few in the Australian business community were more influential than Abeles. Later, Abeles was a witness to Hawke's famous stepping-down pact with Keating.

While Abeles' responsibilities at TNT were increasing, doubtless he felt honoured to be a sounding board for the Prime Minister and gave matters careful consideration. However, the prospect of huge AWAS profits, plus the continued prosperity of Ansett, made it all seem too easy. Abeles became overconfident, many say arrogant.

A fundamental change took place at TAA after James Strong took over and changed its name to Australian Airlines. With the name change came a remarkable motivation campaign for the staff. Ansett watched Australian copy some of its better ideas and, with the benefit of Ansett's experience, do it better. In many ways Abeles' early successes made him less willing to delegate, but the consequent pressures on him made him vulnerable to error. So, although Abeles' whole life had been dedicated to gaining market share, he watched Ansett's decline, not appreciating the seriousness of the situation.

Abeles bought Eastwest Airlines, which was a threat to both Ansett and Australian. If deregulation came, it might have been a launching pad for a third airline. Ansett moved on Eastwest but it was not to prosper under the Ansett umbrella. One reason given was that the aircraft chosen for it suited AWAS rather than Eastwest. Abeles, however, would oppose that view vigorously.

A second serious blunder occurred in New Zealand, where TNT had a close link with Brierley Investments, each owning half of the trans-Tasman Union Shipping Group Limited. Brierley suggested that Ansett come to New Zealand, but there was no firm deal for a joint airline venture. Abeles saw the potential of operating domestic air services in both Australia and New Zealand and eventually connecting the two, but detailed estimates were not carried out, nor was any account taken of how the dominant carrier, Air New Zealand, might respond to a challenge. Air New Zealand upgraded its services substantially and then the New Zealand recession hit, sending Ansett's New Zealand operations into heavy losses. Meanwhile, Brierley Investments had its own internal revolution and ended up on Air New Zealand's side.

In 1987, the Government announced the two-airline policy would end in 1990. By that time, middle-ranking executives in Ansett were said to be unhappy about Abeles' failure to appreciate the threat posed by Strong's Australian Airlines and the lack of a long-term plan. Ansett did a variety of studies (as did Australian) about what deregulation would mean, but essentially, the company went into deregulation ill-prepared.

Abeles finally admitted his error in ignoring Strong's threat, and moved to rectify it. But before there was a chance to take advantage of the new seating arrangements, the pilots dispute hit. Then came deregulation and Compass, the new cut-price airline. Abeles joined the price war with Compass in a way that slashed his overall yields and sent the company deep into the red. There was little attempt to manage the number of discount seats available and to introduce a sophisticated yield policy because Abeles had not set out a clear strategy to cope with the change and had not delegated enough authority to allow executives to do it themselves. He also substantially upgraded Ansett's first-class and business-class seating; this, at least initially, further hit his yields as the discount price war sent many business passengers to the back of the aircraft to take advantage of the low prices.

Abeles has always been good at assessing a situation and making a decision. He applied that principle to buying aircraft and the end result was a series of purchases with no apparent overall plan. Ansett and its various arms have ended up with a multitude of aircraft types, making running costs higher than they should be.

Australian Airlines' costs tended to be lower than Ansett's because it had fewer aircraft and it attempted to retain a business class with three seats grouped instead of two, as in Ansett business class. In the end Australian was forced to follow its competitor, which showed Abeles had won market share.

The losses Ansett incurred after deregulation made it clear that the kind of profits enjoyed in the 1980s would not return for a long time. At the same time, the AWAS bonanza was ending with the collapse of the international aircraft market. But News Corp's British satellite television operation was headed towards success and TNT's joint venture with European post offices also was looking good. Instead of being the saviour, Ansett was now the problem.

There is nothing more devastating for a company operating deep in loss—$2.2 billion in debt—than to find its opponent is about to gain a great advantage. That is what happened when the Government announced that Qantas would take over Australian Airlines. This forced Ansett to end its domestic passenger carrying service for Qantas and to compete against a domestic airline that had the advantage of a strong international operation. At the same time, although Ansett was given the opportunity to become an international airline, Qantas moved to make that harder, by tying up overseas routes and even making it difficult for Ansett to fly the Tasman. Ansett's losses in 1991–92 totalled close to $100 million, even though Compass had been out of the market for half the year.

As the Aspen meeting approached, a 1992–93 loss was expected and a revived Compass was emerging with lower costs than the original. The case mounted by News Corp's young turks—that Abeles had blown it and that News Corp might be required to inject substantial sums into Ansett—was a strong one. If Murdoch was not prepared to get tough with Abeles, then at least general manager Graeme McMahon had to go. The prevailing view at Aspen was that although Abeles should remain, News Corp should look for a way out of Ansett, which had served its purpose. News Corp's Australian chief Ken Cowley should take a closer interest in the situation.

It is now more than ten years since Abeles, in that pre-flight phone call, talked Murdoch into staying with Ansett, but age has not dented Abeles' powers of persuasion. He was prepared to admit that during the previous eighteen months, while he was negotiating the TNT post office deal in Europe, he had not spent enough time looking at Ansett. But now it would be his number one priority. As luck would have it, Ansett went into the black in June and earnings began to rise. The trend continued in July and August looked good. Abeles pointed out to News Corp that he now had a really professional team at Ansett managing yields and income on a day-to-day basis. As demand rose, there was no intention of matching it with extra capacity but rather profits would be allowed to rise with higher yields.

The balance sheet has shown too much borrowing, but about $1.6 billion of the $2.25 billion in Ansett debt is secured on aircraft and that will halve over four years with cash generation. Another $650 million is in general debt, but the company has about $400 million of assets not essential to the business that can be sold. No new aircraft are planned for domestic routes until 1996, so cashflow can be used for debt reduction. The group is gradually disposing of AWAS leases in order to lessen the pressure on Ansett of guarantees. But a domestic airline facing an opponent that is operating internationally needs more than just debt-reduction and a trading turnaround.

As Ansett sees it, the first glimmer of opportunity in the Keating measures came in the way the deal was structured. These days Abeles and the Ansett people have a healthy respect for the abilities of the executive administration of Australian Airlines and John Schaap, its managing director at the time of the merger announcement. Ansett is relieved that Australian Airlines did not buy Qantas. The plan to shift most of the Australian Airlines administration to the Qantas offices in Sydney means that the Australian Airlines team could well go through the trauma of being a takeover victim. In addition, it will not be easy to master the industrial relations aspects of the deal, given the differences in the Qantas and Australian Airlines awards. On the other hand John Schaap has worked tirelessly to try and stop Australian Airlines being minced. It will be well into 1993 or 1994 before we know how the merger really works out.

Ansett staff once looked at those working for Australian Airlines with envy. Now the roles are reversed. Ansett realises it has the excitement ahead of creating a new international airline, whereas its competitors face an uncertain time until the situation settles, and this might take two or three years. The Ansett camp reckons there must be a good chance that Qantas/Australian Airlines' problems will provide short-term opportunities.

However, with its arrangement to carry Qantas passengers domestically ended, Ansett needs to reorganise its overseas airline links. A close alliance with Air New Zealand makes a lot of sense because both sides would get a huge boost in New Zealand by rationalisation. Air New Zealand has been interested in an Australian domestic base and had discussions with Compass before its collapse. But Qantas owns 19.9% of Air New Zealand and is unlikely to agree to Air New Zealand joining the Ansett camp. Brierley may well find it attractive to swap Air New Zealand shares for Qantas-AA shares if it is allowed to. Brierley has always strenuously denied it is warehousing its 35% stake in Air New Zealand for Qantas.

Ansett's view is that, irrespective of what happens with Air New Zealand, the Qantas/Australian deal means that Ansett becomes the only domestic carrier with sufficient size for international airlines outside the Qantas ring to deal with. Of course, should the new Compass grow as planned, it would be in a similar position. At the same time, it is becoming inevitable that Australia and New Zealand will allow much more travel across the Tasman and Ansett will participate in that. Its New Zealand domestic arm will become more valuable.

The real game, therefore, is not so much New Zealand, but the establishment of an Asia-Pacific regional airline. Ansett sees the Qantas advantages in a very different light from the way they have been presented in the press. Qantas has five-year rights over the number of flights to particular destinations, negotiated before February 1992. But rights to additional flights to the same destinations, negotiated since then, carry only a three-year tenure and if those rights are not used they will disappear. Ansett believes that these three-year tenure rights represent a great opportunity, because it will take Ansett two or three years to establish the facilities and connections for an overseas airline. It hopes that within about three years it will be able to fly to most of the important cities of the region: Bangkok, Singapore, Taipei, Hong Kong, Tokyo and Seoul.

So, for the first time since the early 1980s, Abeles has a clear strategic goal for Ansett to work towards instead of spot decisions aimed at making money. Even the lavish expenditure on domestic terminals that are much bigger than required for present capacity has the potential to make sense rather than being another drain on the company. Nevertheless, Ansett will need to overcome enormous hurdles, including the Government's desire to make Qantas successful so it can get the best price, Ansett's mix of aircraft in the domestic market, the need for capital to develop an overseas airline, and the hazards of airline route negotiation. But the challenge is there.

The decision that Ken Cowley should fill Murdoch's shoes as joint managing director of Ansett was not part of the Aspen deliberations; it was taken later. On taking the post, Cowley committed News Corp to developing Ansett and endorsing the position of Graeme McMahon. Indeed, Cowley became excited about the possibility of creating a regional airline. But having two managing directors only works if one is silent and Cowley was not the silent type. To make matters more difficult McMahon was an 'Abeles man' and Abeles was no longer head of TNT. Relations cooled and the young turks who lost at Aspen got a second chance.

And if a substantial offer for News Corp's stake comes from an unexpected source, the pressure will be on from the young turks to grab it.

Murdoch's family fortune

Never in Australia's history has one family accumulated so much wealth over twelve months as have the Murdochs. By any measure, $1.56 billion is an enormous increase. Expressed another way, it is $178 000 an hour, based on 24 hours a day, 365 days a year. You don't need a vivid imagination to hear the cries for new taxes and new restrictions to limit such accumulation of wealth when there are unemployed in the streets. Yet the rise in the number of unemployed in this recession, as in previous ones, is closely linked to the fall in private wealth, which plays a key role in employment. New people will only be hired when businesses are sure of their basic survival and can see a potential increase in their wealth.

The most important feature of the Murdochs' wealth accumulation is that although the family is based in Australia the main success has been achieved abroad. Indeed, in order to facilitate expansion and thus generate wealth, the head of the business, Rupert Murdoch, has had to adopt US citizenship. Many Australian fortunes will be linked in the future to international business, so Australia's taxation, government and employment rules will need to be in tune with the rest of the world, or we will not get the normal benefits that flow from greater wealth generation.

Murdoch discovered a low-cost, high-circulation publishing formula on the streets of Sydney in the 1950s and 1960s. When he exported this formula to Britain, it formed the base of his huge media empire.

Many people, when they have accumulated enough wealth to last them and their families a lifetime, tend to take it easy. But Murdoch has been constantly prepared to risk the family's entire empire on the next achievement. The family has gone along with this policy, sometimes reluctantly. Thus, his fledgling Adelaide base was put on the line when he went to Sydney to take over the *Mirror*; the whole lot was put on the line when he went to Britain; it was the same story when he launched the Fox television network in the US with the aid of, dare we say, junk bonds; and, finally, the empire was put at risk again with the launch of the Sky European television service.

Those final gambles might not have been possible but for the period of unlimited credit that world banks were offering during the 1980s. Past *BRW* rich lists are full of people who availed themselves of that period of bank madness and later lost everything. Murdoch went close; no one could ever forget the personal approaches he made to his bankers, asking for more time to pay. And banks are unlikely to repeat their unlimited credit for a long time. But Rupert came through, News Corporation shares skyrocketed—and with them the Murdoch family fortune. Of course, if something goes wrong and the shares fall, the fortune will decline as quickly as it rose; Murdoch's bets are not hedged.

Risk-taking must always be a part of a vibrant capital society and inevitably there will be winners as well as losers. In Murdoch's case the biggest loser is possibly the Sydney stockbroker who, having short-sold shares in the Bond and Spalvins empires, went for broke on Murdoch and is now a much poorer man. The business communities in Australia, Britain and the US are studded with people who underestimated Rupert Murdoch.

CHAPTER 4

More Lessons From Business

THE BANKING, finance and insurance industries provided some of the great casualties and losses of the 1980s. But out of those mistakes is coming a new look at board and management procedures that will benefit the business community.

THE TRICONTINENTAL TIME BOMB

LATE IN 1984, a month after he was appointed chief executive of the State Bank of Victoria, Bill Moyle made the best decision of his life: to sell the State Bank's 26% interest in Tricontinental. Moyle made the decision without realising that all the elements were already in place to bring about Australia's biggest corporate disaster and whoever bought Tricontinental would be acquiring a time bomb.

In September 1984 the State Bank's partners in Tricontinental included Rural & Industry Bank of WA, Security Pacific of the US, Credit Lyonnais, Mitsui Bank and Sir Ian Potter. Mitsui and Credit Lyonnais were both seeking Australian banking licences in Australia and were potential bidders for Tricontinental. Mitsui told the Tricontinental board that it would buy out the other shareholders. But it made the wise move of calling in Touche Ross to survey the acquisition target first.

The Touche Ross report was a brilliant document because it went right to the heart of the Tricontinental problem, which was already beginning to emerge. It revealed that:

> Tricontinental had several major client groups whose loans constitute a major portion of the company's portfolio.
>
> A significant amount of total loans is provided to the Jewish community, and in loans for property development.
>
> There are a number of loans which have been in arrears for some time and

which have not been closed because of concern that action may endanger the underlying security.

Information on loans, particularly those loans in arrears, is not always completely documented on the files and significant reliance must be placed on senior staff.

Mitsui realised it did not have the ability to fix the situation and saw the trap. Mitsui withdrew and Bill Moyle, realising that Tricontinental could suffer severe consequences but not appreciating the significance of the Touche Ross report, switched from being a seller to a buyer.

On 20 March 1985 Moyle went to the then Victorian Treasurer, Rob Jolly, and explained that the bank was prepared to buy all of Tricontinental. Jolly expressed surprise at Mitsui's decision but agreed that the State Bank stepping in was the 'proper course in the circumstances'. Neither Moyle nor Jolly realised that they had both just committed one of the biggest errors in Australian business history.

With remarkable foresight, the man who was to be appointed chairman of Tricontinental, Neil Smith, raised with the State Bank board 'the frightening aspect' that if one of the major Tricontinental loans failed, the company would be in a 'negative situation'—with liabilities exceeding assets. However, it seems that neither the board, nor even Smith himself, appreciated the significance of his observation and directors appeared to believe that the appointment of retired State Bank executive Jack Ryan to replace Geoffrey Redenbach as managing director of Tricontinental would solve any problem.

The royal commission on Tricontinental reveals that each of the directors of the State Bank had different reasons for wanting to buy Tricontinental. The board never came to grips with these differences. Moyle's appointment to the State Bank was part of a plan to widen its role in commercial banking, a move some directors believed should have been accelerated. Others thought Tricontinental was being bought below asset backing and could be sold later at a profit. Because the board did not set out clear objectives in the purchase, conflicts were to arise between the State Bank's chairman and chief executive that were not explained to the directors.

The key decision the State Bank board needed to face was how the new acquisition of one of Australia's largest merchant banks should be managed. Moyle wanted the Tricontinental board to include State Bank and Tricontinental executives, who would report to the full State Bank board. He believed the State Bank divisional heads would then be able to exercise direct control over functional areas of Tricontinental. In other words, Moyle would control it.

He expressed his views to State Bank chairman Arnold Hancock, who responded that the nomination of directors was 'his prerogative'. Hancock wanted a very different composition of the Tricontinental board to the Moyle proposal, which meant that Tricontinental would operate entirely independently. Moyle would not control it.

Hancock put his recommendation to the State Bank board but, incredibly, Moyle did not speak against it, 'having already made my views known to him'. The board of the State Bank was therefore unaware of the conflict between its chairman and chief executive over the proposal to effectively turn its chief executive into a director of the bank's main subsidiary who would not be involved in day-to-day management control—in effect a non-executive director. We will never know whether the State Bank board appreciated that was the effect of their decision. We will also never know whether a Tricontinental under Bill Moyle would have avoided disaster.

All boards in Australia need to consider whether they have the systems in place that will reveal a difference between chairman and chief executive in case neither man reveals it. An exhaustive debate should expose it. At the State Bank the only way it could have happened was if Moyle was prepared to take on his chairman—yet Arnold Hancock was one of the people who had been influential in his appointment some nine months earlier.

If there was division in the State Bank board, down at Tricontinental there was confusion. Executives were mystified as to why the State Bank had bought Tricontinental given there was no melding of product mixes or delineation of areas in which the two banks would, or would not, operate.

Jack Ryan regarded his appointment to Tricontinental in March 1985 as a caretaker role and told Moyle he wanted to finish by the end of the same year. The board of the State Bank appointed Ian Johns managing director of Tricontinental and Ryan stayed on as deputy chairman. No one seemed to have noticed, despite the formation of an audit committee prior to the purchase of Tricontinental, that between June 1983 and the publication of the Touche Ross report, the person responsible for the problems raised by Touche was the general manager, lending and corporate services, Ian Johns.

Other appointments included Neil Smith as chairman. State Bank director Ian Moreton joined the board. Bill Moyle and the head of the State Bank's treasury operation, John Rawlins, were effectively non-executive directors. All the management structure board decisions required for disaster had now been made.

Tricontinental set itself a budget at the beginning of the 1985–86 financial year, which provided that lending would rise 20% to $1.3 billion. That figure was reached within a month. So in December the board set a new budget, this time allowing for lending to rise to $2 billion by June 1986. As it turned out, Tricontinental lent $2.4 billion during the financial year, 89% more than the previous year and 5.5 times the budgeted increase.

The Tricontinental management had blown out all the gearing guidelines set by the board at the beginning of 1985–86. Clearly the board had lost control. No one believed it necessary to regain it—particularly because management reported an enormous 175% rise in profit, from $4.7 million to $12.9 million. Extraordinary items helped lift the profit to $17 million.

The State Bank directors must have regarded their $30-million outlay to buy Tricontinental as a bargain and were prepared to make a subordinated loan to restore the gearing. But a list of Tricontinental's loans of more than $5 million at 30 June 1986 showed that the group's four largest borrowers owed $489.5 million—seven times Tricontinental's capital base and more than the capital of the consolidated State Bank group.

Tricontinental's biggest client exposure was $190 million, equivalent to almost three times its capital base, or 43% of the capital of the State Bank. There is no evidence in the royal commissioner's report that Smith repeated his warning at the time of the State Bank acquisition or that anyone recalled the warnings of Touche Ross before the acquisition. Indeed, Australian Ratings increased Tricontinental's credit rating.

As the 1985–86 financial year came to a close, Ian Johns set out a three-year plan for the Tricontinental board, one that forecast a much slower rate of growth and a more selective approach to lending. However, the State Bank group itself planned a big increase in property loans.

The Tricontinental board also set out a description of the group's business philosophy that helps explain the rapid growth, given the buoyant feeling and government encouragement at the time.

> Tricontinental has a philosophy of supporting entrepreneurial starters and growing with them. When people have an idea, cashflow and potential, and the idea makes sense, Tricontinental will support them. Tricontinental is different from most other merchant banks in that it stays close to its clients and 'gets its hands dirty' by being supportive.

As a statement of aim, that proposal would inspire any director. But the implementation meant that the group funded the family companies of Alan Bond and Christopher Skase, plus other now-failed groups or entrepreneurs such as John Avram's Interwest, Abe Goldberg, Allan Hawkins in New Zealand, Spedley, Thompson Land, Quatro,

Pro-Image, Bob Ansett, Hartogen, Crestwin, George Herscu, Duke Securities and Barrack.

Unlike the State Bank's carefully managed lending approval system, Tricontinental's managing director dominated the credit committee and had wide powers, including the ability, with 'all available directors on the day' to approve loans of more than $6.5 million. The board never collectively implemented systematic checking of loans before making a deal, either in management or together as directors. In any board the chairman has a vital role, as was shown when Arnold Hancock overrode his chief executive.

During his chairmanship of Tricontinental, Neil Smith was too busy to do the job properly. He continued to undertake significant other duties, including that of chairman of the Gas and Fuel Corporation of Victoria, chairman of the Australian National Airlines Commission (Australian Airlines), chairman of the Bush Fire Appeal Trust Fund that gathered and distributed more than $27 million of public donations to victims of the 1983 Ash Wednesday bushfires, and many other public tasks.

'I regret that owing to my other business commitments and an underlying belief (that) at the proper time SBV would sell Trico, I did not consider it necessary to learn more about merchant banking', Smith told the royal commission.

> I took no part in the day-to-day running of the company. I did not attend meetings that the managing director had with clients, nor did I attend management meetings. My fellow non-executive directors understood that they were free to call directly on the managing director or senior management staff to obtain such information as they may have required from time to time.
>
> I do not think that my lack of regular attendance at the office was of significance to either the board or the company as the deputy chairman, Mr Ryan, gave unstintingly of his time and talents by visiting the office up to three and four days a week.

Johns presented a budget for the year to 30 June 1987, which projected Tricontinental's operating profit rising to $34 million; total loan commitments were budgeted at $3 billion, of which $900 million would be undrawn. Although growth slowed, by the end of that year Tricontinental's loan commitments had reached $3.4 billion, once again over budget and 43% more than the previous year.

But, with the over-budget commitments, again came a higher profit. Operating profit rose to $48 million, or more than 40% above the budget. However, $21.9 million of the profit came from gains in equity investments, i.e., profits from the company share portfolio, which included many speculative situations. Those profits could not be expected to continue.

In July 1987, as happened a year earlier, the board was told that Tricontinental had become even more exposed to a small group of clients. The four largest borrowers now owed a total of $631.6 million, an increase of around $140 million from 1986. The largest exposure to a single client was $246 million, which represented 35% of the entire State Bank group capital.

There were commitments to 26 clients which exceeded 30% of Tricontinental's capital base. The list was studded with operators who were to fail, although it included many good borrowers such as Solomon Lew and John Gandel.

The board realised it was a great time to sell Tricontinental and began moves towards a public share float, but the share crash four months later overtook events. Nevertheless, in the year to 30 June 1988 operating profits jumped from $48 million to $61 million, although the net result was down because of provisions. But Tricontinental management had put in place a deadly game of converting those who could not pay into 24-hour cash advances, which slashed potential problem loans. At the same time a significant split had taken place within the Tricontinental board. Once again it would seem that the parent, the State Bank of Victoria, was unaware of the dissenting opinion.

After the share crash State Bank treasury executive John Rawlins began to be dissatisfied with the standard of information coming before the Tricontinental board and told his chief executive, Bill Moyle, that unless the Tricontinental managing director, Ian Johns, was 'made to change his attitude' he no longer wished to be on the Tricontinental board. That ultimatum had followed some vigorous clashes on the board, occurring when Rawlins expressed concern at the quality of equities that were being given as security for loans. Rawlins told the royal commission

> My concern in relation to Tricontinental's loan portfolio was based on the fact that some of the equities provided by borrowers as security had lost value. Some were likely to lose more value. Some were illiquid. During my final months on the Tricontinental board I had a number of disputes with Johns on lending and treasury matters. At the February 1988 board meeting I said that management had a cavalier attitude to bad and doubtful debt management. I thought that the board was not being kept adequately informed by management. I continued to harbor deep concerns about the quality of the security given for many loans and the attitude of Johns.
>
> Some days after the March 1988 board meeting I spoke to Moyle and told him that unless Johns' powers were restricted I would resign. As Moyle was

> unwilling to restrict Johns' powers I resigned and that resignation was based on my views in relation to the equity-secured portfolios.

Moyle replies: 'Mr Rawlins asked me to do something that was not within my power to do. I do not know how I would have curbed Mr Johns any more effectively than he could have curbed Mr Johns'.

Arnold Hancock says he was not aware of the reasons for Rawlins' resignation or his discussions with Moyle. The situation illustrated the impossible positions the executives were placed in given the way the State Bank had set up Tricontinental board. Of course, with the benefit of hindsight, the fate of most of Tricontinental's clients and Tricontinental was already sealed by June 1988, although what was to happen in the next nine months was to be the biggest blow of all.

Unaware of the pending crisis, the bank board saw the continued high profit and began to look at other ways of disposing of the company, including the ill-fated scheme to backdoor list it through Pinevale, an investment company in which it had a share interest, and the attempt to sell Tricontinental to a new company that incorporated the Australian bank licence. The Australian bank proposal floundered because the independent accountants and proposed directors wanted a guarantee that the assets the bank bought in Tricontinental would yield full value.

While all this was going on, the continuing lack of a proper process for making decisions meant that not only were Tricontinental's clients crumbling, but the bank was pouring good money after bad. In the nine months to 31 March 1989 the amount lent to Tricontinental's thirteen biggest clients (most of whom went broke) rose by an incredible $552 million to $1.7 billion.

The largest sixteen clients involved total loan facilities of $2 billion, representing 50% of Tricontinental's total loan portfolio. It is likely that the losses in those nine months made the cost of saving the State Bank too high.

Although the royal commission made no conclusions, it is clear that the board mistakes included: failure to understand the impact of Tricontinental and the total bank operation; failure to plan a proper board role in Tricontinental to limit and evaluate lending; failure to heed the Touche Ross warning; failure to bring out everybody's different views on the Tricontinental purchase so that a co-ordinated strategy could be reached; failure to make sure that the chairman of the high-risk Tricontinental operation, with its entrepreneurial managing director, had sufficient time and knowledge to do his job; over-reliance on retired executives.

Those board mistakes may not have been as bad had Bill Moyle not allowed himself to be browbeaten by his chairman. Given his experience, it should have been Moyle, not Rawlins, who questioned Johns. Had the Rawlins position been fully brought before the State Bank board during 1987 it still might have been possible to save the bank and prevent the huge losses incurred in that last nine months. It was the final blunder by the board.

THE BLUEPRINT FOR BOARDS THAT AROSE OUT OF THE COLLAPSE

WHEN, in 1990, the Victorian Government appointed Bill Clendenin to the board of the State Bank of Victoria, he walked into a boardroom in crisis. Within two weeks all the other directors were sacked. The board of the State Bank had included people who had been successful in other areas. It had been structured with a balance of independent directors and had always been conscious of ethics. Clendenin, who has been a long-term observer of the role of boards, concluded that the State Bank board failed mainly because it had not fully understood its functions.

It is apparent from other public inquiries that many bank boards have had similar difficulties in understanding their functions. Given that bank boards include directors of the top companies in the country, it is likely that we are looking at a serious Australian problem which goes well beyond the banking community.

Clendenin's experience with the State Bank led him to link with the international consulting firm of Booz Allen & Hamilton, which also had a deep interest in the functioning of Australian boards. They decided, as a first step to setting out a blueprint for the functioning of Australian boards, to undertake a survey of Australia's leading directors. The AMP and CML sponsored the survey. More than 250 of Australia's top directors completed detailed questionnaires and another 60 were questioned closely about how their boards operated and where there was room for improvement.

The backing of the institutions in this exercise coincides with their support of the Australian Investment Managers Group in establishing a majority of independent directors on boards and the dominance on the audit and recommendation committees. Even if the board structure is right, there is no certainty that the board will then operate to the maximum benefit of the enterprise.

Onerous conditions are being placed on non-executive directors that go far beyond their normal areas of responsibility and that is interfering with decision-making in many boards. But the Booz Allen & Hamilton/William Clendenin Associates survey showed that there are also fundamental flaws in the way boards operate in Australia, which confirms that the board difficulties that arose in the finance and banking industry have much wider application.

The survey showed an incredible 77% of the directors agreed that substantial scope existed for improving the practices of boards; 78% said boards should reallocate their time to focus more on strategy and policy; 65% believed board information systems needed to be streamlined and upgraded; and 60% believed more time was required for directors to fulfil board responsibilities effectively.

Comments from leading directors, under the cloak of anonymity, included:

- We have no clear sense of priority as to how the board should spend its time–*independent director*
- I estimate that 95% of boards—including mine—are not doing what they are supposed to do–*managing director*
- Most of our directors have little or no real understanding of our various businesses–*executive director*
- It's pretty easy to manipulate the board's role by the agenda and the papers we give them–*company secretary*

And to emphasise the defects of many boards, when the performance of Australian companies is viewed over a decade there are often considerable differences between the performance of enterprises in the same industry. In most situations the differences reflect the quality of strategic long-term decision-making by a board. The current boards, of course, must grapple with the repercussions of decisions made many years ago.

The managing director of Booz Allen & Hamilton, Paul Kocourek, believes that although the concentration on the composition and ethics of the board have been worthwhile, it is far more important for boards to examine what they are doing and how they should act. He believes that the basic Australian board structure is far healthier than in the US, however, where the vast majority of companies combine the roles of chairman and chief executive. US boards are often populated by non-executive directors who are in fact chief executives of other companies and do not have the time to reflect and work through strategic issues.

Kocourek says a board's effectiveness is determined by the appropriate balance of four inter-related areas: function, structure, information, and practices. The survey highlighted problems in each of these areas. For example, in the function area there was inadequate recognition of the multiple roles and responsibilities of directors and a lack of understanding that boards were the drivers of shareholder value. All too often boards concentrated on internal operational and short-term issues rather than the external and long-term factors.

In the board structure area, a large number of boards failed to select directors according to the unique needs of their company and did not develop and use the skills around their boardroom table. In the practices area there was a failure to link board compensation with the financial performance of the enterprise, and an inadequate system for recognising and rectifying poor performance by directors. Clearly Australian company boards are having difficulty removing unsatisfactory directors.

The survey provided some other interesting responses from the Australian director community. For example, 81% of the directors said they believed that a board should consist of between six and eleven people, with most (48%) opting for between nine and eleven. Yet the survey shows that only 52% of the top 90 company boards consist of between six and eleven. A massive 30% of those boards have twelve or more people, including 7% that exceed sixteen.

Obviously not all boards have these shortcomings, but Booz Allen & Hamilton and Clendenin clearly believe there is a serious problem in Australia. They recognise that the specific requirements of every board are different but there is a general and pervasive need to improve board effectiveness. Accordingly, they have prepared the 'Diligent Dozen'—12 questions every board should ask itself to determine its own effectiveness. In addition they have prepared a model of the way a board might allocate its responsibility and time.

In the model the board has a series of tasks and a range of relationships with management. For example, when setting corporate objectives it must actually make the decision; with strategic direction it needs to define policy guidelines for management; in allocating the resources of the enterprise, the board's job is to approve management recommendations.

In the corporate policy area the board must decide dividend payout; define policy on balance sheet structure; approve management recommendations on capital spending and executive compensation. On industrial relations the model sets out the board's task as advising and counselling the chief executive. In accountability, the board must decide the profit and the reports to shareholders and define policy guidelines on the audit. Of course, overriding all these functions is the primary responsibility of appointing and rewarding the chief executive. As we saw in the Coles Myer case it can be very dangerous to combine chairman and chief executive.

Clendenin and Booz Allen & Hamilton believe that although a

Booz Allen & Hamilton/Clendenin questions that every board should ask itself

1. Past and present performance: What has been the company's financial and market performance compared to history, plans, and business competitors?
2. Underlying causes: What specific competitive strengths and weaknesses, market forces, or drivers of profit dynamics determined these results?
3. Performance potential: What are reasonable objectives and limits to the company's growth, profitability, and appreciation of shareholder value?
4. Strategic direction: Does management have a comprehensive strategy and operating plans for the company to realise its performance potential?
5. Resource allocation: Are the necessary human, financial, physical and other supporting resources provided and properly allocated to achieve success?
6. Management organisation: Does the chief executive provide the leadership required by the company and does the organisation provide for his succession?
7. Financial accountability: Are financial information systems, control processes, decision delegations, and reporting responsibilities established and audited?
8. Operational controls: Does management utilise an effective system of key performance indicators to monitor and control operating performance to plan?
9. Constituency protection: Are mechanisms in place to ensure conformance with legislation and regulations protecting customers, employees and the community?
10. Litigation and disputation: Does management report, control, and provide for all material disputes of a legal, financial or regulatory nature?
11. Crises and contingencies: Are effective management processes in place to anticipate, prevent or correct physical and financial risk management crises?
12. Management priorities: Does the board adequately understand and support resolution of the short-term, intermediate and long-term priorities of management?

board of directors has responsibilities to customers, employees, creditors and the community, its primary responsibility is to shareholders because it must aim to provide them with capital value appreciation and dividend return. To do so it must have a clear understanding of the determinants of shareholder value and tailor its role, its relationships with management, and its practices accordingly.

A LESSON FOR JANET HOLMES À COURT OUT OF TRICONTINENTAL

Straight-talking Irishman Olaf O'Duill brought home to Australia's richest woman that she needed to move much faster to bring her Heytesbury Holdings on to a better business footing for the 1990s. The banker had won the contract to recover as much as possible of the merchant bank's $3.5-billion loan portfolio on behalf of Victorian taxpayers, $40 million of which has been lent to Heytesbury.

It was the morning of Friday 8 November 1991. Eleven bankers to Janet Holmes à Court's Heytesbury Holdings were filing into a conference room on the 31st floor of Perth's Allendale Square building. Waiting inside the room, which, incidentally, was the same one in which the Rothwells' merchant bank 'rescue' was announced, were Heytesbury executives. The company was not in trouble but changes were required to its financial arrangements. It was a time for decisions.

Most of the bankers were the Perth representatives of overseas or eastern state banks, but in the front row sat Olaf O'Duill, who had flown from Melbourne. The Heytesbury executives were entrusted with explaining the finances and operations to the bankers. They included Jon Elbery, who had been right-hand man to the late Robert Holmes à Court; pastoral chief Darrel Jarvis; John Holland construction group head Graham Duff and London theatre group manager Richard Johnston.

Heytesbury managing director Janet Holmes à Court and her other directors (including Katherine Burgherd from New York), were watching the performance of their executives with great interest. More than a year had passed since her husband died, but Janet Holmes à Court still headed an operation that was very much his creation, although she was gradually moulding it to suit her expertise and to meet the changing times of the recession.

Heytesbury, by any measure, had substantial shareholders' funds. A string of changes had been made, but there was still a long way to go.

The bankers were told that even though there was a small operating surplus for the year, asset write-downs had cut shareholders' funds from $480 million to $400 million.

Many credit lines were due to be rescheduled. The bankers' meeting had been called partly because the group had to change to conventional, secured lines of credit instead of the (unsecured) negative pledge borrowing that Robert Holmes à Court and so many other big borrowers of the 1980s had negotiated.

The banks had not singled out Heytesbury for special attention (most companies are now required to offer security), but the loans were due to be rescheduled just as Heytesbury was predicting that in the year ahead it would not cover its interest bill with cash profits, excluding asset sales.

Although its main operating divisions—theatres, pastoral, construction and transport—were profitable, the company had well over $200 million invested in non-income-producing assets including its art collections, studs and the massive Grove House property that occupies almost a hectare beside Regent's Park in the heart of London. Some assets had been sold since Robert Holmes à Court's death in September 1990, but there had been delays and management had been preoccupied with buying and improving John Holland.

Holland was acquired in 1990 for a token consideration, but pushed up Heytesbury's borrowings and loan guarantees enough to more than offset the effect of any asset sales.

In the previous decade Heytesbury had never covered its interest with operating income, but relied on Robert Holmes à Court's ability to reap profits from deals, something he had done with great regularity. For example, in the year before his death he had made $30 million for Heytesbury buying and selling shares in Christie's auction house, enabling the family company to cover its interest bill and make a profit. Janet's talent was not asset trading so, wisely, she closed off all the trading positions Robert had in place.

Janet Holmes à Court says that in the months leading up to her husband's death he had realised it might not be possible to keep producing such deals in a recession. 'I think if he'd lived, quite frankly, he would have had to do exactly what I'm doing, because all those spectacular deals were drying up.'

Janet Holmes à Court was well aware of Heytesbury's structural defects before the 8 November meeting, but for a variety of reasons the company had not acted to correct those problems. It was inevitable the bankers would be critical.

Of the three main Australian operating executives who made major presentations, Elbery, Jarvis and Duff, only one, Jarvis, would survive the coming shakeout. Jon Elbery had been the man who over the years had implemented many of the founder's decisions. He was the driving force behind the acquisition of Holland. Graham Duff lived and breathed John Holland and had assisted in the transfer of the business from the defunct public company to Heytesbury, despite some flak from the Tricontinental and O'Duill's team, owed money by the previous owners. Duff must have been surprised when he walked in to make his presentation to see O'Duill in the front row.

Holland had been able to write substantial contracts in the nine months before the Heytesbury takeover—work Heytesbury had to finance. When it took over John Holland, Heytesbury had considered replacing Duff with a new chief executive who would have a better concept of the restraints of the Heytesbury balance sheet and who might have operated on a lower cost basis. Heytesbury stayed with Duff and he took that as a vote to go out and win new work in Australia and Asia. Although his pricing was aggressive his success at the Great Southern Stand showed he was a good judge of costs. But he did not understand the strains he was placing on the Heytesbury balance sheet.

When Heytesbury acquired its pastoral operations it conducted an international executive search to find Darrel Jarvis. Janet Holmes à Court has always preferred operating businesses to investments and has long had a personal interest in the pastoral holdings. She became an admirer of the hard hitting Jarvis style of management.

In any family company the operating executives' relationship with the owner and managing director always take on extra significance when the business is at a crossroads. And in the three days beginning on 8 November, Heytesbury was in just such a position.

Elbery had the task of explaining the group's overall position to O'Duill and the rest of the bankers. In all, Heytesbury owed about $400 million to the bankers and had guaranteed $100 million in Holland performance bonds. The London theatres, including the Colisseum, were earning about $18 million a year; John Holland $15 million; the pastoral operations $6 million and transport and other activities about $2 million—a total of about $41 million. However, in the absence of asset sales, these profits would not cover the expected interest bills of about $45 million.

Elbery set out his plan to reduce debt to $240 million during 1992 and to $140 million during 1993. It was apparent to all that some of the banks regarded this as either too slow a program, or that the plans were not definitive enough. Apart from O'Duill's Tricontinental, other banks were also under pressure from their boards to reduce outstanding loans: they wanted cash, not promises. Elbery was questioned and his answers did not always please the banks. Elbery's supporters say his warnings had not always been heeded and he would not have had a problem if the Grove House sale for $50 million had gone ahead in April 1991.

Olaf O'Duill worked with the Irish Development Bank before coming to Australia to join Capel Court and later National Mutual Royal Bank. After the ANZ takeover of the National Mutual Royal, he teamed up with former ANZCAP executive Bill Bessemer to form Bessemer O'Duill Pty Ltd, and they obtained a contract to look closely at the accounts of the Pyramid Building Society. That examination revealed the true Pyramid mess.

Pleased with their work, the then Victorian Treasurer Tom Roper gave Bessemer O'Duill the job of sorting out the $3.5-billion Tricontinental debt collection problem. O'Duill's approach has been anything but conventional and his famous drinking session with Becton principals Max Beck and Michael Buxton, which allegedly broke a deadlock, stamped him as no ordinary banker.

O'Duill's mixture of ruthlessness and constructive business-rebuilding programs, looks like working for Tricontinental. At the Heytesbury meeting, O'Duill was dealing with one of the few clients of his bank that did not have a big problem. He wanted to keep it that way so that his bank would recover the $40 million it was owed, plus interest.

O'Duill did not fly out of Perth straight after the Allendale Square meeting. Instead he had further meetings with Janet Holmes à Court that extended into the evening. He gave her a very realistic assessment of what had happened on that day and told her how, if she failed to make the right moves or hasten the asset sale process, she might fall into the hands of bankers like himself.

O'Duill has always been skilled at delivering messages with great impact and clarity. Although Janet Holmes à Court had come to a similar conclusion herself, she could not have been unaffected by what he told her.

During the 1980s she had sat alongside her husband as he built their wealth to levels they could not spend in two lifetimes. Money was the score in Robert's game. Janet was also beside him after the share crash in 1987 when the whole empire began to crumble and he fought desperately to avoid going under. With the help of asset sales to WA Government arms, Holmes à Court faced his problems and came out on top. No one who survived that kind of crisis would ever want to risk the same thing again.

Janet Holmes à Court is reluctant to talk about O'Duill. 'I won't even deny or confirm whether I have had a meal with Olaf,' she says, but concedes 'I think he is a very smart banker', but 'I don't think that he's in a position to dictate policy to Heytesbury and what we do with our staff'. She agrees that the asset sale program was 'slower than we would have thought, slower than the board hoped, the pace was not fast enough for us'. She was therefore very receptive to what O'Duill had to say but, perhaps understandably, did not much like being told. It is not always easily understood by onlookers that Janet Holmes à Court was never as motivated as Robert by the size of her wealth. She is much more comfortable owning operating businesses and is intensely nationalistic.

The Heytesbury directors had stayed on over the weekend and were scheduled to meet on the Sunday morning to discuss the bankers' meeting and other strategies. The combination of the directors' own feelings and the O'Duill message had galvanised the board. Elbury was not the right man for the job.

After the meeting Elbery stepped down and pastoral chief Darrel Jarvis was appointed deputy managing director under Janet Holmes à Court. Eight others departed. Although events like these were taking place in executive suites around the country, it was completely outside the normal Holmes à Court tradition.

Was Heytesbury forced to act by its bankers? Janet Holmes à Court replies in the negative with some passion.

> I don't think it's accurate to say we were in the hands of the bankers. Olaf O'Duill, as good as a banker as he is, and a nice Irishman he is, is not really in a position to dictate what Heytesbury does with its management.
>
> The reason Darrel Jarvis was put in that weekend is that Darrel gets things done. He's turned Heytesbury pastoral around from minus 10 when we bought it. We put Darrel in and we made $7 million the first year.
>
> Practically every manager has been replaced; the training schemes are in place. It's a remarkable transformation. He actually doesn't hang around and talk; he gets on, makes decisions and makes things happen. And Jon's departure really had been unfolding for some time.
>
> It is all linked to 2 o'clock Sunday morning, the 2nd of September of [1990] which was Robert's death. Everything that happened in Heytesbury is linked to that event, not a bankers' meeting or a lightning strike. The one thing that I twigged, within about three seconds of working out that Robert had died, was that things were never going to be the same again and my life had to change very dramatically, but Heytesbury had to change even more so because the skills had gone.

Holmes à Court emphasises that the asset sale program was under way well before the bankers' meeting. The Sturt Creek pastoral property was sold in March; Glentree, the farm in Victoria, was also sold; the Toorak mansion, Miegunyah, was disposed of; the English country house had been sold; paintings had been prepared for sale and warehouses in Fremantle were sold.

'Of course so much of what we inherited was part of another game. The woolstores in Fremantle were bought because he [Robert] was going to set up another newspaper à la the *Western Mail.*' She plans to retain the Australian art collection, much to the relief of many Australian boardrooms (releasing it on to the market would hurt the value of other corporate collections). The rest of the collection included Monet's Hay Stacks, plus paintings by Soutine, Signac, Pissaro and Boudin, Latin American works and contemporary British works. More than $40 million has been raised in sales. Janet Holmes à Court says it is not possible to hang the most expensive paintings in her home without making it like a prison, because of the security precautions that would be required. Jarvis went on to cut the bank lending substantially with sales of property assets, part of the car collection, too pastoral properties, the Colisseum theatre and other assets.

As to the current outlook, Janet Holmes à Court says

> We've accelerated the pace of [asset sales]; we're going hard at it; we are making things happen, but the plan is to go further. We think we might downsize those three operations and get down to $130 million to $140 million worth of debt, but we are continually monitoring our plan.

One of the problems Heytesbury faced was that Graham Duff had built the Holland business and raised its gearing (including guarantees) too quickly, given the slow pace of Heytesbury asset sales. Most bankers regarded the performance bond guarantees as another liability. Three weeks after the 8 November meeting, Graham Duff stood down as head of Holland.

> One of the briefs for the new deputy managing director and one of the things Darrel Jarvis did instantly on coming in, was to say to Holland 'This is a recession, we've got to blend this company in and fit it in with Heytesbury. You can't just go out and grow forever and a day'. But the important thing for the initial period in Holland was to get that pipeline filled up again. It's like having a bubble in the water pipe where there is a little element of nothing going through the pipeline and that's been filled up very nicely now. We can get on with the consolidation. All our guarantees are in place for the work that we've got in hand and there is other work that we've tendered on.

Asked whether she had considered floating John Holland, she said: 'I had 20 years as a wife of a public company chairman, but it's a distinct possibility'. Holland staff were told in December 1991 that the former head of the Victorian TAB, Bob Nordlinger, would be CEO of the Holland operation. Janet Holmes à Court and Darrel Jarvis wasted no time. But they may have been too quick because within six months Nordlinger had stepped down.

On the cattle properties, Holmes à Court says

> What I want to do basically is to have the best-run pastoral operation in Australia. I am not really into it being necessarily the biggest. At the moment ourselves, Stanbroke and the AA company are about the same size, about 300,000 cattle. We've made massive changes since we took it over.
>
> The reason we sold Sturt Creek was that it was not a particularly good property and it was not well located for us to manage. Although it was adjoining some of our other properties, the only arable part of it was about as far away from the management site as possible. I wouldn't mind selling three or more other properties that don't necessarily fit into the scheme. And probably in the long run we would scale down all the operating divisions a little bit, scale pastoral down by selling, maybe selling properties that don't fit in as well, maybe scale down the theatres a little bit. And possibly going into Asia a bit more.
>
> We're already selling about 30,000 cattle into Asia each year for fattening. We are doing a lot of work up there and know the people who end up fattening and selling the cattle. And we might eventually go up there.
>
> I made the decision after Robert died that we wouldn't be doing anything in America, particularly with the purchase of John Holland, because it's been in Asia for so long. We will concentrate on Australia, Asia and Britain. Robert was never really into Asia. I think he thought it was some place he flew over on the way back to Australia.

Janet Holmes à Court's vision is to have operating businesses earning about $50 million and debt about $140 million with servicing costs well below $20 million. If she speeds up the asset sales, the fact that the drought didn't affect most of her pastoral properties will give the group a big boost.

> You know how I've often said that you can only force a certain amount of food down your throat and live in a certain number of houses, and sleep in a certain number of beds, and wear a certain number of clothes, and you don't really need very much more. And if on the way we can produce things for Australia and employ people, then . . .

O'Duill and Janet Holmes à Court are now speaking the same language. Tricontinental wished more of its clients had spoken that language.

LLOYD'S STRUGGLES AS A TRADITION ENDS

MANY Australian enterprises are now experiencing rises in insurance rates—particularly in big-risk underwritings—as the repercussions of Lloyd's of London's problems spread throughout the world. Lloyd's is not like a conventional insurance company; it is a collection of stallholders or syndicates. In 1991, they were backed by the personal assets of 26 000 syndicate members, or 'names'.

At present, there are about 280 stallholders who underwrite and lay off insurance risks each day at a central market. In Australia, big risks tend to be in large mining projects and professional indemnity policies. These are the areas where the Lloyd's marketplace provides much of the world's underwriting capacity. At the end of 1991, 4000 of the 26 000 active Lloyd's 'names' withdrew, significantly reducing the underwriting capacity of the syndicates.

The nature of Lloyd's problems, the close relationship they have to the volatile US insurance industry, and the emergence of European insurance companies as increasingly important underwriters, are factors that are not widely understood in the general community. The City of London, which has led the world insurance market for generations, has realised that if Lloyd's goes into steep decline it will affect what is a major British skills base. As a result, a taskforce was set up headed by the chairman and chief executive officer of Sedgwick Group Plc, David Rowland, to study what had gone wrong and how it could be fixed. Rowland visited Australia in 1992 to explain the taskforce's report to Australian syndicate members.

Rowland says that to understand what has happened to Lloyd's, a study is needed of the industry 30 or 40 years ago when Lloyd's dominance was unquestioned. Rowland comments of that period that 'If underwriters of Lloyd's suffered a loss, the rates would rise and Lloyd's could dictate that because they were the world leader in their classes'.

Traditionally, the insurance cycle involved seven years of good times and seven years of bad. Underwriters enjoyed healthy rates until 1978. A very soft insurance market existed for the following seven years. Then, on schedule, rates increased rapidly in 1985, and underwriters throughout the world, and particularly at Lloyd's, believed they were going to get very rich. But within a few years the world insurance market had changed, a development that was not fully appreciated in the Lloyd's marketplace. Although Lloyd's syndicates were making a lot of money on the 1985 and 1986 accounts, they were also driving a lot of business out of the market. Rowland explains that

> The big American buyers suddenly found themselves unable to get protection for some of their liability business and, if they could get it, it was so expensive that it was, in their view, grotesque. They were also becoming increasingly sophisticated and the risk managers in the big corporations perceived that generally the insurance industry was giving back at least 70¢ in the dollar and using 30¢ on the transaction of the insurance business.

The 1985–86 price rise prompted big corporations to set up offshore companies to virtually self-insure—and in the process took $45 billion in insured assets from the market. At the same time, the European insurance industry started cutting the price of marine and other insurance to capture business from London. The loss of market share by Lloyd's coincided with a huge demand by individuals to become 'names' and join syndicates in a bid to cash in on the bonanza that was expected to follow seven years of difficulties. 'Vast increases in both the numbers of members and members increasing their capacity to underwrite, took place', Rowland says.

> Suddenly, the music stopped and by 1986, rates, instead of being up, were starting to go down. Lloyd's, as a marketplace then of about 400 syndicates, representing 30,000 members of Lloyd's, was not bringing the new business in the way it used to, or the business that they were bringing in could only be placed at a fraction of the rates.

The cleverest underwriters are often those who rate the new business successfully and arrange their re-insurance programs on the most competitive terms so that even if rates are falling they can make a profit and the losses go through to the next layer of re-insurance.'

However, not every syndicate could do that and some started devising innovative high-risk policies to use up their spare capacity. In particular, they promoted excess-loss (XL) policies, under which insurance underwriters took premiums but did not pay anything until damages reached a specified figure. After that they met all losses. The XL contracts were reinsured several times in the market and syndicates that were not careful finished with several layers of the same risk. Lloyd's syndicates that specialised in XL policies did very well up to 1985, and provided some of the highest returns of any of the Lloyd's syndicates. Accordingly, in 1985–86 when newcomers were looking for syndicates to join, the XL groups were very popular. For a time all went well. But then came the huge claims caused by the Piper Alpha oil rig disaster off Scotland, several big storms in Europe, hurricanes in the US and typhoons in Asia. These claims were fed through the market and were magnified for many syndicates because of their basic reinsurance commitments.

'The actual claims paid to each other by syndicate members might multiply so you could get a very considerable concentration of Piper Alpha in one syndicate, and those syndicates were often the glamorous ones', Rowland says. 'If you're writing XL reinsurance, and the layer that you are writing is not penetrated, then it's 100% profit. If it's penetrated, it's 100% loss.'

At the same time another problem was developing—the growth in claims related to environmental issues. Rowland says

> I'm in syndicate 90. When I came to Lloyd's in the 1950s, the underwriter of syndicate 90 was a god in the market who knew more about American reinsurance business, treaty business, contracts and other US insurance matters than anyone else. Syndicate 90 was not flashy and did not necessarily achieve the best results in the market, but year after year absolutely excellent results came forward.
>
> Around the late 1970s it became apparent that the contracts that had been written reinsuring the American insurance companies—Aetna, etc—based the indemnity on the date of the injury or accident, not on the date of the claim being reported. So if a contract existed covering 1955 and it was subsequently shown that workers contracted lung disease through working with asbestos, they might bring claims in 1980, and it was the 1955 policy that paid. The American courts established this principle, although it was in doubt in terms of the wording and from that time onwards all old-year policies drawn on a current basis were vulnerable.

This development proved particularly awkward for Lloyd's because syndicates are normally closed off after three years. As a result, new members of syndicate 90 took on board past risks after adjusting for provisions. At the start of the 1980s Lloyd's tried to find a way to provide for the claims that might arise from US court decisions. A successful underwriter in the marine business, Dick Outhwaite, decided that the market had been unduly panicked and there was still a lot of money to be made. He proceeded to underwrite the old-year liabilities of other Lloyd's syndicates. For example, for a premium, he wrote a contract for syndicate 90, taking 50% of the risk of all old-year liabilities prior to 1973. Outhwaite's view turned out to be horribly wrong and members of the Outhwaite syndicates suffered big losses.

Accordingly, the big losses in Lloyd's were incurred by 'names' in syndicates that followed Outhwaite or that were heavily committed to XL policies. Many that suffered huge losses were new Lloyd's members. At the same time, 17 500 of the 'names' have at least one 'open year' and most have three or four. An open year is when there are claims that cannot be quantified and the 'names' have a contingent liability against their personal assets that cannot be quantified. It is not easy to live knowing you can be bankrupted at any time. Many Lloyds 'names' believe that the managers of their syndicates did not look after their interests and so have begun legal action. The cases could establish precedents that mean that there would be an entirely different relationship between the 'names' and the syndicates. Not surprisingly, syndicate members who have suffered big losses have started legal action. This could establish precedents that would greatly change the way the market operates.

The Rowland taskforce has made several recommendations to improve the running of Lloyd's while preserving its character as an insurance marketplace. These include measures to give syndicates access to corporate capital, establishing a fund to cover big losses by particular syndicates, substantially reducing the costs of the market—which have ballooned in recent decades—and giving syndicate members greater rights. Rowland hopes the recommended changes will enable London to maintain its strong position in the world insurance market, but the insurance companies that operate alongside Lloyd's in London have their own problems. Most of the big companies, including Royal, Guardian, Sun Alliance and General Accident (but not Commercial Union) have been incurring huge losses. In addition, their sharemarket capitalisations have contracted.

Rowland says 'Back in the 1950s or 1960s, Royal was a great business and it might insure Unilever. Unilever was a giant company and its factories would work in risk-exposure sums that related in some way to the capital base of Royal'. But today, Royal has a much smaller capital base, prompting big companies to look at different means of managing risk.

The British insurance industry may be facing plenty of problems, but according to Rowland, difficulties in the US industry will be much more severe. 'When the music stops, the pain and suffering in the market will be worse than anywhere else'. US insurance companies are still producing profits and have adopted aggressive pricing policies.

> The view from outside America is that the majority of these companies are producing profits by under-reserving, whereas quite a number of European companies, particularly Lloyd's, are very substantially reserved. It is known, for example, that no American insurance company carries any pollution reserves which, in one sense you would say, is absolutely crazy, but they are

> petrified about discovery. If you carry a pollution reserve, you are almost admitting in a court that you actually believe you may be liable for pollution losses. Lloyd's underwriters clearly take a different view.

German, Swiss, Italian and French insurance companies have come through the recent difficulties in better shape than British and US firms because they did not write US business and their tax rules enable them, over generations, to establish tax-free reserves. This is a practice that is not allowed in Britain and Australia. Lloyd's focused on its traditional markets in Britain and the US, which together account for two-thirds of its business. It does not have a significant stake on the European continent.

Premiums are rising in Australia where mining companies, for example, are becoming concerned that they cannot get the insurance limits they want. 'Generally speaking, there are far too many insurers and brokers and much too little business—insurance companies in Australia are rather like lemmings hurtling over a cliff', Rowland says. 'Occasionally they see the stop sign right at the edge, but they choose to ignore it and they hurtle over the cliff again and the rates fall even more.'

Rowland says underwriting losses have been very painful in Australia, but adds that few business people visiting Australia believe that the country is not a good place to do business. He says many decide that Australia is such a wonderful country that 'it must be good' and that it is 'going to come right'. 'Insurance companies have been doing that forever, so have brokers', he says.

The Rowland taskforce is designed to take Lloyd's into the next century, leaving behind the mistakes of the 1980s.

WESTPAC'S THREE LESSONS

ON 1 OCTOBER 1992, Westpac chairman Eric Neal, deputy chairman Neil Currie and three other directors resigned over past errors. Many of us wonder what we would have done if we had been on the Westpac board in recent years. Every director or manager of an enterprise needs to understand the lessons of Westpac's experience, and the opportunities that lower property values and rents will open up for good businesses. These trends will be assisted by the upturn in the US economy.

Being a Westpac director during the period from 1987 to 1992 would have been a challenging experience. With the benefit of hindsight, it is now clear that during the 1980s the bank had significant weaknesses, and that the final outcome of its actions might have been much worse. For example, in the mid-1980s, as it was setting out to be a big regional bank, it had an accounting system that provided infrequent profit reports and insufficient monitoring of risk. It was able to get by with this in a regulated environment; indeed, it was one of many banks in that position. But deregulation left Westpac's board badly under-informed.

The first lesson for all boards is that if they are not happy with the data produced by an accounting system, they should be very wary of expansion. When Stuart Fowler took over as managing director just after the sharemarket crash of 1987, he began to improve the bank's accounting systems, a task which took some years.

In 1988, the property boom hit, and the bank and its various arms all participated. Everyone worked independently and there was no total-risk assessment. Westpac acquired the minority interests in Australian Guarantee Corporation (which had big property exposure), to fully own what was expected to be a profitable asset. AGC went on to report good profits, and all those involved were heroes at the time.

This brings up the second lesson: boards tend not to probe too deeply into areas where profits look good; understandably, they concentrate on those that are obviously causing problems. Directors need to understand the amount of risk being incurred to generate profit.

By 1990 there was a greater appreciation of the dangers Westpac was facing. Yet there must have been frustration among some of the directors about problems with overseas ventures, answers to board questions and possible future bad debts. One long-serving director told *BRW* writer Ali Cromie that anyone would have to have had 'rocks in their head' to say the board was particularly satisfied with the bank's performance. The remark was unprecedented. After that article former chief executive Bob White demanded the board review policies. When he was knocked back he resigned from the board.

The traditional attitude at Westpac towards problem property exposures (as duplicated by almost every other big bank in the world) was to make no provision if the property was a new development. The bank relied on the replacement value of the property to advance with inflation and income to rise as tenants were found.

Westpac's directors continued along this course in the year to September 1991, although it was becoming more controversial as many feared the property market was changing. The directors consulted the Lend Lease subsidiary Civil & Civic to make sure that the value of new buildings as recorded in the 1991 balance sheet did not exceed reasonable construction costs. That entailed some write-downs because of the excesses of the 1980s. The bank's 1991 balance sheet showed clear signs of strain as the level of problem loans rose. Its formula also meant that it made fewer provisions than some other banks, even though it was boosted by the allocation of about $700 million in superannuation surpluses to general debt provisions.

On 1 October 1991, the day after balance date, Frank Conroy became Westpac's managing director. He had no desire to have his first three or four years tarnished by the need to recoup past losses. It must have been difficult for the board, which had just signed a set of accounts using its traditional policy, to have a new chief executive advocating a completely different policy that would inevitably result in severe criticism of those accounts.

But Conroy had a lot on his side. Westpac's economists were saying that the property market slump was very different from previous ones, and there might not be a recovery before the end of the century. Any director contacting Lend Lease's Stuart Hornery would have received the same advice. Hornery believes that the shrinking numbers of corporate administrators and a likely decline in the amount of office space allotted per person will affect demand for commercial property throughout the 1990s. The AMP Society's representatives, who joined the Westpac board after the annual meeting, would have confirmed the problem.

Thus, we reach the third lesson from Westpac's experience: that directors should question their basic assumptions each year, and that a new chief executive should not be expected to take the same attitude to the problems of the past as the previous one, even if he was on the board.

The job ahead

Since its write-downs in early 1992, Westpac has become a very different business. Shareholders' funds total $5.4 billion, which represents $3.75 a share (previously $5.66), including 74 cents in future tax benefits. Asset backing, without the tax benefits, is $3.01, or approximately the price shareholders were asked to pay in the three-for-ten share issue. The issue, which was underwritten, lifted shareholders' funds to $6.6 billion, despite a huge shortfall.

The group's underlying profitability before tax and bad debts in the half-year to 31 march 1992 (excluding the superannuation contribution) equalled an annual rate of about $1.4 billion. This meant that shareholders' funds were almost four times underlying earnings. After the issue, would rise to about 4.8 times, without allowing for the profit on extra capital.

At 31 March 1992, Westpac had problem loans totalling $10 billion that have been effectively written down to about $6.4 billion. In other words, shareholders' funds after the issue and net problem loans are about the same. One of Conroy's most important tasks is to set management procedures in train to manage those problem loans so that they yield at least book value and, it is hoped, much more. The NAB's Don Argus has about $4.2 billion in problem loans, with a specific provision of about $1.1 billion, so his bank has half as many net problem loans as Conroy's, although its provision is smaller.

Conroy and Westpac also had to counter some of the ill will created in the market by the September 1991 balance sheet. Six months later, Westpac had to claw back $95 million of the claimed $700-million 1991 superannuation surplus. The general provision of $1.1 billion for doubtful debts was reduced to $700 million in the latest changes, and future European tax benefits of $55 million were reversed. US accounting standards once again proved a better guide to the 1990–91 results than did the Australian outcome.

One of the reasons for Westpac changing its policy was the new accounting standard 1010. Every company in Australia is now required to look closely at the market value of all its assets when preparing a balance sheet. The market was nervous that Westpac would be hit again by this policy and after the issue was announced the shares fell below the $3 issue price making directors very thankful they had arranged an underwriter.

The new environment

If we look past the problems of Westpac and other companies that have made write-downs, we will see emerging a very different business environment: one in which there is a lot of money to be made if you have a good business. In the past, the big fortunes were often made because of rises in property values, rather than in the value of a business. But what the Westpac assumptions indicate is an environment in which the value of a business will be a prime asset.

Leaving aside the low level of economic activity, the actual business climate has never been more favorable. As we know, interest rates are down. It is possible to rent property at a fraction of former costs and lock in low rates for most of the decade. Wage outcomes are restricted through lower inflation, and managers who are doing their job are eliminating unnecessary work practices. If you can hold your business's revenue at a reasonable level, then the outlook for profits is good. And, as the sharemarket is showing, as rates fall, so the value of those profits is rising. If your shareholders' funds are being hit by the property downturn, the value of your goodwill and brands might compensate.

How the Big Boys Work

THE WESTPAC–AMP DEAL IS SWUNG

WESTPAC'S former chairman Eric Neal and AMP chairman James Balderstone are not traditional banking or life office people, yet their roles were pivotal in changing a decade of management strategy, in 1991 making the AMP–Westpac strategic alliance possible. The alliance of Australia's biggest life office and oldest private bank created a force of unprecedented power in the Australian capital and savings market. The two chairmen took a fresh look at the adversarial strategies of their organisations adopted in the 1980s and their far-reaching discussions set the framework for the alliance. What made this a rare event was that it owed its origins to an arrangement between two chairmen rather than the top management of the companies. It would therefore never be easy to implement. Of course in 1990–91 neither Eric Neal nor James Balderstone understood the extent of future Westpac problems which have tended to obscure the remarkable deal.

The paths of Neal and Balderstone have crossed many times over the years. Balderstone made his name in the meat trade and as chairman of BHP during the Holmes à Court battle. Neal made his name in building products by developing Boral into a major force in the industry.

Balderstone became a professional director in 1970–71 when he joined three boards—AMP, BHP and the CBA Bank. After the CBA Bank merged with the Bank of NSW, he became a director of Westpac, but in 1984 had to choose between the board of Westpac and the AMP; the AMP had decided to go into banking against Westpac. Balderstone chose the AMP and left the Westpac board—the same year he became chairman of BHP. Neal joined the Westpac board in 1985, and three years later went on the BHP board under Balderstone's chairmanship.

Neal might have become chairman of BHP to replace the retiring Balderstone had he not been headed for chairmanship of Westpac. When Balderstone took over as chairman of the AMP in February 1990, he and Neal had unique chairmanship positions.

The AMP and Westpac chairmanships are not usually at the forefront of change, but during 1990 Neal and Balderstone were shouldering burdens of responsibility much greater than most of their predecessors, and those pressures played an important role in the alliance.

The pressures for Neal at Westpac have been well documented. When he joined the bank's board in 1985 he could not have conceived the number of dangerous loans that the bank was granting. But he would have noticed that the bank's accounting system (in common with other banks) was out of date and well below the standard he had set at Boral. Stuart Fowler, then Westpac chief executive, had been modernising the system but it was a slow process and the system doubtlessly contributed to the more than $6 billion of problem loans and sharply reduced profits at the bank.

Westpac's adventure into life assurance was a direct response to the AMP entering banking. Whereas the AMP was not successful at banking, Westpac clearly showed that a bank could win at life assurance. Although Westpac Life was doing well in the marketplace, its growth was draining cash at a bad time for the bank. Later, more capital would be required for life assurance, competing even more strongly with the group's banking requirements.

The problems Balderstone inherited when he took over the chairmanship of the AMP were not as well understood as those faced by Neal but were more demanding. In his first year as chairman, Balderstone watched the AMP's reserves fall sharply as a result of the decline in share and property values. Although the AMP remained very strong, the impact of the fall was made more severe by a war with the National Mutual that had forced the AMP to provide high-reward capital-guaranteed products for industry superannuation funds. The AMP had invested a lot of the new money into long-term equity positions, so it was vulnerable in a fall. (The National Mutual had also suffered.)

At the same time, the AMP's costs had risen sharply and this would affect long-term growth, particularly as the industry superannuation funds it had wooed could easily migrate to other managers who offered a better deal. As 1990 rolled on, the Gulf War loomed and the Australian sharemarket continued to be depressed. Balderstone could not have predicted in the final months of 1990 that Australian and world sharemarkets would have a big rise in the first three months of 1991 to replenish the reserves. Indeed, there seemed every chance it would fall further.

Not only had the AMP's move into banking been unsuccessful, but it had been demonstrated that banks were an efficient way to distribute life assurance products. The distribution system the AMP had developed over generations and in which so much had been invested during the National Mutual war, would not provide the growth the AMP hoped for during the next twenty years. Clearly, these were great concerns for the AMP board. Balderstone's clear mind in simplifying problems had been important for BHP during the takeover battle in the 1980s. It was required again at the AMP.

Against a background of strategic questioning in both organisations, late in 1990 the two chairmen started the comprehensive talks about where their organisations were going. Balderstone faced the most immediate problem at that time so he initiated the discussions. Not only did some people at the AMP Society realise they needed a bank distribution outlet, but the managing director, Ian Stanwell, had been ill and the society was then looking to appoint Ian Salmon. The timing was right for both Balderstone and Neal and the talks went well, partly because neither man had played a role in the war between the two organisations.

In the 1980s both managements believed they were invincible. By November 1990, the two chairmen knew better and saw that an alliance would bring overwhelming advantages. Neal reported to his board and it was decided to form a management taskforce to negotiate with the AMP. Neal and the board chose Frank Conroy and David Morgan, the key Westpac bank executives who worked under Fowler, plus the general manager of group strategic planning, Vernon Harvey. Nevertheless the absence of the Westpac managing director Stuart Fowler from the team must have seemed strange to the AMP people.

The AMP's choice would also have seemed strange to the Westpac people if they had not been tipped off about the pending reorganisation. The AMP's chief general manager international, Ian Salmon, headed the taskforce with the support of the chief funds manager, Ray Greenshields, and strategy planning executive and chief economist, Ian Campbell. Within a few weeks Salmon would be told that he would take over as managing director with the brief to undertake a big reorganisation. So the Westpac talks became a crucial part of strategies.

For secrecy reasons, the first meeting of the taskforce was held at Melbourne's Regent Hotel, which is part of the Collins Place development owned by the AMP. This was a fitting setting for Salmon, considering that at that time he was probably still best known for his Collins Place victory over Norm Gallagher in the 1970s.

High on the AMP negotiating team's agenda was the aim to secure bank outlets for its life policies. If the AMP could produce life and personal super products under the Westpac and AMP names, it would leave its competitors trailing. On the Westpac agenda was the need for capital, the prospect of higher profits and the attraction of having a long-term relationship with the AMP. It was soon clear that beyond these early agendas a strategic alliance between the two groups would change the face of the capital markets in Australia. Security was kept tight until it was necessary to inform Canberra.

The final deal delighted both boards. The AMP would buy the life assurance and personal superannuation business of Westpac, but would not handle Westpac's corporate superannuation. A jointly-owned company would distribute AMP life and personal superannuation products throughout the Westpac banking system. Life assurance would immediately become a source of profit for Westpac rather than a drain. Westpac would become the main banker for AMP (a position it had lost when the two groups began fighting) and the AMP would take a placement of Westpac shares to lift its position to 10%, and then later, in March 1992, to 15%.

With the placement, life office sale and other moves, more than $300 million would immediately be added to Westpac's capital base. A further $200 million was added when the AMP reached 15% of Westpac. There were also other smaller parts of the deal that were significant. They included:

- The AMP will underwrite a range of Westpac-brand general insurance products to be distributed through the bank's branches.
- Westpac will provide the AMP with a series of bank transaction products to be marketed to AMP policy holders under an appropriate brand name.
- The two groups will join the BLE capital group, which specialises in venture capital and provides loans and equity for smaller businesses. The AMP will inject $24 million and will become an equal partner with Westpac and 3i Group Plc.
- It is proposed that the AMP obtain treasury and financial services from Westpac on a non-exclusive basis.
- The two groups agree to develop associations overseas, where a common interest can be developed profitably.

At the AMP Salmon moved to implement some of the biggest changes the society had made since its foundation. As part of those changes the AMP has effectively become a contract supplier of life office products using two market outlets—its agents and the Westpac joint marketing company. It has two brands—AMP and Westpac—possibly the two best in the country.

A report from management consultants McKinsey & Co recommended extensive internal changes to the AMP as part of a program to reduce costs by a staggering $200 million. The report also discussed the problem of the group's marketing. It said there was an important role for independent life agents, but that like similar institutions around the world, the AMP commission-based selling systems were wrong. At that time, when an agent sold policies which needed little input or policy tailoring, the agent's compensation structures were too high. On the other hand, when an agent was required to spend a lot of time setting up a policy and continuing to service the client in subsequent years, the compensation was too low.

Accordingly, Salmon told his life agents that their commissions were too heavily geared to the sale and not sufficiently geared to the service. He pointed out that life agents would become much more professional and receive less for start-up sales and more for honouring continuing obligations but overall fees would fall. Because clients have a choice of where they buy AMP products—either through an agent or, by using the Westpac brand, through a bank—agents' commissions are a sensitive matter. It is likely that people who know that they want will get the best deal at Westpac, but those who require special products and counselling will tend to deal through a life agent and pay slightly more.

When Westpac embarked on the project to create a new life office, it did so in an environment of increasing profits and the vision of growth unbounded. However, building a life business adds value to a balance sheet, but any profits recorded are required to be re-invested in the business and often are insufficient to fund the growth. It is not until a life business is 20–25 years old that it begins to mature and provide a cash benefit to its shareholders. The MLC is a classic illustration. The company was not popular on the sharemarket because it handed out so few benefits to shareholders. It took Ron Brierley to realise the store of wealth that existed in the maturing MLC, although it was Lend Lease that capitalised on the opportunity.

These days banks need to supply revenue to shareholders and their credit rating is determined by their basic profitability and gearing. Had Westpac continued to fund its life company, shareholders would have had to wait well into the next century for the benefits.

But many Westpac people were unhappy with the deal because they believed the bank would have been better placed to press on alone in the life business. But a year later they were glad of the AMP backing when the bank announced a staggering $1.7-billion loss and asset write-down plus an issue of capital to cover the losses. It was then the turn of the AMP people to mumble about its role. The Society had bought its shares in Westpac above $4.60 and watched them fall below $3 after the loss.

At the time, Eric Neal was proud to add the AMP to his list of directorships, which included Australia's biggest company (BHP), biggest life office (AMP) and biggest private bank. The 1992 Westpac and AMP resignations were a deep personal blow. James Balderstone was equally pleased to resume his seat at the Westpac board table—the position he relinquished when the AMP went into banking, although problems he found at Westpac must have made him wonder whether instead of linking with Westpac he should have chosen the National Australia Bank where his friend, BHP's Brian Loton, is vice chairman.

CSR LOOKS THROUGH A FOUR-YEAR TUNNEL

IN MAKING their historic asset write-downs early in 1992, the directors of CSR worked on three important assumptions: that the Australian economy would perform much worse than the US during the four years from 1992; that Australia's recovery over the first three of those four years would be slow and restrained; that unemployment would remain high during that time.

What makes these assumptions so significant is that the CSR board includes people who sit on the boards of some of the biggest and most influential enterprises in the country, including BHP, AMP, Brambles, CRA, Pacific Dunlop and the Queensland Investment Corporation. Each director was personally involved in the assumptions and the valuations although, when presented with a choice, the board almost always accepted the lowest figure.

The entire business and investment community, when assessing future long-term strategies and forecasts, obviously will take into account this pessimistic outlook by such an influential group of directors.

But CSR's assessment of the Australian economy is only one aspect of a remarkable revaluation that breaks new ground in Australian accounting and management practices. CSR began the process when it realised that its management was reluctant to shut down surplus plants because the big write-offs involved would affect the bottom line. This is a problem that many other companies have faced: keeping plants going on a token basis simply to avoid write-offs.

When CSR first proposed to its auditor, Deloitte Ross Tohmatsu, that the plant write-downs be recorded as an extraordinary item below the profit line, it was met with a polite shake of the head. Because it made no sense to keep the plants going, managing director Ian Burgess was prepared to take the write-downs against profit if no alternative was available. The plant problem led the company to look at its entire asset register, including the $680 million invested in goodwill, patents and trademarks. CSR began to consider whether, if the plant write-downs were part of an overall review of asset values, the auditors might possibly treat the whole exercise as below the profit line. Most company boards and the accountancy profession are in debate in this area. The boards want asset write-downs (or write-ups) completely separate from yearly profits so they don't affect dividends and obscure year-to-year trading results. Accountants want them classed as abnormal losses (or profits).

CSR's chief finance officer, Don Murdon, hit on an idea to execute a write-down without affecting the dividend. Perhaps the parent company's share premium reserve, which had been created by issuing shares above face value, could be used for a dividend if shareholders and the courts approved the move. It was unprecedented but the lawyers agreed and Deloitte's Rob Freeman went one further by accepting the principle that a huge one-off asset review, including the plant write-downs, would be treated as an extraordinary item below the profit line. But Freeman was not allowed to buck his profession and his advice was later opposed by other leading accountants and the Australian Securities Commission, forcing CSR to write the assets down above the profit line. Later the accounting standards were changed forcing a regular review of assets and the charges treated as abnormal items. CSR's approach was followed by many others.

In its review, CSR wrote down assets by $696 million, which was reduced by a write-up of land and buildings totalling $188 million, making a net asset reduction of $508 million. Tax benefits on the plant closure and other items, plus minorities' share of the write-downs, brought the net reduction to shareholders' funds to $372 million.

In all, CSR shut twenty-eight plants in Australia and the US, with write-downs totalling $194 million. This was the first part of the exercise. The next area to be examined was CSR's brand names and trademarks, which were in the books at about $180 million. Although the company's main brands are CSR, Bradford, Readymix and Gyprock, none of these was in the balance sheet because they were not part of a recent acquisition.

The brands valued in the books included Formica, Monier, Hydro Conduit, Humes and Rinker in the US. In the various CSR takeovers, these brands had been given values, usually based on a value added to profit. Most of CSR's recent acquisitions involved substantial goodwill payments, which needed to be amortised against profit. But brands do not have to be amortised, so there was a clear incentive to maximise brand values and reduce goodwill by a corresponding amount.

The company asked Paul Espie of Pacific Road Securities to conduct the brand and trademark valuation; he chose a 'comparable royalty basis', which means that he estimated how much an outside party might pay for the use of each brand. This produced a very different result from past methods: brand and trademark values were cut by $120 million to about $60 million.

The group's largest intangible was goodwill, which was valued in 1991 at just under $500 million, including $350 million in US assets. The valuation of US intangibles was obviously a key item in the total review, so it was preceded by a strategic assessment by the board of the company's US strategy. Most of the CSR directors visited the US independently to satisfy themselves that the group's US investment was still a correct strategy. The board was unanimous that the investment was sound and decided it was likely to perform much better than Australian investments in the years ahead.

Forward cashflow estimates were prepared for all Australian and US operations, based on assumptions agreed to by the board and management. The ten-year projections by CSR's US chief, Keith Barton, were discounted at an annual rate of 10.5% to reach a current value. The first Barton estimates vindicated the $350 million goodwill valuation. The board then asked Barton to prepare his most pessimistic case.

Half of CSR's US investment is in Florida, where CSR is one of three companies that dominate the state's aggregate and ready-mixed concrete market. Florida's population is rising by 200 000 a year (the annual rise has been as high as 500 000). Although the recession has hit sales of the company's products, there is huge latent demand. Barton's pessimistic-case forecast was that recovery would begin at the end of 1992 and proceed steadily. In any current valuation based on discounted cashflow, the rate of cashflow in the first two or three years is vital to the final outcome. The pessimistic view cut $100 million from the US goodwill, reducing it to $250 million. Directors accepted the low figure.

In Australia, directors agreed to assume that inflation would stay low (about 3%), making it difficult to achieve substantial price rises. The board's view was that the amount of business destroyed by the recession and the severe cost-cutting still being undertaken by

Australian companies, plus continuing unemployment caused by the number of young people coming out of the education system, would dampen consumer confidence. Accordingly, recovery in growth would be modest in CSR's financial years to 31 March 1993, 1994 and 1995. A bigger rise was expected in CSR's 1995–96 year as the problems worked their way through the system. However, the 1995–96 boost did not greatly affect the March 1992 numbers because, reflecting higher interest rates in Australia, a discount rate of about 13% was used on the projected cashflows to determine today's value. As a result, the value of Australian goodwill fell from $120 million to $20 million.

In fairness, much of the Australian goodwill was invested in timber, and CSR had taken on its competitors in a price war. The value of timber and log licences was cut by $45 million. Slow growth in Australia also cut the value of quarry and other raw material reserves by $69 million. If the company had not written up any assets after the write-down, the group's gearing would have come out at about 35%, compared with 29% before the adjustments.

The CSR board does not want the ratio of long-term borrowing to shareholders' funds plus long-term borrowing to exceed 35%. Although the company had the ability to write up the main brands, it chose not to, because it might need to amortise them against profit. Assets such as the group's aluminium interests could have been written up, but this would have involved a new asset class valuing all CSR's plant and equipment—a huge job.

CSR had never written up its real estate during the boom, but it would have been required to make a revaluation in 1993 under new regulations, so this valuation was brought forward. Properties were revalued and all valuations were based on current zoning (the Sydney Pyrmont refinery site was zoned industrial). This resulted in an increase of $188 million.

The cost of the total asset valuation was about $2 million. But future profits will increase by about $15 million a year because amortisation and depreciation charges will be reduced.

LESSONS FROM MIM SHOCK

A DIFFERENT approach to mineral development projects by federal and state governments will be an important part of recovery in Australia. However, just as Canberra was beginning to understand what was required, one of our biggest mining groups, MIM, was downgraded by S&P-Australian Ratings. Although credit downgradings have become common in Australia, the reasons for the downgrading of MIM will reverberate around a large section of Australian mining, manufacturing and service industries.

Mount Isa has been one of Australia's great low-cost mineral resources in the post-war years. But with those riches came bad work practices, high government charges and several unsuccessful attempts at diversification by MIM's board. Managing director Norm Fussell and his team slashed MIM's costs, but at the same time some other high-cost producers went out of business, MIM's rivals around the world cut their costs and new low-cost mines such as BHP's Escondida (copper mine) in Chile entered the market.

The ratings agency says MIM's transport (partly provided by the Queensland Government), milling and processing facilities are high-to-medium cost and the overall operation has moved up in the world cost scale. Accordingly, MIM's credit rating is being assessed on a world-competitive basis and this practice will be extended to other Australian projects.

Australian institutions and bankers, as well as the owners of mineral deposits, must now assess everything on a world basis as they determine whether to invest. If they are tempted to invest on the basis of political or national sentiment, then the credit rating agencies will quickly haul them into line. I am not sure Australian management and governments fully understand what this change means.

But there is another significant aspect of the downgrading: S&P put little weight on MIM's long-term strategic investments. Most Australian companies focus on short-term performance because of the pressure exerted by institutions that are somewhat like children with a short concentration span (many of the problems experienced by US companies stem from the attitude of their institutional shareholders).

MIM has about $1.2 billion in borrowings, and almost the same amount has been used to build up a series of strategic investments. These include minority stakes in European zinc and copper treatment plants in partnership with the German Metallgesellschaft: 3% of Metallgesellschaft (the AMP owns 5%), 22.5% of the Canadian-based metal miner Cominco; and 25% of Asarco in the US. In turn, Asarco owns 18.5% of MIM and Metallgesellschaft owns 14%. Returns from MIM's $1.2-billion investment portfolio are very poor; the company yielded only about $42 million in the year to 30 June, disregarding a windfall gain. In addition, the investment plays havoc with debt-servicing ratios in a time of low commodity prices.

Should MIM quit its investments, pay off its borrowing and enjoy a leap in its credit rating? When I spoke with Norm Fussell at the end of January 1992, (before the credit rating came out), he was adamant that participation in the Metall-MIM-Cominco network—one of the biggest forces in the world zinc and lead market—is one of MIM's great assets and the stake in Asarco's US copper operation complements it. Interestingly, Cominco is one of the world's lowest-cost zinc producers. Fussell will have to take the credit-rating downgrade on the chin.

Downstream thoughts

I have selected a few quotes from Fussell's thoughts on investing in downstream processing plants that I think many resource enterprises (including agriculture) might ponder. The strategic thinking behind MIM's investment has wide application.

> Our strategy is that today we are in a market world where you can no longer live behind the mine fence and expect that the people downstream are going to take care of your interest. Therefore you have to follow your product to the market . . .
>
> In a sense, it is no different from a General Motors now owning its distributors and dealers—Toyota, anybody in that sort of game. The market today is much more about quality and hence, premiums on good-quality metals in all the markets. It is much more about just-in-time inventories—critically about just-in-time inventories in a lot of cases. It is much more about bi-product disposal markets, because bi-products are becoming a much more important component of the economics. All of that is not necessarily good news for Australia because in some ways it is dragging processing closer to the market . . .
>
> No, Metall didn't screw us. [Many of MIM's stakes in processing were bought from Metall]. If we hadn't got an entry into Europe, what we were receiving for our metal at Mount Isa would be a lot worse today than it is. So you can't look at the investment profit contribution simply as a contribution . . .
>
> Copper miners are hurting at the moment because treatment charges are double those of 12 months ago. They will stay that way for four or five years because there is a smelter bottleneck. Out of that we will get two or three new smelters in the world, so in five years there will be a glut of smelting capacity . . .
>
> We were doubling our zinc capacity at Mount Isa in the early 1980s. We had a situation where Japan had been our only customer for 25 years and we had no interest in zinc smelting/refining anywhere. We took the view that if we were to continue in that situation in the midst of doubling our capacity while at the same time the Canadians were bringing on additional capacity, our economics in terms of what we got as net back to the mine would become catastrophic. So we had to diversify our market and we had to find new capacity.

It was that that drove us into buying 50% of Ruhr-Zink in Germany, locking up contracts for 130,000 tonnes of concentrate. They would not have put one-third of their total intake with one group without some other connection . . .

To build a zinc refinery today would cost you $500 million. We have half of the zinc refinery for $25.6 million. We've just expanded Ruhr-Zink from 120,000 to 200,000 tonnes. To finance the expansion there was money from the EC for environmental reasons, there was money from the German Federal Government for environmental reasons, there were low-interest loans guaranteed by the state. Because it was creating jobs, the equity that had to go towards the plant was very small.

Of course, that is one of the difficulties you have when you look at building a stand-alone plant in Australia versus building it in markets where there is not a level playing field . . .

We are shipping the equivalent of 250,000 tonnes of zinc metal and concentrates at present. We arguably have got about 150,000 tonnes' capacity in plants that we've got in joint venture. This is one reason we look to Japan for an extra one . . .

Secondary processing in Australia? You don't always get a role in the secondary processing in Australia because we are not big enough. The big secondary markets are going to be Japan and South-East Asia.

An issue for Australia is energy cost for heavy industry. We tend to want to sell electricity and gas to industrial users at the same price as we sell them to household consumers. We really have to change that policy to the Japanese and Western European policy of special rates for industry, to attract industry on a long-term basis. If we do that, there are opportunities in Australia.

BHP

The plunge into beer

Chairman Brian Loton was probably the most cautious of all BHP board members about going deeper into Foster's Brewing Group. Although Loton was not opposed to BHP effectively spending $1.5 billion in additional cash to acquire 37% of the brewer, he has a most unpleasant memory of his period on the Elders IXL (now Foster's) board.

During the late 1980s, Robert Holmes à Court's buying of BHP shares was countered by John Elliott's Elders, and BHP, in turn, took a placement of Elders shares. In the truce that followed, Elliott and Holmes à Court went on to the BHP board and Loton joined Elders. During his time at Elders, Loton saw Elliott and his team in full flight, creating an empire that was expanding, apparently without bounds, and creating a culture that would prove dangerous in the 1990s. Some of the 1980s Elders traditions were still implanted in parts of Foster's and Loton needed to make sure everyone at BHP understood what they were getting into.

Many in the stockmarket believe BHP is skipping a few pages in the corporate rule book by going much deeper into a business that is foreign to its own operation. To succeed, BHP and the Foster's board will need to make changes in the culture and operations of the company, as well as countering some threats to the business.

It is not surprising that the market is asking whether BHP should go back into Foster's and risk another $1.5 billion, and suffer a share price fall. In the end, after weighing up the risks, BHP has decided to invest in the brewer because of the potential rewards. It also found it very hard to walk away from the $1 billion that Elliott's International Brewing Holdings owed BHP, even though that amount was in the BHP books at $583 million at 31 May, and Foster's shares have been trading at levels that indicate that most of the money is lost.

Yet any loss from supporting Elliott is the only bad point in what was Loton's most brilliant single deal when, after the 1987 sharemarket crash, Holmes à Court became a forced seller of his huge BHP share parcel and Elders also agreed to sell its BHP shares. About half the combined parcel was purchased by BHP for the current equivalent of about $6.40 a share and was cancelled. The other half was bought by a newly created company called Beswick Pty Ltd, owned 50% by BHP and 49.9% by Elders, and the balance by the ANZ Bank as trustee. But the capital structure was organised so that 88% of any increase in the value of BHP shares went to BHP and only 12% to Elders.

BHP was making a paper profit of about $1.7 billion on its investment in Beswick as a result of the rise in BHP shares, and the purchase and cancellation of the shares theoretically yielded an even bigger sum: a total of $4 billion when the Foster's decision was made.

In 1988 when Elders, BHP and Beswick entered into their deals, BHP's shares in Elders were sold to a joint company called Harlin, which was similar to Beswick but with one important difference: the main gain on any increase in Elders' share price was to go to Elliott and his co-shareholders rather than to Elders itself. (Harlin's name was later changed to International Brewing Holdings.) That gave Elliott a much bigger stake in the Elders operation and also revealed the difference in attitude between the two men: Elliott was the entrepreneur; Loton was the professional executive.

Unfortunately for Elliott, he was unaware of the difficulties his rapid expansion would create. International Brewing was not content with the stake in Elders it obtained from BHP. He ultimately made a bid for the entire company at what turned out to be too high a price. The subsequent decline in Foster's share price wiped out Elliott's equity and those who had lent unsecured money to finance the bid.

The so-called Vextin banking syndicate had first charge on International Brewing's shares in Foster's and BHP had second charge. The Vextin syndicate appointed a receiver to that part of International Brewing that owned 32% of Foster's (Citicorp controls another 116 million Foster's shares). BHP has now bought the Vextin syndicate's Foster's stake for $2 a share, at a cost of $1.44 billion. It is also paying an additional $60 million to take up two sets of options, but the actual cash cost to BHP of the Vextin 32% is only $1 billion because BHP's position was also supported by a series of guarantees that Elliott obtained from a syndicate of banks to persuade BHP to allow him to bid for all of Foster's.

Now that those guarantees have been exercised, about $1 billion of the cash BHP paid for Foster's shares has gone to the banks. The balance of the $500 million went back to BHP itself. In addition, BHP must subscribe $300 million to the Foster's new issue, bringing the total outlay to $1.3 billion.

But BHP also revealed at a news conference in September 1992 that it had been required by the Vextin bank syndicate to offer $2 a share for 100 million Foster's shares held as security for Citicorp's loan. This is a very expensive purchase because BHP is not pocketing the money over $1.40 a share. And it will bring BHP's total outlay to $1.5 billion and its average price prior to the rights issue up to $1.46—the market level on the day of the announcement. A price of $1.46 is very close to a level at which BHP would lose all its equity and would be rescuing the banks.

Therefore, the only way to look at BHP's bid for Foster's is to regard it as a new investment, and to determine whether this is the best way for BHP to spend between $1.3 billion and $1.5 billion. Other international breweries looked at Foster's and reckoned BHP's overall price of $2 was too high (bearing in mind that they were obliged to make a full bid, whereas BHP could limit its purchase to 32%). BHP had two choices: walk away or take Foster's shares at a cost of $1.40, plus the new-issue commitment. Directors concluded it was a good investment despite Foster's problems.

However, in July 1992, BHP called together brokers and institutions from around the country to explain that BHP's new corporate strategy was to 'become the world's best resources company'. The board had authorised the outlay of $6 billion during the next few years on projects spread over the group's three main divisions: steel, petroleum and minerals. Included in the total plan was the spending of between $1.5 billion and $3 billion on the acquisition of an additional minerals enterprise. It was a confident BHP with a clear sense of direction that faced the institutions, and the market knew what it was about.

BHP is an incredibly strong company, with cashflow from operations even in the depressed 1991–92 year totalling $3 billion. In the previous year it generated cash of $4.2 billion. The company's new projects coming forward, particularly in the oil sector, and the better returns expected from the Escondida copper operation in Chile, are expected to lift cash generation substantially in coming years. Against that background, investing another $1.3 billion to $1.5 billion in Foster's is not regarded as a big allocation of funds. However, by putting new cash into the brewer, BHP is making a much deeper commitment to the company than it ever has in the past. Until now, it had always been an option for BHP to take its loss on Harlin (International Brewing Holdings) and offset it with a healthy profit on Beswick, which would have reasonably satisfied BHP's shareholders.

Foster's has gross assets of $8.2 billion, making it bigger than any of BHP's single divisions, and equal to more than one-third of BHP's total assets of $24 billion. Ranking ahead of BHP's equity in Foster's is some $6.8 billion in liabilities, including more than $3.6 billion in borrowings. BHP's borrowings total $8.3 billion. Of course, with less than 40% of Foster's, BHP will not consolidate the Foster's debt and assets on to its own balance sheet, but it will almost certainly equity-account the Foster's profit into its own. On the other hand, it will be very difficult for BHP to retreat from Foster's, so the company must perform and service its debt obligations or there will be huge pressure on BHP to inject further capital. In effect, the position of Foster's is similar to that of a partly owned BHP subsidiary.

Two years ago it was becoming obvious that Elliott's International Brewing Holdings would collapse. BHP began a detailed study of Foster's, so that if and when the time came to decide whether to buy out the bank lenders to International Brewing and take control of the 32% of Foster's, then the facts would be available so directors could make a considered decision. Those studies have revealed the depth of the Foster's problems, but also the opportunity to transform the company if management is able to overcome them.

Some of the worst problems at Foster's are in the beer operations in Australia, where the business has been neglected while executives spent time worrying about board battles. Most of the publicity has been directed towards the company's problem loans, which are the subject of this week's big write-offs and subsequent new issue.

But Foster's more serious long-term problems involve its base beer operation.

During the 1980s, Foster's was too good for a Castlemaine Tooheys managed by Bond Brewing. But now that Doug Myers' Lion Nathan is in charge, Foster's rival is much more aggressive. It caught Foster's napping in its home town of Melbourne and took market share away through the launch of Tooheys Blue. During the decade ahead, Foster's faces a formidable foe in Australia. Myers told institutions in September 1992 that Castlemaine Tooheys' productivity per employee was 40% better than Foster's and profitability per employee was 60% better.

Last December, SA Brewing's Ross Wilson commissioned the international management consultant LEK to study all the Foster's operations. It identified huge cost savings available within the Foster's group; it was these savings that made Wilson anxious to proceed with his merger proposal. BHP has done its own study and come to similar conclusions. The Melbourne plant has poor productivity, Queensland is not much better and the NSW plant needs heavy investment. Confirming these conclusions, Castlemaine Tooheys earned $220 million before interest and tax in 1991–92, whereas Foster's managed only $190 million from 4–6% more market share.

BHP sees the waste at Foster's as an opportunity to boost profitability substantially. It is encouraged by the appointment of Ted Kunkel as managing director. It did not take Lion Nathan long to transform Castlemaine Tooheys so, presumably, the same thing can be done to Foster's with even more dramatic results. Of course, beer is completely outside BHP's area of expertise and it must rely on the Foster's management. But it has appointed four line managers to the Foster's board.

One of the attractions of committing itself to Foster's was BHP's belief in the ability of Kunkel, who impressed with his management of costs at the Canadian operations of Foster's. In Australia, his first move was to acquire virtual control of Queensland's Power Brewing, which is an efficient operation, and opens the way to transferring much of the Queensland brewing operation to it. In the longer term, it is an option to supply other states from Brisbane.

Over the years, Foster's has never had good relations with its hotel customers and its suppliers. The dramatic ending of SA Brewing's can contract was a typical example. It is always dangerous to tackle a new competitor when relations with customers and suppliers are uneasy. The company has now embarked on a customer-service training program.

But the Foster's problems in Australia go deeper than costs and customers. Its flagship brand, Foster's, has become a relatively small player in the Australian beer market, considering the big promotion it has had. The company's management always believed that Foster's beer could be promoted like soft drink, but the strategy does not seem to have worked. It is possible that the Foster's name became too tarnished by Elliott's plan to 'Fosterise' the world and became too identified with him as a symbol of the 1980s.

To direct so much advertising expenditure at a flagship brand that is not performing, at least in its full-strength form, is a big long-term problem. Kunkel has tried to cover the gap by introducing Victoria Bitter on tap into hotels, and in NSW he has resurrected the Reschs brand. The new Foster's Bitter is being used as the counter to Tooheys Blue, a move that carries an extra risk by using the Foster's name.

BHP advisers were dismayed recently when the Australian management of Foster's began describing the company publicly as a beverage group, with a hint that it might one day go into soft drinks. With so much work to be done in the beer area, Foster's is a long way from diversification. It is the last thing shareholders want, particularly given the group's debt. The remarks showed how difficult it is going to be for the new Foster's board, and Kunkel, to remove the old traditions.

Foster's has excellent businesses in Britain and Canada, but both are under challenge. In Britain, all the existing brewers are being forced to end their hotel ties, which will change the rules of British brewing. Courage has the advantage of a bigger share of the packaged beer market and this will assist it during this process. It also has been a successful marketer. Nevertheless, from next November, about 2500 of the 6800 hotels in its joint-venture company, Inntrepreneur, will no longer be tied houses.

Many other changes are likely in brewer relationships in the next few years and it will require expert management from the Foster's group to gain best advantage. But BHP knows that if the going ever gets tough in Britain, there are buyers for the Foster's interests there.

In Canada, Kunkel did an excellent job bringing the Foster's and Molson breweries into a joint venture, which is likely to enjoy increasing profitability. To date, the Canadian beer market has been highly regulated and US brewers have found it difficult to penetrate the market. But from the beginning of 1994, possibly earlier, the brewery-owned beer stores in Ontario will be opened to US competition, although the provincial government will set a minimum price to deter dumping. Nevertheless, it represents a serious challenge to the Molson–Foster's joint venture. On the other hand, the full benefits of the rationalisation have not yet been reflected in profits, and the worst-case scenario is that Molson's profits could fall 10–20%.

The Molson group lost heavily in supporting Elliott in his bid for Foster's. It looked hard at buying part, or all, of International Brewing's Foster's parcel but was not prepared to match BHP's price. The other obvious buyer of Foster's shares was the Asahi brewing group of Japan, but it has its own problems.

When BHP announced it was appointing a receiver to International Brewing and was prepared to buy out the Vextin banking syndicate, the market took the move calmly, but then it realised the extent of the asset write-downs and the fact that Foster's would need to make a share issue. It was apparent that BHP was going into a problem situation. In general, brokers tend to the view that BHP is motivated in part by its past statements that it would not lose from its investment in International Brewing.

Overseas investors have always been nervous about Foster's, going back to the days when they were well ahead of Australians in predicting Elliott's problems. Other brokers take the view that there is clear long-term value in Foster's and that to walk away would be to effectively sell at the bottom of the market. The BHP board concluded that, with the right management changes and cohesive board supervision, Foster's could emerge as a strongly performing company.

The war between Foster's and Castlemaine Tooheys will require marketing innovations on both sides. It will be difficult for small brewers to survive, leaving the two majors to fight it out. Both companies are dedicated to profitability and each knows it cannot wipe the other out. On BHP's sums, assuming the written-down Foster's outstandings are collected during five years, the company could be debt-free in three years. Capital expenditure commitments may delay the event, but the company has the potential to be a cash powerhouse.

It is not easy to find mineral investments in Australia because of the myriad restrictions and bans on mining, so most of BHP's mineral development work will be overseas. Accordingly, an investment in Foster's increases the group's stake in Australia and is an offset against volatile commodity markets. But at this stage, with so many problems ahead, BHP would be delighted to sell and recoup its money.

However, if and when the problems are solved, BHP may get a taste for beer and it is always possible that with its 'Fresco' options, which are to be exercised in eighteen months' time at $2.09 and the 'Faversham' options, which are exercised in April 1993 at $2.19, BHP will decide to go into Foster's more deeply.

Looking to the future

BHP's decision to move deep into Foster's in an attempt to recover a bad investment is of great concern to those who saw little downside risk in BHP's medium-term outlook. After BHP announced the bid its shares fell sharply. If it can overcome the Foster's problem end then, despite its present setbacks, BHP still has the potential to earn $2.5 billion a year by the mid-1990s as a result of the work of the company's prior years. A clear aim looms for BHP executives: the attainment of a $2-billion profit. Although 1992–93 will again be tough, the following year looks much better. The structures are in place to begin earning at the $2-billion target rate in 1993–94, and by the middle of the decade BHP has the potential to begin earning at a $2.5-billion rate. The reason for the optimism is BHP's commitment to long-term projects in past years.

For the past few years BHP has been spending $2 billion a year on its businesses, building up future capacity. It has reduced costs in steel (although not as far as it had hoped) and built an export business, launched the remarkable Escondida copper mine in Chile, increased efficiency in other parts of its minerals business and, after a successful round of exploration, now plans to bring on stream a succession of oil and gas fields that will be commissioned in the first half of the 1990s.

The recession has delayed the flow-through of these moves by slashing the profitability of the steel business. Nevertheless, BHP has performed better than most other large companies in Australia and its individual divisions have outperformed most companies in similar businesses overseas.

BHP's share price has more than doubled since the dark days just before the reconstruction in 1988 that saw Elders IXL and Robert Holmes à Court sell their stakes although in September 1992 it was hammered back.

Like CSR, BHP itself is taking a very conservative view of the Australian and world economies, and is not budgeting for significant upturns in economic activity for the 1992–93 financial year. But its minerals and oil divisions will lead the charge towards the $2-billion profit target. BHP Minerals' profit growth will come not only from Escondida and the expected recovery in commodities prices as the world swings out of recession, but also from cost-cutting and productivity increases in existing projects. Particularly exciting is the plan to produce copper metal at Escondida as part of a 25% rise in output. As well, the business will grab a bigger share of world markets through more effective marketing and efficient delivery of its products.

A key to the future of the group is business in the emerging nations of North Asia, which have become important markets for iron ore and coal and will become increasingly important to the company during the 1990s. The company is also exporting steel to mills in Korea. BHP believes that although the Japanese economy has slowed down and the US is emerging from a trough, the newly-industrialised Asian nations will maintain reasonable growth during the coming twelve months and will continue to grow rapidly, in the medium term at least. BHP will supply this demand either from present capacity or from incremental capacity which can be added at low cost.

In oil, the group has brought into production the Skua field in the Timor Sea and the Kutubu field in Papua New Guinea, the first tangible result of the group's global oil search. And in 1993–94 production will start at oil and gas fields on the North-West Shelf, as well as at the Bruce gas and condensate field in the North Sea.

When BHP began planning the additional output, it assumed Bass Strait production would continue to decline. But changes in the tax system mean it has become economic for BHP and Esso to institute a new round of development there. This will put a floor under production at the 1991–92 level, which will be slightly lower than that of 1990–91. The Bass Strait joint venturers will spend almost $1.5 billion developing fields that could contain more than 250 million barrels of oil. All these developments should take oil profits to $1 billion by the middle of the decade given reasonable oil prices.

In 1989 BHP bought a refining and marketing business in Hawaii, Pacific Resources, essentially for experience. But there have been disappointments along the way, most notably the acquisition's inability to pass on increases in the crude oil prices to its customers.

The profit potential in BHP's main processing operation is not nearly as high as it is in minerals and oil production. For almost ten years the company has poured vast sums into steel making, yet no end to the painful period of reconstruction is in sight. In 1991 profit was savaged, dropping from $560 million to $190 million. During 1992–93 the group is planning substantial changes to the way its oldest steel plant, in Newcastle, is organised.

The company has established a network of overseas operations that will enable it to emerge as a world player in the steel export business, so improving the economics of its steel business by insulating it from the domestic economic cycle. But to make the export business successful it will need to improve margins by changing the range of its export products, with the main target markets in coated steel products.

But the fundamental strength of BHP Steel is still its dominance of the domestic market. That is why what BHP really needs is a big increase in steel demand in Australia, where the margins are higher. Ron McNeilly, who took over the steel division when John Prescott became chief executive, believes there is some 'slight evidence' to support the belief that the domestic market has turned the corner, but a recovery in earnings in the steel division is still going to come over the long haul, rather than immediately.

However, BHP believes that when the domestic recovery does arrive, its steel division will be well positioned and will once again be a big contributor to group profits. The changes in the company have been staggering. In 1983 it sold 3.1 million tonnes of steel on the domestic market and exported 1.3 million. Ten years later in 1992 its domestic sales were the same but exports had risen to 2.4 million tonnes. Whereas it had 40 300 people in 1983 numbers were down to 28 600 in 1992 and tonnes per employee had risen from 178 to 400.

BHP has been trying to counteract this country's unpopularity in world share markets by promoting itself as a global resources company that happens to be based in Australia. However, the concept will not be embraced by investment analysts overnight, considering that BHP has traditionally been seen as a means of investing in Australia even though more of its activities are based offshore. And Foster's adds an extra complication.

Links of steel

BHP did not shop around for its banking during the 1980s, even though the practice was then fashionable. The ANZ may have made a lot of mistakes during the decade, but when BHP needed money the bank's chief, Will Bailey, provided it instantly. The result is an interesting long-term relationship: ANZ Trustees is the key shareholder in the joint Elders-BHP company Beswick, which is the largest shareholder in BHP.

The ANZ preferred not to sell its equity in New Zealand Steel, and the Big Australian was ambivalent. So BHP's banker now has a small equity in its steel business, further strengthening their links. NZ Steel should do very well because its costs are comparable with those of BHP's Port Kembla operation. In addition, New Zealand's stevedoring costs are less than a quarter of Australia's outrageous waterfront charges. As a result, BHP will export from New Zealand whenever possible.

RALPH MUST BE BOLD AS BRASS

JOHN RALPH at CRA chose a very different approach to the same problem that Philip Brass was combating at Pacific Dunlop. Brass's simple approach at Pacific Dunlop's Edgell operation—closing vegetable processing plants at places like Cowra that could not be made world-competitive and giving towns like Bathurst and Ulverstone a choice: agree to competitive practices or accept that their plants will shut down just like the other three—was undertaken because Brass knew he could very easily replace Australian plants with ones in Asia or New Zealand.

Ralph knows even better than Brass just how good New Zealand's individual contract labour laws are, at least as applied at Comalco's aluminium smelter at Bluff in the South Island. Comalco's agreement with workers, negotiated on an individual contract basis, not only slashed the cost of aluminium but made for much happier employees and better base rates of pay. No one was forced to resign. Everyone was a winner, except the union.

Comalco's Bell Bay aluminium smelter in Tasmania has many factors in common with Edgell's Cowra vegetable plant: it has old technology and the recent rise in productivity in New Zealand proves that it is ridden with poor work practices.

But Ralph has not announced Bell Bay's closure because Comalco has a large investment there. There is a chance it can be fixed if power charges plus labour rules are changed and, more importantly, Ralph has not yet negotiated extra power supply in New Zealand. It is even possible he still thinks that the Bell Bay managers and workers can be brought up to New Zealand standards.

If you were a smart union, interested in the long-term future of workers at Bell Bay, you would appreciate the dangers posed by the New Zealand improvements. You would work with middle managers to show how you could duplicate the amazing improvements in productivity in New Zealand and berate Ralph for holding you back by not installing the latest technology. And you would press the Tasmanian Government hard for alternative power prices.

But protecting the long-term future of the Bell Bay community is not the unions' top priority. One of the unions at the plant, the Federation of Industrial Manufacturing Employees, reckoned that the best way to answer the New Zealand challenge was to file for a 'preference clause' in the company's award. The metal and electrical unions then joined the game. Members of the Industrial Relations Commission went to the Bell Bay plant's nearest town, George Town, to investigate whether union members should be given priority in employment and employment opportunities, including overtime and promotion, plus preferential treatment in retrenchment situations.

The unions clearly have no concept of the long-term threat posed by New Zealand. Perhaps that is the fault of Comalco's management. The practical effect of the claim is to insert union power between managers and workers and appears to have been a response to the company's policy of wanting to deal directly with its own staff, including the elected delegates of the union.

What the New Zealand experience teaches Ralph and all other managers is that simple 'enterprise agreements' are not enough; Bluff had an 'enterprise agreement' for years. Increases in cost-competitiveness come about when management and workers adopt the same goal and realise that their survival and prosperity is linked. Traditionally, managers of large companies in Australia have found it very cosy to deal with their staff through unions rather than discuss issues directly with their workforces. But the cost has been high; the big gains being experienced by companies like Comalco in New Zealand are showing it is much higher than had been realised. Enterprise bargaining will not work unless it incorporates direct operating cohesion between workers and managers, and if unions are to prosper they will have to find a way to help that process.

The failure of Australian unions to understand the position of Australian companies will result in many more worker retrenchments and plant closures than would have been necessary under normal circumstances. The Bell Bay unions are gambling the jobs and livelihoods of the Bell Bay community against the belief that John Ralph will not act like Philip Brass. But Ralph has shareholders to look after and has no choice but to do the right thing by them. What Ralph should do is encourage people with houses in the Bell Bay area to go to Cowra (via New Zealand) and come to understand who the union is really representing.

Worker protection

The Comalco New Zealand agreement puts 'workers' on the same conditions as people classified as staff. Uniform conditions embrace annual leave, sick leave, superannuation, tenure and other staff provisions. The deal also includes a sentence in the staff employment contract that says

> The usual hours of work for this position are in accordance with Roster 1, but rosters may be varied to suit the needs of the business. Notice will be given of any impending changes to rosters. However, in order to perform the job effectively you may be required to work additional hours as appropriate. The salary specified in this letter of offer is inclusive of overtime.

The NZ flexibility in hours and jobs and the common motivation to achieve improvements has been responsible not only for a remarkable productivity transformation, but a substantial rise in the quality of production. It seems that when New Zealand workers were given staff freedoms, flexibility and responsibility, they responded by finding ways of improving their work. The amazing outcome will be studied by employment behaviour experts for years. If the Comalco experience in NZ is duplicated in other large organisations, Australian workers really should be concerned.

Telling the Politicians What's Happening

MOST FEDERAL Government ministers spend too much time in Canberra and are remote from what occurs in the real business world. From time to time *BRW* tries to help them with insights from the business community. Over the years sometimes politicians have listened—like the period when Paul Keating put his 'killer tax' on small and medium business which, as a result of *BRW* pressure, was deferred. But despite article after article, we failed to convince Paul Keating to lower interest rates until it was too late. Here are some more hints for our politicians.

A FORECAST FOR GROWTH

AUSTRALIA'S two big political parties are now heading in remarkably similar directions. Both are aiming for growth and see this as the only way out for Australia. For the Labor Government, this means a stunning reversal of its longstanding policy of placing restrictions on new developments. The land-use criteria it is now adopting are the ones the mining industry has wanted for years. Early in 1992 the parties had relatively small differences in targeted growth projections, with Paul Keating calling for a rate above 4% and John Hewson making forecasts just below 4%. In the 1992 Federal Budget documents the Government was reluctantly forced to reduce its target to 3%.

Neither party has any real hope of achieving 4% or even 3% on a sustained consumer demand basis. Indeed, if consumer demand rises too much, the result will be a blowout in the balance of payments, a slump in the dollar and rekindled inflation. A substantial amount of the called-for growth must come through productivity improvements. Hewson says his Fightback package will deliver those gains. In One Nation, Keating was predicting productivity rises of only about 1.5%, a figure that seemed too low, although he was seeking to convert predicted growth into higher employment.

But that's not easy—at least among big companies. We are seeing company after company report enormous cost reductions and the ability to increase production dramatically without hiring additional labour. At the same time, many large businesses are about to take their cost-cutting and labour-shedding to new levels, and the latest statistics show that stocks are being wrung out of the system, either to generate survival cash or as an efficiency measure. There is a chance that Keating may be right about overall growth in the five years to 1997, but not about its long-term employment implications. My guess is that the Treasury will probably have a similar view.

ACTION IS NEEDED TO MAKE JOBS

In May 1992, when Bill Kelty and Paul Keating sat down with the intention of discussing unemployment at the meeting of the Economic Planning Advisory Council, the main subject of their conversation was tariffs. Australia's free-trade stand at the Gatt talks means that higher tariffs are not among the Government's options. Even if they were, they would not change the unemployment situation greatly.

In the years after World War II, tariffs were used to create jobs for low-skilled workers (often migrants). They led to work practices that are totally unacceptable today. Modern manufacturing needs a flexible, highly-skilled workforce. Now the service industries provide the employment equivalent of the car assembly lines of the 1960s.

Unfortunately, Australia has rules in place that restrict the number of jobs in the service industries. If our leaders are really interested in easing unemployment, instead of just mouthing slogans, they could take some obvious steps to make employing people, particularly young people, more attractive.

The abolition of shift penalties and weekend loadings would open up a whole range of new jobs that young people are best able to fill. Those penalties operate to keep young people out of work and to give extra rewards to those with jobs. Not only is it uneconomic to keep many labour-intensive businesses open for longer hours; Australia's better architects and engineers are now building hotels in Asia because such projects are no longer viable here as a result of shift allowances and other add-on costs.

Payroll tax is closely linked to the issue of shift allowances. Abolishing payroll tax and replacing it either with a different tax or cuts in government wastage would enhance the attraction of employing labour. And of course, an end to demarcations and other work-practice rorts also is essential.

These moves are so obvious that in a sense all of us must share the blame for high unemployment. It is community policy to put other interests ahead of those of the unemployed, so we must not complain about the social repercussions of our actions.

But if we were really serious about unemployment we would go beyond the obvious. For example, my guess is that the greatest unsatisfied demand for labour is from two-income couples, whose personal lives are made very difficult as they try to raise families. Those who use home help usually pay cash, which means that the beneficiaries often stay on the social service register and do not pay tax.

Why not make home help a tax deduction, provided it is paid to people with tax-file numbers? This would boost youth employment, and the cost would be offset by the creation of taxable income and a reduction in social-service costs.

A second possibility to boost skilled employment, one that would be much more effective than higher tariffs, would be to offer special depreciation allowances for the introduction of electronic data interchange (EDI). The way Australian clothing and textile companies can beat imports is to supply replacement goods to stores within a week. By linking bar-coding machines at checkouts with terminals at their plants, local manufacturers could not only save retailers a fortune in stock costs, but also boost their turnover by quickly refilling shelves with fast-selling goods.

THE ONLY WAY TO JOB CREATION

PAUL KEATING and John Dawkins have made it clear that Australia's voters should judge them on their ability to reduce unemployment. To have credibility in a 1993 election, more than a token reduction is needed, so they have set themselves a difficult and dangerous task. Even in a conventional recession, unemployment falls significantly only when profits have recovered and the economy is beginning to build up steam. With many other countries now also in recession, it will not be easy to create those conditions in 1992, although short-term employment will rise as a result of the big spending by the Government in the August 1992 budget.

And, making the task more difficult, this is not a conventional recession. The management revolution taking place in Australia and around the world has meant everyone working in an enterprise is frightened of losing their job. This holds back consumer spending and the retrenched workers add to the pool of unemployed.

Keating and Dawkins will be aware that it is much easier to achieve such a revolution if there is growth in the economy. On this front, the signs are not all bad. It seems clear that the US and Japan will give their economies a boost, and further rises in German interest rates are unlikely. Given the level of our interest rates and the fall in the dollar, many Australian companies lifted their level of profits in the half-year to December 1992 although whether it will be of sufficient magnitude to cause them to hire staff before the 1993 election is doubtful.

Although there are moves that will help, the only measure that will deliver on unemployment is to lower the currency further and hope that the recession and better productivity will cushion the inflationary impact. The fall in the dollar after the 1992 Federal budget offers that chance. Malcolm Fraser came to a similar conclusion when he was PM, but our debt is higher now and we have deregulated, so dropping the currency carries greater risks. However, in the circumstances existing around the August 1992 budget, the chance of a lower dollar and low inflation was worth going for.

A public service

One move that will increase employment and prosperity is John Dawkins' decision to revamp the Industry Commission and bring it to Melbourne under its new head, Bill Scales, rather than keeping it remote in Canberra.

The shift to the real world will enable the commission to be much more effective in combating the problems of non-competitive government services, and sets a precedent that other departments may follow. An incredible feature of the March quarter CPI figure was that in the year to 31 March 1992, the rate of increase in government charges was four times higher than that for non-government charges. Even allowing for statistical variations during the preceding eighteen months, government charges have risen at two and three times the private-sector rate. Meanwhile, all those industries that the old Industries Assistance Commission ordered to be flexible will be amused that the Canberra-based public servants are not taking easily the order to move.

NO DOLLARS WITHOUT THE DETAILS

SOME ASIAN leaders have privately expressed great surprise that, when he became Prime Minister, Paul Keating went out to seek advice from the community. Asian leaders set goals and priorities and then perhaps seek advice within those parameters. One of Paul Keating's greatest problems was that he was given an overload of ideas and criticism. Although he stated he was making unemployment his top priority, in fact there could be no long-term improvement in employment until the basic business infrastructure has been repaired. To do that, Keating must restore the capital structure of small business, take steps to improve the international competitive position of Australian enterprises and increase the savings rate. Every new measure taken by the Government needs examination using these criteria; only if business is satisfied that the mistakes of the past are being reversed will confidence rise and long-term employment improve.

The destruction of the small-business infrastructure has been the most damaging result of the recession. Small businesses are not only our biggest and most efficient employer of labour, but are also the most vulnerable to a policy of high interest rates. From 1989 to 1991 there was little conception in Canberra of the harm being done to this vital part of our society. Even if Canberra now understands the situation—and that is doubtful—the problem is not easy to fix.

The banking system was damaged by the collapse of small businesses. The boards of banks send out instructions to their managers to lend, but the managers fear for their jobs and are more likely to pull the plug than give assistance. It is not easy to provide a circuit-breaker, but clearly much greater incentives need to be provided for banks to lend to smaller businesses at interest rates that do not cripple the client.

The array of taxes and the extent of the bureaucracy need reducing. The plan of the Minister for Small Business, David Beddall, to make the sale of small enterprises free of capital gains tax if the proceeds are reinvested in another small business, should attract long-term equity capital to the sector.

In terms of making Australian businesses more competitive, the most obvious move is to devalue the dollar, although this is one of the more difficult policies to control—and perhaps the most dangerous. If the dollar falls too far it will create a momentum that will be hard to stop, which will skyrocket inflation and lift interest rates. A safer policy, but one that brings benefits more slowly, is to significantly increase depreciation rates so that most items can be written off over three years and some over five.

It is important that any new depreciation system be simple. At the beginning of 1991 equipment suppliers were thrown into confusion when orders were held back in expectation of what the March statement might hold. Orders were then delayed even further waiting for new depreciation legislation. As it turned out, the Treasury spiked what was an essential reform, and the whole exercise was a waste of time.

Keating's plans to inject money into roads, bridges and other projects will provide some help, but they are attacking symptoms rather than problems and will not change confidence levels. Because of the deficit, the Government can spend only limited amounts of extra money on such infrastructure projects so rules to encourage private investment in this area need to be established quickly. Unfortunately the August 1992 budget did not tackle the issue.

Spending half a billion dollars to improve Australia's rail network is a high-risk investment because in today's environment less businesses want to rely on so inefficient an organisation. It is much better to use door-to-door road transport. Fortunately, Treasurer John Dawkins was not prepared to spend the money on the rail system until its Melbourne hub adopted better work practices but they will need to be very good to get transport companies to switch containers from trucks to trains.

In terms of increasing savings, Keating has always resisted pressure to take an axe to the superannuation grand design and dividend imputation—two of his greatest achievements as Treasurer. The Federal Opposition proposes a superannuation model under which executives without the benefit of income-splitting or other business-related advantages will be able to save far less via superannuation. But Hewson proposes, as an offset, to limit capital gains tax to 30%—making equity investment more attractive—and to lower personal income tax at the top level.

Until savings are substantially increased we will be at the mercy of overseas borrowing, which will affect confidence levels. Unfortunately, increasing savings goes against the grain of a Prime Minister trying to stimulate the economy.

INVESTMENT STRATEGIES

AUSTRALIANS might ask themselves why Japan and many other Asian countries are short of skilled labour when we have such a surplus of labour. Part of the reason is the bungled economic policy but just as important is the lack of capital investment in Australian industry in the 1980s. The Government blamed business for the lack of productive investment but, unfortunately, once again Canberra got it wrong. The Government did not understand that its policies had the effect of making overseas investment more attractive and that our work practices made large-scale investment in Australia uneconomic unless it was based on low-cost commodities.

BRW has been campaigning long and hard for proper investment policies but until 1992 no one in the Government, or the public service, has been prepared to listen. Many proposals sit in public servants' pigeon holes. It is not hard to work out what must be done. Our depreciation rates are way out of line with the rest of the world and need to be accelerated to make Australia a more attractive place to build plants aimed at the export market. It makes sense to subsidise the training of additional staff, particularly people who are not wedded to a particular craft but have multi-skilling.

The virtual black ban on development projects imposed by the Hawke Government to appease environmentalists and Aborigines needs to be reversed. The green movement's policies have cost jobs for many thousands of Australians.

On this front, it was encouraging to see the Resources Minister, Alan Griffiths, prepared to give Greenpeace a kick in the rear end by allowing BHP to explore for oil in the Otway Basin in Bass Strait. Naturally, he imposed strict but realistic environmental controls.

A CRUCIAL TEST

ONE OF the more significant statements on the environment in Paul Keating's One Nation plan says: 'The Government has decided to improve the process by which it establishes new parks and marine parks by more fully integrating economic and environmental considerations'.

Just as the ban on mining at Coronation Hill told the world mining industry that the Hawke Government was not serious about development and was prepared to take the unemployment consequences on the chin, so the new proposal to make a national park of the Kimberleys, an area that has enormous potential to contribute to our future wealth, will test the meaning of Keating's words. Rightly or wrongly, the mining and agriculture industries have set great store on them.

But many more decisions like this are required for the Government to show that it is serious about job creation. A good place to start would be for it to tell the WA Government it would get no help on jobs until it gave the go-ahead to Hamersley's iron ore deposit at Marandoo and removed the threat over Australia's iron ore exports.

WA MUST STOP ITS NONSENSE

STATE GOVERNMENTS have the power and ability not only to make life miserable for their own residents, but to do great harm to the rest of the nation. The classic illustration of this was the Cain/Kirner Government's bungling of economic and education policies in Victoria during the 1980s. Residents of New South Wales and other states thought at first that they could be insulated from Victoria's mismanagement, but they were wrong: Victoria was too important to the nation.

Now Western Australia is building a record of serious policy mistakes. Australians therefore need to take a much closer interest in WA and to exert full pressure on the delinquent Government to act in the interests of its own population as well as the nation's.

The standard of government in Western Australia was abysmal for much of the 1980s, but WA Inc's antics did not affect the rest of the country, apart from some notable eastern states investors and banks who took big risks and lost.

But Western Australia is one of our power houses for resources, so when the political process there goes seriously wrong, Australia's long-term export outlook is affected. WA Premier Carmen Lawrence has a sound understanding of the relationship between strong export industries and the welfare of West Australians and Australia as a whole. But she has been ill-advised in her selection of Cabinet posts and the power to determine the future of vital projects has fallen into the hands of people who do not have a similar appreciation of the importance to Australia of exports.

One of the most important of these projects is Hamersley's Marandoo iron ore development, which is required to fill the gap as Mt Tom Price runs down. The Japanese steel industry, which has placed great faith in WA, has been stunned at the seemingly endless series of inquiries held into Marandoo by the assorted bodies to which Lawrence has given too much power. The final straw came in January 1992 when an obscure body, the WA Museum's Aboriginal Cultural Material Committee, discovered it had the power to jeopardise Australian iron ore exports. Although the Premier has stated that the mine will go ahead, clearly great harm has been done to the nation by this thirteenth and most bizarre inquiry into Marandoo.

The Marandoo hold-ups should have been no surprise given what happened earlier to BHP and a large Japanese group that wanted to develop separate mineral sands projects. Rather than Aborigines, the problem that time involved transport and power routes. As with Marandoo, no one could make a decision and in the end the projects simply could not go ahead (the developers are probably grateful in the short term because of what has happened to the mineral sands market).

In another example, CRA spent $30 million looking for coal at Mt Lesueur, north of Perth, only to have its right to mine whipped away to appease environmentalists. The combination of Mt Lesueur, the mineral sands fiasco and Marandoo has sent clear messages around the world.

Many would also remember that when Peko-Wallsend wanted to expand Robe River, the Aboriginal issue was trotted out and the move was blocked. And last year, when Western Mining wanted to rid itself of uneconomic work practices at Kambalda, the WA Government backed their retention (in fairness, changes made at other WMC sites will enable expansion to take place).

The people of Western Australia are starting to cotton on to the fact that, although they would inevitably have had high unemployment as a result of Canberra's blunders, their own Government has made their dole queues longer.

Smarting from criticism, Premier Lawrence issued a press release in January 1992 claiming that nineteen big projects worth close to $6.6 billion had either started or were about to be constructed in WA. The list owed much to the wisdom of previous WA governments: $2 billion was connected with the North-West Shelf, a development that, these days, probably would never have got through the myriad environmental and Aboriginal bodies that have been set up; another $500 million involved extensions and adjustments to existing plants. (Imagine trying to erect the Kwinana oil refinery in WA today.) The biggest new project was the $2-billion Collie power station, which took five long years to clear government-imposed obstacles only to run into financial obstacles.

The most exciting part of the statement was the Premier's commitment to change. If Lawrence can muster the political courage to regain control of her Government and disembowel those powerful bodies dedicated to unemployment in the state (while ensuring that any new project meets the highest international-standard environment tests), then she will do a great service to her own state and the nation. But unless WA is prepared to help itself, why should it receive special help?

PROTECTING PRODUCERS

In 1991 I praised Carmen Lawrence for having the political courage to underwrite a minimum price (set at a low level) for the state wheatgrowers as a temporary measure to protect the industry while European and US governments were subsidising their industries, trying to remove low-cost producers like Australia from the market. Lawrence's foresight convinced WA growers to plant reasonable acreages and, as it happened, they were able to sell at good prices.

Premiers of the eastern states didn't have the courage to fill the void left by the Commonwealth's inaction. Accordingly, Australian wheatgrowers elsewhere, who didn't plant as much as they should have and had the added problem of the drought, were hit hard—exactly what the Europeans and Americans wanted.

If you are in a long price war, you either take steps to protect your best producers or go out of business. Australia will lose its wheat industry, despite its efficiency, because the boffins in Canberra don't understand the nature of a business environment in which strong players use government money to eliminate weaker, low-cost competitors. This is the only situation in which subsidies are acceptable.

HOW ASIA WILL USE OUR SKILLS

For the past twenty years Japan and some other Asian nations have seen Australia as a vast quarry. As we move deeper into the 1990s, this concept is taking on an entirely new meaning. For as well as being a source of valuable minerals, Australia is now being recognised as a reserve of unused human talent that is available to be tapped.

Other nations are coming to understand that an array of skills in architecture, construction and other areas is vastly under-utilised because the 'backward' Australians have not made their investment conditions internationally competitive. Asian countries have a much better understanding of how business and investment capital can be mobilised. The problem is that at present they lack the skills to carry out their plans. But our skills usually come cheap, so Australians can be hired to create wealth and jobs.

It is important to emphasise that it makes good sense for Australian architectural, building, engineering and other service groups to extend their operations into Asia. But this time around the expansion is taking place when there is little or no work at home, because investment capital finds conditions abroad better than in Australia. In effect, many Australians are going to Asia to survive.

Prime Minister Paul Keating did not take the chance to alter the capital rules and make it worth considering investing in Australia. It was not easy to do, given the forces in Canberra who are too remote to understand what is happening.

Of course, work practices are the main impediment to development and job creation in Australia. But, while current union problems are not to be underestimated, the situation has improved in many areas.

The completion of the Great Southern Stand at the Melbourne Cricket Ground in time for the cricket World Cup was an international signpost in this regard. But any improvement in union behaviour is being offset by uncompetitive depreciation allowances, environmental regulation difficulties, crazy permit requirements and the high cost of government services. The accountancy firm Ernst & Young surveyed forty-seven of our top 100 companies and confirmed that the present write-off provisions were holding back investment.

Keating must attack on all fronts if he is to rekindle investment. Other nations will be tapping the experience that built many of Australia's tourist facilities. For example, Australian skills will probably be used to vastly increase the tourism capacity of some Asian countries, particularly Malaysia.

This shift of skills comes at a time when domestic tourism operators can see that Australia will be short of capacity in a few years. However, it is not economic to build new facilities here because our depreciation policy, work practices and other conditions are out of line with those of our competitors. The tourism industry's depreciation rules are particularly archaic. Not only are basic allowances out of line, but a vast number of essential items are excluded altogether from the deductions: these include golf courses, car parks, footpaths and aircraft runways.

In a strange way, this mirrors the situation in the resources sector. It is possible to mine in Australia, but when companies try to build secondary processing plants (to replace industries lost following tariff reductions) they run into a wall of constraints. As a result, the projects go to countries that understand what is required.

Keating tried to win short-term points in his 26 February economic statement by announcing big hand-outs to the states. But the real test will be whether he changes the rules so that Australia can compete for investment dollars and become more than just a quarry for minerals and skills. If Keating, or his successors, do not understand what is happening, and most of Australia's skills go to creating jobs in countries to the north, rather than at home, then crazy as it might seem now, we will have to think about sending workers to places where labour shortages are emerging (such as Malaysia). Obviously, work conditions in Asia will not match those in Australia.

Quite rightly, all Australians will regard with horror the idea of sending our unemployed to Asia as guest workers. This is why we cannot afford to have our investment rules out of line with those of our competitors. But if we continue to stick our heads in the sand . . .

VICTORIA IN FOR BIG CHANGES

WHILE THE Greiner affair in NSW was attracting the publicity in June 1992, an even deeper crisis was taking place in Victoria. For the first time in sixty years a government was forced to admit it couldn't pay its debts as they fell due. Creditors to the Government's Public Transport Corporation had to wait until after 1 July, to get their money. This confirmed the warnings I first gave in 1990 that the sheer incompetence of the Kirner Government meant that all who dealt with it did so at their own risk.

The inability of the Kirner Government to pay its debts on time is an important issue for the whole country. The Kirner Government tried to sell off property by offering to take up space at exorbitantly high rentals that would cripple future state finances.

At the same time, the Government rushed through building contracts the state could not afford to suit its political agenda, knowing this was its last chance. The contracts were sped up so a new government couldn't overturn them. Like any negotiations done in a hurry, the inevitable cost over-runs will further cripple the state.

As you will remember, in 1990 I advised Victorians, if possible, not to have their Year 12 children educated under Joan Kirner's VCE. Many of those who were not able to take that advice are now being forced to help their children in often mindless project assignments whose outlines were conceived when the Premier was Minister for Education.

NSW has avoided the worst of Victoria's problems because its Government acted to cut costs while Kirner and Cain kept spending. The Greiner Government also took some tough decisions on education. Victorians will have paid an enormous price for electing the Cain/Kirner administration.

Meanwhile, the reforms planned by Jeff Kennett go much further than any government has attempted in Australia before. Almost every activity outside the courts and police will be considered for privatisation, often on a contracting-out basis. The result may well be the most efficient state in Australia, but the turmoil on the way through will be without precedent and it will not help employment in the short term. Just how the Victorian problem will affect Australia's rate of recovery remains to be seen.

HEWSON'S ESSENTIAL TASK

JOHN HEWSON and the Liberals could do with some friends. Originally, what was so good about the Fightback package was the leadership it displayed in contrast to a tired Hawke Government. Effectively, it removed Hawke from office. But now it is pitched against a Labor Government with a flexible Prime Minister whose leadership qualities have given the party a second wind. The Wills byelection showed how a future election campaign might be conducted.

Instead of being regarded as a package, specific parts of Fightback were being scrutinised and they proved vulnerable. The most public thrust of the package is the goods and services tax, which will fund the abolition of payroll tax and lower income taxes, with the aim of boosting employment. In the Wills byelection there was no sign that the Liberals had devised a way to sell it against determined opposition.

Perhaps it is not saleable, especially as another group of Liberal supporters, the elderly who do not draw the pension, are vigorously opposed to it because it would reduce the purchasing power of their investment income. As if this is not enough, the Fightback package alienates slabs of the Australian population, for debatable national gains. The Liberals' plan to abolish tariffs is a good example. Most of the 'hard work' on tariffs has already been done by Labor.

The final abolition is a relatively minor matter, given other national priorities. But Toyota and Ford have indicated that they will restrict investment, and even consider closing down in the long term, if tariffs are cut out. Keating realised he was on a loser and reversed his position, so isolating Hewson and alienating what would otherwise be a Liberal business support base. Phil Cleary won Wills on an anti-tariff-reduction policy with the aim of providing employment—a simple winner.

On a second front, the combination of the GST and enterprise bargaining is worrying many normally staunch Liberal supporters. Management in Australia has a lot to learn about enterprise bargaining and will face a baptism of fire at the same time as GST is introduced. The combination of those two events may require a clamp on the economy if it has started to recover.

Labor started Australia on an extensive program of industrial reform that virtually demanded that our enterprises work towards being the best in the world, or close down. Such a policy inevitably causes carnage if it is not accompanied by similar efficiencies in Government administration, the wharves and the transport system. It costs three or four times more to export steel from Australia than from New Zealand.

Despite his flexibility, Keating has shown no signs of having the political courage to tackle these problems, although the better ministers in his Cabinet know that if they cannot fix the waterfront before polling day—so that BHP's stevedoring costs in Australia are the same as in New Zealand—they should not be returned to office.

If anything, the result in Wills makes it even harder for Keating to fix these problems, so the community badly needs a Hewson to perform this essential task, to avoid an avalanche of avoidable closures. But Hewson's policies drew 7% fewer primary votes in Wills than the previous Peacock campaign achieved. If Hewson is a good politician that will teach him something. But for Hewson it is all or nothing. He has the option of returning to merchant banking if he fails in the Federal election.

Meanwhile, on the other side, Labor virtually had a Centre Right and Left ticket operating in Wills and the Left won. Keating is too smart not to adjust. Accordingly there were many small handouts in the budget to make a much more confident parliamentary Left happy. The way it stands now, if unemployment falls a few points by election time, as economists are predicting, then Keating will still be well in the race.

7
CHAPTER

Fostering Small Business

BIG VERSUS SMALL

THE MANAGING directors and boards of many of Australia's bigger companies have received a warning from the *BRW Top 500*, which shows that while the big companies have been moaning, many of our smaller listed companies have been improving their profitability. Incredible as it might seem, 220 of the top 500 listed companies reported a rise in profit in the half-year to June 1991. Although some important bigger companies are doing well, the better smaller companies are leading the way.

Small and medium-sized privately-owned companies have received a battering in the recession. Many were highly geared and so were hit when the Reserve Bank and the Government raised interest rates to high levels. But the prosperity of Australia will ride on the development of smaller businesses. Indeed, the management and boards of big companies should think seriously about the implications of the Australian Statistician's report, *Small Business in Australia*. Larger companies and governments need to think long and hard about whether there are advantages to their operation in contracting out some of their activities to smaller operators. And small businesses and anyone thinking of venturing into the area need to appreciate that, despite the risks, they have considerable advantages over large companies in certain markets.

The Australian Statistician, Ian Castles, discovered that in May 1989, owners of businesses with less than twenty staff paid their employees on average $11 an hour ($11.50 for males, $10.10 for females). When employee numbers rose to between twenty and forty-nine the pay rate rose to $11.60 and those with more than 100 staff paid employees $12.80 an hour—$1.80 an hour or 16% more than the smaller operators. These statistics were not peculiar to 1989, but denoted a trend which had been developing over a long period and which I believe accelerated over 1991–92.

On the other hand, part of the difference in pay rates can be explained by the fact that the number of hours worked a week in larger companies is greater than in smaller enterprises, and consequently there is more overtime. The report indicates that the greatest differences in pay rates between small and large enterprises occur in mining, manufacturing, transport and communications.

In the retail, wholesale and finance business areas, those employing between twenty and 100 people appear to pay more than the very small or the large. And there are two categories, 'recreation, personal and other services' and 'community services', where workers in larger enterprises are paid less than in smaller ones. Perhaps not surprisingly, given a labour cost advantage, Castles concludes that smaller businesses appear to yield more profit from a dollar of sales than larger ones.

In Australia we have the strange situation in which small businesses are being starved for capital even though they are able to employ labour more cheaply than larger groups and, I suspect, use workers more productively. Smaller businesses must rely much more heavily on bank borrowings and so inevitably have a higher failure rate—especially when the wooden heads in Canberra use interest rates rather than government surpluses to bring on a recession.

In general, large companies are experiencing exactly the reverse situation. Most have as much capital as they could want, owing to the strong sharemarket prices, which are being chalked up despite the bad results being recorded.

Large companies—and governments—need to look closely at every aspect of their work practices and decide whether it is possible to do things differently, perhaps by contracting out some tasks to cut costs and take advantage of Castles' conclusions.

Many smaller groups were able to move more quickly into the growth markets of Asia, often because they were not saddled with big commitments in Europe and the US. Large companies should look more closely at forming alliances, cemented by equity, with smaller groups that can perform functions they themselves do poorly.

Quite correctly, great attention has been paid to the destruction of small and medium-sized businesses, but the *BRW Top 500* shows that the viable ones can quickly make themselves more productive without going through the tortuous processes that larger companies must contend with. They will lead the recovery and provide additional employment.

If yours is a small enterprise needing inspiration then think of the Federal Parliament canteen, which produced good savings by contracting out. If contracting takes off in the Public Service and in large companies, we are looking at huge cost savings. At the same time we will create a vibrant small and medium business sector which will greatly add to national prosperity. The most valuable asset any small and medium business can have is a long-term contract—i.e., a source of cash flow. Our bankers are just starting to understand that they can lend on such deals much more safely than on property. Those who contract to provide public services will have a wonderful base from which to expand.

On the other hand, we will need to assist those made redundant by cost-cutting to find jobs, either by lifting the economic growth rate or making it easier for people to hire. The present retrenchment rules make every hiring a high-risk operation and start-up pay is also a big barrier to job creation.

Our banks' dilemma

The shortage of bank capital for employment-generating businesses in our community, at a time when we have too much labour, is easily explained. The interest cuts that have occurred in the bank bill rate have not flowed through to most small businesses. The simple fact is that because of past loan losses, most banks find lending to small business unprofitable, in spite of higher gross margins. Bank executives almost put their jobs on the line every time they make a loan to a small business. The result is that most small businesses financed by the main banks are paying almost twice the bill rate while, by contrast, there is a price war among the major banks to lower housing rates. There are indications that some banks are starting to understand that their long-term future lies in small business lending.

THE GOVERNMENT'S CONTRIBUTION

EARLY IN 1992 Prime Minister Paul Keating and Treasurer John Dawkins knew that Labor's re-election depended in large measure on the delivery of improvements in employment—and unemployment—by polling time. Although specific infrastructure projects would help, they would be offset by further retrenchments in large enterprises.

The Government's recognition that the smaller privately-owned businesses will be most likely to lead an employment recovery, and that these are disadvantaged in the capital market, will necessitate the provision of a remarkable array of aids. But the trouble is that there is little detailed knowledge in Canberra of privately-owned business, and every time Paul and John have attempted to help they have either messed things up or failed to get full value for their initiatives.

Then Dawkins got the idea of helping small businesses by providing relief from wholesale sales tax, giving Opposition Leader John Hewson a GST backhander on the way through. Once again, here was a well-meaning initiative with potentially unfortunate side-effects. The scheme allows enterprises paying less than $10 000 in sales tax to opt out of the system. If they wish, they can charge for their goods and services without adding sales tax—but they get no sales tax exemption on their purchases.

If we assume that a business is required to charge 20% sales tax on its products, then a $10 000 exemption limit converts to a turnover below $50 000. That figure is relatively small, but if the business operates in more than one name, perhaps with a husband and wife as owners, it will not be long before the effective limitation will be increased by two or three times. If an enterprise already has plant or buys it second-hand, then the only sales tax payable will be on most—but by no means all—of its raw materials. The system encourages 'backyard' enterprises to stay small and not hire additional people. A rash of backyarders with a 20% cost advantage now threatens the existence of slightly bigger companies. Taxes that have artificial cut-off points rarely work.

A second area of help comes through the proposed pooled development funds (PDFs) They are a good idea, but would have worked even better had they not been designed in Canberra. The plan is that a PDF can only subscribe direct capital to a business with assets of less than $30 million. Dividends from such funds are tax-free, and there is no capital gains tax on the sale of PDF shares. Each PDF, which must be incorporated as a company, pays tax at a 30% rate rather than the 39% for normal companies. The idea is to attract capital for privately-owned enterprise at a concessional tax-rate tax.

The rewards from PDF investments can be very attractive if the right businesses are selected, as was shown when the Greenchip Opportunities Fund (which had been launched as a tax-deductible fund in a management investment company scheme) lifted net tangible asset backing by 17% during the first nine months of 1991–92.

If the Government wanted a quick response, it could have set straightforward rules to enable existing funds to embrace the new proposal. It could also have set the $30-million asset limitation at $50 million to encourage institutions to back the scheme. But the public servants writing the rules confined the PDF investments to trading companies (not property investment groups) with what are defined as total assets of less than $30 million. Many enterprises carry inflated assets on their balance sheets relating to a previous era, but do not want to write them down. The rule-writers should have based their limitation on the capital value being established by the new shares under issue. At the same time, the pooled funds must buy 10% of the company, which might mean a $3-million injection—often more than is needed.

The third so-called area of aid concerns the earlier successful efforts of the Minister for Small Business, David Beddall, to reduce the paperwork for small businesses. One of his achievements was the quarterly, rather than monthly, payment of pay-as-you-earn tax. Guess what the new compulsory superannuation rules have in store for small business in 1993–94: monthly superannuation payments with terrible penalties for inadvertent non-compliance.

They never get it quite right

The One Nation and Fightback packages are further examples of how the politicians never get it quite right when dealing with private business. Prime Minister Paul Keating promised that 50% of the goodwill profit on the sale of a small business would not be subject to capital gains tax. When a small business is owned by a single person, such a system could work well. But the same may not be true for many substantial small businesses that are within corporate structures.

In theory, if a private company sells a business and, after indexation, there is a $200 000 profit on goodwill, under the Keating plan $100 000 would be taxed for capital gain and the balance would be tax-free. However, accountant William Buck tells me that this is not the great advantage it might at first seem. Owners of private businesses usually see their rewards in terms of what they eventually can put into their pockets. If shareholders want to get their hands on the tax-free cash that is generated either by the indexation gain or the goodwill profit, then it must be paid out as a dividend. Buck says that a dividend from such funds cannot be franked, so it attracts the top personal tax rate of the shareholder. In other words, in the long term, shareholders of privately-owned businesses in corporate structures would get no relief from indexation or the One Nation concession.

One option is for a shareholder to sell the corporate structure. However, buyers are much more prepared to pay the full price for a business rather than risk the hidden liabilities, such as tax, involved in acquiring a corporate structure.

In his Fightback package, Opposition Leader John Hewson offered full capital gains relief to a business when it is sold as long as the funds are reinvested in a similar business. This also does not appear to assist the withdrawal of funds and it raises this question: what is a similar business?

It is all very well for government to want to assist private business overcome the obstacles that confront it, but the politicians must realise that to do this they need advice from non-public servants. Nevertheless, on the question of capital gains, it seems both parties are moving towards treating smaller private businesses in a manner similar to that afforded home owners. If they maintain this trend, the implications for the structure of the business community are significant, especially now that there is a lot of talent that is no longer employed by larger corporations.

WILL BANKS TAKE THE CHANCE?

THE DEBT–EQUITY swap arrangements announced by Paul Keating in his One Nation economic statement open opportunities for Australian bankers—but not all are champing at the bit to take them up. The measures in the Keating package are a victory for the National Australia Bank managing director Don Argus, who convinced the Government to make the historic change. He was supported by Will Burley of the ANZ Bank.

Under the new arrangements, if a company owes, say, $1 million to a bank but clearly cannot service and repay its debt, the bank can forgive and write off enough of the loan to make the company viable. The amount of the write-off is tax-deductible, yet can be converted into equity in the business. In other words, banks will be able to convert debt into equity and have their cash coffers boosted by a lower tax bill. They will also have the equity running in their accounts at a token value.

Australian banks did not comprehend the consequences either of their overlending in the mid-1980s or, later, their over-zealous approach to debt-collecting when the economy turned sour. They now have a chance to put some surviving Australian businesses on a much better footing, with the Government picking up 39% of the loss. In the longer term, this could transform these companies' business strategies.

The Government's plan is that the banks should sell this equity in about five years, but when a business goes on to succeed, they may be reluctant sellers because they will have to pay tax on the full amount raised. The National Australia Bank does not plan to convert its pure property problem loans into equity; rather, it will reserve the technique for viable businesses that may have problems with property. Exactly how many of NAB's problem loans will be eligible for conversion is not known, but the total could be in the vicinity of $500 million.

ANZ executives have also been instructed to go through the bank's big problem loans, looking for companies that are basically sound but have borrowed too much. If all parties agree, the bank will consider converting part of the debt in the businesses into equity.

Australia's recovery is linked to business confidence, and enterprises that are living on a week-to-week basis at the whim of their bankers represent weight in the saddlebag. It is impossible to run a good business that way. Every time a bank converts a staggering company into a profitable operating structure, it will not only help the nation, but also give the banks better value.

Unfortunately one of the difficulties all the banks face in taking advantage of the proposal is the bizarre situation created by dividend franking credits. If the National Australia Bank were to forgive and write off, say, $200 million of a hypothetical $500 million in eligible problem loans, it would effectively reduce its tax bill by $78 million (39% of $200 million). In theory, the deal is good because it would boost the cash on which the NAB could earn a return by $78 million.

The debt reorganisation would not reduce profit, assuming the right provisions had been made earlier. But when a bank pays less tax it reduces the amount of franking credit available for its shareholders, thus reducing the attraction of NAB shares to investors. This is a very sensitive subject for institutions such as the NAB that have substantial overseas earnings and cannot count the tax paid on them for Australian franking. If there were franking credit relief, many more banks might be interested in the scheme. The banks warned the Government prior to introduction that the facility would not be widely used without franking credit relief.

Meanwhile the NAB does not plan to seek board representation in the ventures it assists. However, approved accountants will be appointed to each of them, opening up many opportunities for alert professionals who are prepared to move alongside smaller businesses and their bankers.

When deals are done, banks will have the opportunity to learn about equity and management, rather than simply driving businesses into the dust. My fear is that the bank managers who contributed to the original crisis will hold us back once again.

It is important that businesses recapitalised in this way be set servicing and repayment schedules that hark back to the traditional banking practice of basing loans on anticipated cashflow. Once the franking credit and other bugs are ironed out of the system, it will offer the opportunity to recapitalise vast numbers of small businesses and, if the banks are willing, may turn out to be one of the important innovations in the Keating statement. The fact that German banks acquired their huge equity positions in difficult times has not been lost on the scheme's supporters. If the banks do not take this opportunity, then Australian prime ministers will be reluctant to take bank-inspired solutions seriously in the future.

Inspiring each other

On the subject of business confidence, one of the problems experienced by people who run really successful privately-owned businesses is that it is hard to compare notes with enterprises that are achieving similar results. In the present economic climate, no one wants to boast.

The *BRW*/Price Waterhouse reception for Australia's fifty fastest-growing companies brought together business people from all over the country; many of them came to talk to others who were similarly successful. The usual farewell line was 'See you next year'.

HOW TO TAKE ON A BANK AND WIN

BANKS AND bank-owned finance companies are still squeezing successful small and medium-sized business operators throughout Australia—particularly where property loans are involved. In effect, the difference between the commercial bill rate and the overdraft rate for such businesses has widened as successful operators are forced to pay for the sins of the unsuccessful.

Most of those affected suffer in silence and hope they might benefit from the new attitudes of some banks towards successful smaller businesses. But two Melbourne accounting firms have decided to allow publication of details of an event that may be a watershed in lowering lending rates to many small businesses. The accountants were successful in slashing the loan rate of a client, who has a successful health-care business, from 15.5% to 12.5%. In addition, the accountants have received an apology from the finance company.

The dedication to detail by CPA accountant Ian Cugley, of Cugley Ciravolo & Associates, and the tough tactics of debt consultant Dennis Goldenberg, may assist other accountants whose clients are in a similar position, and who are looking for a way out. Cugley believes the favourable response by the finance company after its senior staff had understood what had happened is a model for others to follow.

In November 1990 Ian Cugley's client, a partnership, wanted to ensure it had long-term funding for the extension of the business. It negotiated a ten-year loan with one of Australia's leading bank-owned finance companies. Initially, the partners were quoted an interest rate of 17.5%, which compared with a bank reference rate of about 17%. At the time, it was a perfectly fair rate, although interest levels had started to fall.

The loan documents stipulated that interest rates should be reviewed every three months and would be governed by market forces and the finance company's cost of funds. Nevertheless, the finance company had absolute discretion on changes in interest rates. Cugley told the broker who arranged the deal that the terms of the rate revision were vague and gave the financier total discretion. Cugley was told he should not worry: the financial institution had 'standing' and could be trusted to act fairly and properly.

The loan was not actually drawn down until February 1991, by which time rates had fallen again but the finance company's rate remained at the 17.5% negotiated three months before. With the first review in May 1991, Cugley contacted the finance company, pointing out that rates had fallen again and was told that the clients' rate was falling by 0.5%. Cugley protested that this was a small cut given the huge reductions available elsewhere, but the finance company replied: 'That is the best we can do until the client establishes a track record'.

Three months later, and prior to the August review, the finance company contacted Cugley and visited the business. A finance company officer said he was 'most impressed'. The client and Cugley expected a big cut in the rate, but again, all that was offered was a token 0.5%.

Then came the November review. The finance company called again but this time the message was that there would be no reduction despite further cuts elsewhere in the community. Cugley wrote to the finance company, pointing out that the cut of 1% in his client's rate represented a fall of only 5.71% or less than one-third of the fall in the bank's index reference rate. The finance company replied that it would not cut rates until the review in the middle of February 1992. Once again, general rates fell and the bank finance company managed a 1% cut to 15.5%. Cugley responded by pointing out that the total decrease since the loan was established was only 11.43% of the original rate compared with a 23.29% fall in the bank reference rate.

What was happening to Cugley's client was no different from what was happening to successful businesses around the country.

Fortunately, the client's business was doing well—it had met all payments on time; its gearing, based on a February 1992 valuation, was only 59% and the profit (after deducting directors' emoluments) covered interest and principal payments 1.71 times. At this point, Ian Cugley had done everything that could be reasonably expected of him. Nevertheless, he had a well-documented case and decided that in the interests of his clients a tougher approach was required. He consulted Dennis Goldenberg who specialises in handling difficult situations involving debt.

Goldenberg went straight on to the attack. After setting out the security of the loan, he tried to prove that the finance company had acted unconscionably and unreasonably in not cutting rates in line with the general market.

He threatened to haul the finance company's senior executives before the Australian Society of CPAs and use the matter as the focus of a debate on the ethics of the accounting and business community. The company realised the charge of unconscionable conduct was serious, prompting a review by senior staff. Immediately the finance company cut the rate to 13.8%. But Goldenberg and Cugley had set a target of 12.5% and attacked again, this time with more data about the fall in the finance company's target lending rates and data from the bank and finance company's treasury departments showing the extent of the overcharging. It was made clear that Cugley's client had relied on the good intentions of the finance company. Goldenberg wrote another blistering letter to the finance company.

> The fact that rates didn't fall is inexcusable and highlights the advantage taken of clients by some officers of institutions where clients are either not vigilant or naive. The subsequent history of this loan is riddled with disadvantage to our clients in that the indicated targeted rates were not applied, which has cost our client dearly.
>
> Mr Cugley now seeks that the interest rate on this loan should not exceed 12.5% p.a. and that that rate be backdated to the last interest review date [February 1992]; to at least partially compensate his client for excess interest paid. He also requests that future interest rates be related to an agreed margin over a mutually agreeable indicator . . . might this be a case where Politik Real should prevail?
>
> Would you agree that the small interest rate adjustment needed to arrive at an acceptable 12.5% could bring this whole time-consuming and potentially messy business to an end, without loss to either the company or our client?

In the end, the finance company reduced its rate to 12.5% and apologised to Goldenberg in what is a remarkable precedent-setting letter:

> Your comments in your letter are acknowledged and we regret the vague and ambiguous method of rate reviews conducted in the past.
>
> In an endeavour to formalise future rate reviews, the facility will be indexed by a margin of 4% over the top . . . quarterly debenture stock rate at the time of review.
>
> We regret that our client had to resort to the actions undertaken to establish a more structured rate-review process and advise that we have recently reviewed this process internally so that this situation does not occur in the future for all our clients.
>
> We thank you for bringing this matter to our attention and we sincerely apologise to Mr Cugley for the inconvenience in the past.

Cugley says many financial institutions and their executives are under great pressure in the present environment and it is understandable that some situations are overlooked.

> I have nothing but praise for the bank-owned finance company. It's not easy to admit you are wrong and then correct the mistake in a way that is fair to both the finance company and my clients. I will again consider recommending other successful clients to them—particularly now the rates have been set.

Newcomers to the Stock Exchange

WHEN A COMPANY joins the Stock Exchange lists it files a prospectus which reveals a great deal about its operations. But usually that information is couched in language that is hard to understand. Two prospectuses, the Commonwealth Bank and John Fairfax have attracted enormous attention and the reports on their prospectuses help to explain what they are doing today. Other issues that are of keen interest are by GIO Australia, Southern Cross Airlines—the new Compass—and Rupert Murdoch's Pacific Magazines. Once again their prospectuses provided valuable guides to the challenges ahead.

THE BIG FLOAT

THE COMMONWEALTH BANK's then managing director, Don Sanders, and his deputy, Ian Payne, first began preliminary preparations for Australia's biggest public float in 1991. The profit draft they were examining would have been very different from the final document. Behind the numbers and revelations in the prospectus is the story of a board and its management coming to grips with great changes. The manner in which the bank's current management copes with these challenges will determine the level of success enjoyed by shareholders in the years ahead.

Australians know from practical experience how strong the bank's base has become. It is clear that most banks see retail or personal banking as the main source of profit growth in the 1990s, and no bank is better placed in this area than the Commonwealth. The issue capitalised the bank at $4.5 billion, compared with the 1991 share market capitalisations of $8.1 billion for the National Australia Bank, $5.3 billion for Westpac and $3.8 billion for the ANZ.

The Commonwealth has a much larger market share and retail network than the other banks, so the potential is enormous. The challenge facing the bank is to convert that magnificent market share and size into a more profitable Australian bank. But, as the prospectus indicates, that task is not going to be as easy as it might have seemed on New Year's Day 1991, when the Commonwealth bought the State Bank of Victoria. Indeed, if directors call the shots wrongly, they could end up with a Sydney-based bank that has almost half its assets in Victoria which are not producing proper returns because of management mistakes. If that happens, the shares will be a bad investment to all those who bought Commonwealth Bank shares after the Float at prices well above the public issue.

To understand the significance of the challenge posed by the State Bank of Victoria, it is necessary to understand the changes that took place within the Commonwealth Bank in the first six months of 1991. On 31 December 1990, the day before the acquisition, the Commonwealth's profit and balance sheet looked very different from what appeared in the prospectus six months later. The prospectus shows that the bank earned an after-tax trading profit of $209 million (before deducting minority interests) for the half-year to 31 December and was looking at a profit of about $400 million for the year to 30 June 1991. That was down on the $494 million recorded in 1989–90, but still respectable. Moreover, directors and management knew they had two other pluses under their belt: the Commonwealth's problem loans and bad debt provisions at that stage appeared much smaller than those of the other banks, and it was sitting on a huge abnormal gain as a result of a surplus in its superannuation fund.

In the six months that were to follow, the debt situation deteriorated markedly so the bank had to rely on that 'abnormal' superannuation gain to carry its stated profits in the year to 30 June and justify pricing the shares at $5.40. Significantly, the investigating accountants, Arthur Andersen & Co, refused to endorse the directors' policy of treating the gain as an abnormal profit for 1990–91, but, rather, reversed the bank's superannuation contribution over the past five years.

For many years the Commonwealth Bank had been paying about 18% of its staff salaries into the superannuation fund so there would be enough available to provide an indexed pension for all retired bank officers. The actuarial calculations were made on the basis of a relatively small difference between salary rises and investment returns. But during the 1980s not only were salary rises lower than expected, but investment returns were much higher than forecast, thus creating a large surplus. In addition, the Commonwealth Bank offered its employees the chance to go into a new scheme where, instead of an indexed pension, much greater emphasis was placed on a lump-sum payment and vesting of the bank's contribution.

Because Australians prefer lump sums to pensions and like the security of vesting, more than three-quarters of the Commonwealth's employees (and all new ones) chose the lump-sum-based scheme. As lump-sum schemes are much cheaper to finance than indexed pensions, the surplus in the fund grew. Even after part of the surplus was allocated to present and past employees, that still left about $850 million available to the bank. After tax, that became a net gain of about $520 million—not far short of the $790 million the Commonwealth paid for the goodwill of the SBV. In effect, it paid for the equity required in the acquisition.

The bank's profit for 1990–91 was further boosted as it did not have to contribute to the super fund. The bank's actuaries are assessing when the bank will need to start contributing again, which will mean an annual bill of about $130 million. Meanwhile, the bank will write off the State Bank goodwill over twenty years as an 'abnormal item'.

The 1990 half-year net trading profit of $209 million turned out to be almost all that was earned for the full year, because the next six months added little more than $60 million to the result, despite the purchase of the SBV. The $270-million profit for 1990–91 would have been reduced by a further $80 million after tax if full superannuation contributions had been paid. Without the $520-million abnormal gain from superannuation, there is no way the Commonwealth could have priced the issue at $5.40 a share.

The bank earned only token profits in its second half-year because of much higher bad and doubtful debt provisions in its own operations as well as in the SBV, and because it had to carry so many loans for which interest was not brought to account. In the first half, the bad-debt write-off was $385 million. The second half-year provision was around $740 million, to bring the total for the year to at least $1025 million, compared with $462 million in the previous year and only $298 million in 1988–89.

Most analysts believe that in view of the heavy responsibility placed on directors issuing prospectuses, a very conservative view was taken of the bad debts and problem loans. This is undoubtedly so, but it is interesting to reflect on how Payne describes what happened to the bank during the first half of 1991.

> We have a system of scrubbing out our loan portfolio four times a year. The larger accounts are, of course, handled month by month and the decision as to when and how much more provision is necessary is taken at those key points. I don't think that as at December we anticipated the problems that were going

> to emerge in the first six months of this calendar year. We really did not. I think 1990–91 is going to go down in history as probably the worst year for Australian banks for a long time.

Like all other banks, the Commonwealth has a list of 'non-accrual' problem loans: it does not credit interest owed on them in the group's profit. It makes an annual provision against these loans (which is included in the $950-million total bad and doubtful debts write-off) in the expectation that they will not be recovered in full. At 31 December 1990, 'non-accrual' loans amounted to $1.6 billion and directors, partly reflecting past years' provisions, had provided $851 million, or 53%, against their not being recovered. By 30 June non-accrual loans had doubled to $3.2 billion, and although the provision was increased to $1.4 billion it represented only 44% of the total. Some analysts have queried the sharp reduction in the provision rate in the second half-year, but the bank stood behind its sums, which were more conservative than those of many of its rivals.

The Commonwealth (including the SBV) was exposed to most of the big crashes, so it is not surprising that its problem loans have increased. But the future is what counts. The prospectus shows that the bank has exposure of more than $950 million to one group and more than $600 million to another: its two largest loans. The press has concluded that these exposures refer to News Corporation and TNT, where the Commonwealth is the lead banker.

The $270-million expected net trading profit for the year to 30 June 1991 equalled just over 30 cents a share, which meant the bank was issuing on a price/earnings ratio of 18 based on capital after the issue, and about 14 on pre-issue capital. Both figures are much higher than other banks, which is why those abnormal gains from superannuation (equivalent to more than 60 cents a share) were so important.

The abnormal gain is available to enable directors to pay a dividend of, say, 40 cents a share, which would yield 7.4% even if trading remained tight. In the original draft prospectus directors forecast a 45 cents-a-share dividend but they amended it to forecast a yield 'comparable with those of the industry'.

Most brokers believed at the time of the float that the bank would be able to reduce substantially its bad-debt provisions in the 1991–92 year and earn better returns from the SBV, so the brokers predicted that net trading profit would recover to $500 million, or 60 cents a share. But Potter Warburg forecast that the overhang of problem loans would continue in 1991–92 for all banks and accordingly predicted a profit of only $400 million, or 48 cents a share for the Commonwealth. When the 1991–92 numbers were announced the bank earned $416 million or

51.5 cents a share—very close to the Potter Warburg estimates of a year earlier. The market continues to price the bank shares on the basis that there are substantial cost savings ahead to lift profits.

Meanwhile, one of the bank's great assets is that as a result of paying tax on the superannuation surplus and earlier trading profits it has tax franking credits of $650 million—which means that in better times it will be in a position to pay high levels of franked dividends.

Leaving aside short-term problems, there is no doubt that the SBV acquisition gives the bank the opportunity in the medium term to mould a national enterprise of unique strength and profitability. But it is one of the toughest management tasks in the country and made the prospectus difficult to follow. For example, the bank constantly quoted figures setting out the position of the Commonwealth Bank in one table and the State Bank in another. It was as though the Commonwealth had become a two-headed monster. Because management was constantly looking at two sets of tables, many executives did not fully understand what the SBV acquisition had done to the combined operation. Without doubt, the future success of the Commonwealth Bank depends on its ability to integrate the two arms of its operation in Victoria into a highly profitable business.

There are two basic methods of merging banks. In the early 1980s the National Australia Bank acquired the Sydney-based CBC and the Bank of NSW acquired the Melbourne-based CBA to form Westpac. The method adopted by the new Westpac was a slow integration and careful blending of both sets of staff. In contrast, the National Bank went in with the clear goal of completing its rationalisation swiftly and brutally—despite pools of blood and personal anguish. Many in Westpac now believe their approach was not as good as the NAB's because the drawn-out affair created tensions and affected the bank's ability to take advantage quickly of opportunities that became available.

The Commonwealth has taken a route similar to Westpac's, and Westpac managers warn privately that those involved may suffer the 'death of a thousand cuts' instead of the swift action of the sword. Indeed, Westpac, who initially over-bid the Commonwealth, had planned a swift process of integration for the State Bank, although in fairness to the Commonwealth it must be said that Westpac would have been helped by the fact that its operation in Victoria is much smaller than the Commonwealth's. The Westpac people believe that because the SBV is so much larger than the old CBA, there is a danger the Commonwealth will encounter much more serious problems. The Commonwealth rejects such criticism and says integration is on track.

The Commonwealth moved to gradually remove the SBV logo so that the whole operation would come under the Commonwealth banner. Westpac, on the other hand, had been considering centralising the Westpac-SBV bank but operating the State Bank of Victoria as a separate brand in Victoria, in much the same way as AMP life policies are being sold under two brands as part of its strategic alliance with Westpac. (The Reserve Bank might have objected to Westpac's plan, but it would have been hard-pressed to sustain a persuasive argument against it.)

When the Commonwealth Bank took control of the SBV, naturally it immediately established centralised financial control and moved to develop technology to integrate the data-processing networks of both organisations. These two moves alone yielded substantial savings. The way the Commonwealth Bank directors described their moves in the prospectus is interesting.

> Successful integration of these two large organisations will take a considerable time. Although significant rationalisation benefits are expected to commence in 1991–92, the complexity and scale of the integration mean the bank does not expect the rationalisation process to be completed for two to three years.
>
> . . . Because the SBV was an independent organisation, many staff were employed in policy-making and head-office functions. The merged bank therefore initially contained many duplications of function, which are being rationalised as the need for separate administration disappears under integration. The rationalisation process is under senior management control and the objective is to retain the most suitable staff to maintain the effectiveness of important functions in SBV as integration proceeds.

There is a danger that half of the bank will be in turmoil for an extended period, enabling predators to gain market share as internal squabbles affect service.

At the time of the prospectus Payne vigorously rejected the suggestion that the option of using the swift sword to effect a quick merger was available.

> We've got a timetable in place that shows us what we can do. The problem with our merger is that it is so concentrated in Victoria. We have paid a very large amount of money in goodwill for the retail franchise of that bank, and that depends on the people staying in this part of the team and on the customers. The last thing we want to do is move in a way that jeopardises that franchise.
>
> We believe we can meet the objectives of integrating the units, bringing the staff numbers down or rationalising the staff between two organisations in a way that doesn't expose us to a death of a thousand cuts, just by managing the process properly.

> Our state manager . . . has had to adjust to a position of reporting to Paul Rizzo, the man responsible and accountable for getting those operations together. I can't speak about how Westpac did it, but it's a discrete thing. We've just completed a very significant opinion survey of both customers and staff, and will be doing those regularly. It showed a much better situation than we contemplated. While the customers' view of the State Bank has clearly changed because of all that happened, they appear to have accepted the role of the Commonwealth Bank in the whole process.

Payne said attitudes among the staff as to whether the merger and its outcome had been a good thing 'have now swung strongly to the positive, and that was not the case when it first happened'.

If, during the next few years, the Commonwealth's management can pull off a successful SBV integration, they will achieve a remarkable rise in profitability. The prospectus shows that the old Commonwealth Bank was much more successful in reducing the cost of its staff in relation to net income than the SBV. In 1986 staff costs for both the SBV and the Commonwealth absorbed about 47% of net income. By 1990 the Commonwealth had reduced that to 35%, while the SBV's figure had risen to 51.6%, partly as a result of a fall in net income but also because of higher operating costs.

Payne described the way the Commonwealth reduced costs:

> We have turned all our systems upside down and got projects in the branches that have enabled us to run the business more tightly out there and in head office. Undoubtedly, further economies are available in the future—for example, from remoulding and reshaping the way we do business through the branches. This is all blue-sky stuff to an extent, but in talking to bankers in this country and elsewhere you know costs are really going to be critical.
>
> The big issue for the Commonwealth Bank is, of course, that the profile of our business in important areas is different and more labour-intensive than the other banks. We have a much higher volume of labour-intensive transaction-based business through our branches.

The Commonwealth Bank's ability to be a leader of the banking industry in operation efficiency provides good grounds for believing that it will solve the problems of the State Bank acquisition. However, at the same time it is facing a very determined thrust from the National Australia Bank and from smaller players like the Bank of Melbourne. All the banks have been working on new technologies to enable much better integration of bank accounts and provision of services at lower costs. The NAB adapted its existing system and, although its rivals say that eventually they will have better systems, it has introduced a range of products that led *Personal Investment* magazine to rate it 1991 and

1992 Bank of the Year. Previous winners were the Commonwealth and Westpac.

Payne recognised the threat posed by the National and the correctness of its strategy.

> He [former NAB chief Nobby Clark] took a very sensible route. Our system handles a great volume of transactions, which is the nature of our business. It was also the first system on line in the country. We've worked at keeping it ticking over, but the time has come to revamp it; but it is going to be revamped on a very careful basis. It will happen progressively according to functions over a couple of years . . . You take advantage of what you've got there at the time. But I don't disagree that there has been a range of approaches, and I think the approaches offered by the National Bank have probably been the best.

Banking analysts will be closely watching the market share each of the banks achieves, particularly in Victoria. However, Payne pointed out that in the months leading up to the takeover the Commonwealth deliberately built up its liquidity so it could pay the $1.6 billion on 31 December; it managed its deposit-rate structure to attract extra funds. 'Our deposit levels were artificially inflated and that's why, by some indicators in Victoria, anyway, they have come off since then.' After 30 June that process will have ended, so market-share figures from 1 July will be an important test.

The Commonwealth board's summary of the outlook in the prospectus was: 'While present economic circumstances are depressing bank earnings in general, the board believes the bank is well positioned to share in the benefits of future economic growth and to consolidate its position as a major participant in Australia's financial markets'. However, the 1991–92 profit showed that the profit benefits of that strength is further away than most people thought at the time of the prospectus.

THE STRENGTHS AND WEAKNESSES OF FAIRFAX

THE FLOAT of John Fairfax Holdings Ltd reveals an enormous amount about the company. There are similarities with the Commonwealth Bank float—Fairfax's mastheads are also household names and the prospectus has been widely advertised—but unlike the Commonwealth Bank, the Fairfax directors have made forecasts of future net profits. And the assumptions behind them are important.

At the same time, the unusual accounting treatment of staff redundancy costs, masthead values and possible payments to Kerry Packer as compensation for his withdrawal from the Tourang consortium bid, are not only of interest to shareholders but they also carry a wider significance. In particular, a way has been devised to use the unique Fairfax conversion from receivership to public company to pay staff redundancy and other costs without affecting the profit-and-loss account. One could argue they are being paid out of revalued masthead values.

Fairfax operates in three main media markets. The first is the Sydney region, where the *Sydney Morning Herald* is the flagship, supported by the *Sun-Herald* on Sundays. Its flanks are secured by ownership of the daily newspapers in Newcastle and Wollongong, and the group has a string of Sydney suburbans. The second media market is Melbourne, where the *Age* in past years has been subjected to attacks by papers of the Herald & Weekly Times, now part of News Corporation. The *Age* has rebuffed the challenges very well, although it was required to launch the loss-making *Sunday Age* to make sure News Corporation was not able to attack the base *Saturday Age* classified advertising market via a dominant Sunday newspaper. The *Age* has 72% of Melbourne's classified market and the *Sydney Morning Herald* has 76% of Sydney's. The News Corporation inroads on these classified markets has been very small over five years, showing the strength of both Fairfax titles. The third main market in which Fairfax operates is business publications, where its two key mastheads are the *Australian Financial Review* and *Business Review Weekly*.

The company also has big printing plants in Sydney and Melbourne. The prospectus says the Sydney plant will require considerable expenditure, but financing this has not been allowed for in the forecasting period to June 1993 covered by the prospectus for the 1992 share issue.

The Fairfax company must surely be one of the few enterprises in modern times to go to the public in Australia without either a chief executive officer or an executive on the board. Indeed, a CEO did not take up an appointment until September 1992—ten months after the Tourang syndicate won the bid for the company.

The board of Fairfax is structured to offer a different perspective on issues than would be offered by the board of a standard large Australian public company. The five Australian non-executive directors have an extensive range of experience and, according to the prospectus, three of them—chairman Sir Zelman Cowen, Sir Laurence Street and John Singleton—do not hold a directorship in any other publicly listed company. Cowen is a former governor-general, Street is a former chief justice of NSW, and Singleton is a widely-known proprietor of an advertising agency. The other two Australian non-executive directors, former CRA chairman Sir Roderick Carnegie and present Brambles managing director and Commonwealth Bank director Gary Pemberton, have public company directorship experience.

There are three overseas directors: deputy chairman Conrad Black and Daniel Colson, both representing the Telegraph group in London, and Brian Powers of the US private investment firm Hellman & Friedman. After the float, the Telegraph owned about 12.5% of the voting stock. The Telegraph and Hellman & Friedman each have convertible debentures and options, but the Hellman & Friedman debentures can only be converted to voting shares if they become Australian-owned and the Telegraph voting interest cannot rise above 15%. It pressed the Federal Government to be able to go to 20% but was rejected.

The Fairfax float is also unusual in that all but 15 million of the 173 million shares to be issued came from shares and debentures issued in December 1991 when Tourang bought the Fairfax operation. (Tourang later changed its name to John Fairfax Holdings Ltd, which issued the shares and debentures.) To support Tourang's December share and debenture issue, a series of financial forecasts was made, and the new Fairfax board and the management had to review the figures in preparing estimates for the latest prospectus.

Although the new forecasts are very close to Tourang's, one or two key situations have changed and placed a different perspective on the sums. It is always hazardous to make forecasts, so the Fairfax directors set out in the prospectus a set of economic scenarios behind their forecasts. They then made a series of key operating assumptions, and explained how any variation in these would affect the bottom line. It is a model for other prospectus authors to follow.

According to the Fairfax economic scenarios, in the 1992–93 financial year there will be a rise in Australian gross domestic product of 4.3%, inflation as measured by the CPI will be 3.5% and the Australian dollar will average US75 cents. Interestingly, the Federal Budget documents which were published about six months later forecast GDP would rise by 3% in 1992–93.

On the basis of operating assumptions derived from this Fairfax scenario, the directors forecast that group profit would be $94 million before tax in the year to 30 June 1993. The share offer price of $1.20 represents a multiple of nine times the forecast 1992–93 before-tax profit. No tax is required because of prior losses, but a theoretical provision of $37 million is made to bring forecast 1992–93 net profit in at $57 million, giving a price/earnings ratio of 14.8 at $1.20.

The $94-million before-tax profit depends, of course, on the board's operating assumptions being achieved. Perhaps the most important operating assumption involves interest rates, because of the company's borrowings. Every 1% change in the commercial bill rate reduces or increases the profit by $7.3 million.

The original Tourang plan still left Fairfax with $700 million worth of base debt, plus additional working capital facilities. In 1992–93, a proportion of the cashflow generated by Fairfax will be required to reduce this debt.

Group profit is also sensitive to changes in advertising volume and rates. Directors forecast a rise of 4% in 1992–93 volume, which is broadly in line with their GDP growth forecast and emphasises the close correlation between the economy and the Fairfax advertising market. Every 1% rise or fall in advertising volume moves profits by about $4 million. Directors say that 10% swings in volume are 'not uncommon'. Every 1% change in advertising rates has a $6-million influence on profit.

Another profit-sensitive factor is newsprint, which is bought in US dollars. A rise of one US cent in the Australian dollar's value lifts profit by $1.3 million. But if the Australian dollar fell from US75 cents to US70 cents, the before-tax profit would fall by $6.5 million, all other things being equal. The price of newsprint depends on the Australian Newsprint Mills rebate and the overseas price. The overseas price has been falling, but could be expected to strengthen if the US economy recovers. The directors also made no provision for a claim by Lady Mary Fairfax, made under a previous agreement before Fairfax changed hands, for a payment of about $7 million a year for life. The matter is before the courts.

These assumptions have been moulded into a set of forecasts that predict gross operating revenue will rise from the $723 million expected in 1991–92 to $782 million in the year to 30 June 1993—an increase of about 8%. Operating costs are expected to rise by only 2.8%, from $578 million to $594 million. With revenue rising at almost three times the rate of increase in costs, it enables earnings before interest and tax to increase by 34%. Although this is an impressive figure, the original Tourang estimates provided for an even greater rise. In addition, Tourang's estimates were based on an inflation rate of 5% compared with the Fairfax directors' forecast of 3.5%. Tourang said salaries would move in line with the 5% CPI estimate.

Given the Fairfax directors' predictions of an inflation rate rise of

3.5%, an increase in newsprint usage and other costs associated with a 4% rise in advertising volumes, and a tendency for newsprint prices to increase, clearly some reduction in staff costs is required by Fairfax to contain total increase in operating costs to 2.8%.

The prospectus says: 'The directors have assessed that some cost savings can be effected over time. The financial forecast for the year ending June 30, 1993, incorporates some of these cost savings to the extent that they have been planned by management'. The directors go on to point out that the associated redundancy costs will not affect the profit of the company but will be treated as a 'pre-acquisition provision'. Given the accountancy standards, this was no mean feat and was achieved in the following way. At the time of the Tourang deal, the then directors assessed the expected staff redundancy payments and other 'contingent acquisition costs and estimated future rationalisation costs' payable after 31 December at $70.9 million. This provision became an important part of the balance sheet that was formed as Tourang acquired the Fairfax assets. Tourang issued $686 million in shares and convertible debentures.

In the balance sheet as at 31 December that amount, with small extras, became $687 million in shareholders' funds. Once shareholders' funds were established at $687 million, plus the special provision at $70.9 million, the rules for the balance sheet were set. All the tangible assets of Fairfax (freeholds, plant, debtors, investments, etc.) came across at book value, while on the other side liabilities to banks and creditors, plus other provisions, were also incorporated at book values. The only two flexible items were two assets: the value of mastheads and future tax losses.

The value of future tax losses was set at $190 million, leaving the mastheads at $1165 million. Had the special provision not been made, presumably the mastheads could have been reduced in value by $70.9 million to $1094 million with shareholders' funds still left at $687 million. The mastheads will not be amortised against future profits.

Although there might be some controversy over assessing the mastheads this way, the whole Tourang exercise was the result of an open auction over many months, and the public issue capitalises the company at $140 million more than the original Tourang deal. This provides an additional degree of conservatism on the masthead values. The auditor of Tourang, Ernst & Young, became auditor of the whole John Fairfax group.

Ernst & Young has agreed that staff redundancy payments and other costs that come into the web of the special $70.9-million provision will never be recorded in the accounts as abnormal or extraordinary items. These costs are virtually being covered by a boost in masthead values.

Directors have declared that $22.5 million of the special provisions was 'current'; that is, it is expected to be drawn on in the 1992 calendar year. The balance of $48.4 million is a non-current provision and may be required in subsequent years.

Fairfax director Gary Pemberton will be familiar with the basic principle behind this exercise because he used a profit on Brambles shares, secretly held by Brambles, to finance the start-up losses of the group's United States expansion.

If all the $70.9 million is not used for staff redundancy and the other costs envisaged for the provision, then conceivably the wording might allow it to be used for a special payment the company is likely to make to Kerry Packer, an original member of the Tourang syndicate. The terms of his withdrawal effectively mean that on 30 December 1993 Fairfax must pay Packer's company, Consolidated Press, 30 million times any rise in the share price above $1. (If the share price in the twenty trading days before that date averages $2, Packer will get $30 million. If it is only $1, he will get nothing.) The funds for this payment will come from the exercise of 60 million options that are exercisable on the same date.

The ability to keep a potential $70.9 million in staff redundancy and other payments away from the profit-and-loss account has greatly assisted the group's ability to charge $1.20 a share to the public, or 20 cents above the institutional price of December 1991. The tax losses that will be created by payments made against the provision do not appear to have been capitalised in the balance sheet. The benefits of tight cost control, helped by lower staff numbers, begin to show up in the Fairfax estimates for the year to 30 June 1993. The prospectus makes no forecasts for 1993–94. By contrast, in the original Tourang document, operating costs were again expected to show only a token rise in 1993–94, even though inflation (and salary rises) by that time was forecast to be 6%. Revenue was expected to rise by a further 7.6%. Tourang estimated that operating profit before tax would jump from $96 million (the Fairfax prospectus forecasts $94 million) in 1992–93 to a staggering $153.8 million in 1993–94.

Tourang had forecast that operating costs would rise by a total of only 3.4% over the two years to 1994 even though inflation was estimated at a total of 11% (5% in 1992–93 and 6% in 1993–94). In the Tourang estimates, interest costs would also fall as a result of bank debt repayment. The 1993–94 cash generation that Tourang forecast was $140 million before bank debt payments and was an integral part of the capitalisation of the company, as were the hoped-for cash benefits if revenue increased faster than forecast.

For a company as highly borrowed as Fairfax and requiring expenditure on plant, cashflow is crucially important. In the six months to 30 June 1992, free cashflow was estimated by Fairfax directors to be actually a deficit of $12 million, even though operating profit before tax and depreciation would exceed $30 million and total gross cashflow was boosted by a further $17 million in new capital raised by the float.

Directors said this $47 million was required for redundancy payments, capital expenditure and pre-receivership creditors. In the 1992–93 full year, free cashflow was still forecast to be only $20 million, even though earnings before depreciation and tax, less dividend payments, were expected to total about $90 million. During 1992–93, further redundancy payments are provided for, along with capital expenditure and an unspecified requirement to begin repaying bank debt. The message behind the differences between forecast cash flows and earnings over two years is that the original Tourang estimates provided for substantial redundancy costs. If those redundancy payments are less than estimated, directors will have a buffer against wrong trading forecasts. They will also have a higher cost base. The Tourang document indicated that $200 million of the $700-million bank facility needed to be amortised, starting in 1992–93.

The prospectus refers to the need to upgrade the Fairfax Sydney printing plant and says

> The timing of the construction of new plant for the Sydney operations is uncertain and the costs and benefits are unclear at this stage. Management believes it is unlikely any significant expenditure in relation to a new plant will occur within the financial forecast period included in this prospectus; further, management believes the book value of the existing plant would be minimal by the time any new plant became operational. However, as an indication, such a new plant could involve capital expenditure well in excess of $200 million.

The existing plant of the company around Australia is valued at only $74 million. The prospectus makes no provision for financing any additional plant, even though News Corporation is upgrading its Sydney facilities, including the provision of colour-printing equipment. The bank covenants allow for dividends to be 50% of after-tax profit but have unspecified restrictions on capital expenditure.

The Sydney plant problem will be one of the greatest challenges for the new board and management. It will be much easier to solve if the Tourang forecast of a before-tax profit of $154 million and free cashflow of $140 million is achieved in 1993–94. The 1993–94 after-tax profit forecast by Tourang was $94 million, giving the company a price/earnings ratio at $1.20 of about 9 on present capital and debentures. But the Fairfax directors do not repeat those original Tourang

1993–94 forecasts in the prospectus and, indeed, the Tourang figures were based on a somewhat different set of assumptions to those used in the prospectus.

The Fairfax float, which predicts an interest cover in 1992–93 of 2.3, capitalises the entire Fairfax operation at about $1.6 billion. After the issue the sharemarket added a further premium to the stock. The company is well placed to benefit from an upturn in the Australian economy but it is vulnerable to any higher interest rates that might flow from the same upturn. A board of the calibre of the Fairfax board is unlikely to leave the plant modernisation decision (and the necessary funding) unresolved until the end of the forecast period on 30 June 1993.

I should point out that I took up my employees' entitlement to the issue. With its wonderful mastheads, the company has great long-term potential, despite the concerns in the prospectus about the long-term effect of interest rates on the Fairfax bottom line; the revenue and cost assumptions; the scheme to keep staff redundancy and certain other costs away from the profit-and-loss account; and the need to make a decision on new printing equipment for Sydney—and how to fund it.

THE WRONG PRICE

FULL MARKS to Rupert Murdoch for negotiating such a high price for Pacific Magazines and Printing. It is useful to reflect on what motivated J. B. Were to underwrite the float at the wrong price. First and foremost, Pacific Magazines was a good company and the market was hungry for good stock. Secondly, the issue had been structured so that most of the profits would be paid out in dividends, to enable a high yield of about 6% (a fully-franked income at that level looked very attractive). Thirdly, everything J. B. Were had touched had been successful so, not surprisingly, they were very confident.

Where they went wrong was that they didn't place enough emphasis on the fact that the high profits were achieved partly by charging a high rate of depreciation in the tax accounts and a low rate in the accounts that go to shareholders. In addition, Fairfax came on to the market much earlier than expected and no one was very happy about a section of the business being sold to Murdoch's nephew.

The long-term performance and value of Pacific Magazines' mastheads depends on the group's ability to make profits. Meanwhile, Rupert Murdoch has the cash in News Corporation's pocket as a result of the Were underwriting and belief in the long-term value of the company.

REBORN COMPASS DEFIES GRAVITY

J. B. WERE's willingness to back their judgement was taken one step further in the float of Southern Cross Airlines—the new Compass. To outsiders, the great surprise about the float of the new Compass airline is that J. B. Were & Son agreed to back the project. But perhaps even more amazing in the light of the Australian Securities Commission's controversial charges against the former Compass directors is the high calibre of the board of Southern Cross Airlines Holdings, which will operate the revived carrier.

The board includes former National Companies and Securities Commission chief Leigh Masel, senior Queensland company director Graham Tucker, former Queensland Treasury head Leo Hielscher, former Federal Government minister Dame Margaret Guilfoyle and former Australian Chamber of Manufactures chief executive Brian Powell. In addition, Geoffrey Cohen is a financial adviser to the board. Cohen is a former Arthur Andersen & Co partner and president of the Institute of Chartered Accountants. Although all the members have options to take up shares, none has any other vested interest in the float.

Behind the planning for the Southern Cross float are several former pilots or executives of Australian and Ansett airlines. They include Leonard Heard (director of operations), Henry Theunissen (chief pilot) and Jim Davidson (manager of line operations). This support from established airline people, plus access to Compass's name, facilities and staff, and forecasts of very low costs all helped persuade J. B. Were and the non-executive directors to put their names, and possibly their savings, on the line. Another crucial factor was the ability to recruit Sam Coats as chief executive. Coats has held high executive positions at Southwest and several other regional airlines in the US.

The new carrier has significantly lower costs than either the old Compass or its rivals. And so the main danger to its existence, an all-out price war, would not only be very costly to both existing airlines, but also would almost certainly end in a case before the Trade Practices Commission.

The new Compass has the same number of aircraft as the old operation but only half the seating capacity because it is using McDonnell Douglas MD80 twin-jet aircraft rather than the wide-body Airbus. The old Compass leased its aircraft when demand for planes was at a peak and prices were high. But that demand has now slumped, and the new carrier's leasing costs will be about half as much on a per-seat basis.

Most of the five aircraft being leased by the new operation are used, which also helped reduce prices. Aircraft lease companies are now desperate to get deals, and so the Apogee group not only offered the aircraft at low rates, but also agreed to sub-underwrite 26 million of the 100 million Southern Cross shares being underwritten by J. B. Were.

The Queensland Government sub-underwrote a further 20 million shares, as well as agreeing to subscribe to 1.5 million shares once the public issue was completed, and General Motors of the US accounted for another 2.5 million. General Motors owns EDS Australia, which will provide information technology services for Southern Cross. The Queensland Government's involvement was conditional on the new company's head office being located in Brisbane and on the provision of flights to Cairns and Townsville.

The support of these groups, plus a 5% commitment from National Mutual, meant J. B. Were only had to find sub-underwriters for 46.5 million of the 100 million 50-cent shares in the underwritten portion of the public issue. Were needed all the help it could get because the issue raised only half the targeted amount and the underwriters and sub-underwriters had to subscribe the rest.

The new Compass aimed at 114 staff per aircraft, and this is expected to fall to less than 100 when its fleet grows to seven planes in 1994. The old Compass had more than 200 staff per aircraft, although this would also have fallen when additional aircraft were leased.

Although staff costs on a per-seat cost will remain about the same, the old Compass achieved its low figure by using larger aircraft. This strategy also meant fewer flights, and so made it harder to achieve good yields.

The average capacity of the planes used by Australian and Ansett is much nearer to that of the 142-passenger MD80 than to the 280-seat Airbus. Yet their per-aircraft staff levels are more than twice that of the new Compass—a fact that would put them at a distinct disadvantage in a price war. Moreover, they have many more types of aircraft to service.

Initially, the new Compass has 1420 seats available daily on its flights between Melbourne and Sydney, (about 20% of the market) plus 850 between Sydney and Brisbane, 568 between Melbourne and Adelaide and 284 between Brisbane, Townsville and Cairns. These are the most profitable routes in Australia. It will not fly to Perth—the service that lost the old Compass a fortune—until it leases additional aircraft and even then may stay in eastern states.

The most important challenge facing Southern Cross is to get through its start-up period and begin trading profitably. Profit projections are important, but the crucial figures are the amount of cash in the company, its fares and its load factor.

Compass fares are lower than those being charged by Australian and Ansett, but the level of discount depends on the basis of comparison. Southern Cross estimates that 10% of its passengers will travel executive class, 40% standard economy, 25% seven-day advance and 25% 14-day advance. Peak-hour travel will account for 40% of the flights. Its directors expect that Compass will sell only 62% of its seats during the first year of operation.

The directors also assume that the company will accept advance bookings and use the cash but insure passengers against loss. (Given the assurances in the prospectus, the directors would almost certainly be personally liable if the insurance policy were not implemented.)

On the basis of these assumptions and the prospectus estimates, the group will start with cash of about $35 million. This is expected to rise to $46.4 million in 1993, $76 million in 1994 and $103.5 million in 1995. In other words, if the estimates are realised, by 1995 the group will have about 63 cents a share in cash plus its existing business. This means that if a price war developed and Southern Cross were forced to discount Compass fares by 15%, the group would still have enough cash to be in business in three years.

Of course, if the fare cut were increased to 20% or 25%, the group would be under much more pressure. However, demand would almost certainly increase its load factor. If the existing airlines were forced to match the Southern Cross fares and then go down another 20%, their losses would be huge. As it turned out when Compass launched they went the other way and announced a fare structure that was higher than that forecast in the prospectus. If they can attract sufficient passengers at that level, they will do very well, but directors are taking a big risk.

WHAT WENT WRONG WITH THE GIO FLOAT

In a mere thirty-two hours 128 000 Australians wrote cheques worth a total of $2.2 billion in a mad scramble to get shares in GIO Australia—$1 billion more than was needed to fill the issue. If the issue had remained open for its full term, another $1 billion would almost certainly have been subscribed. It was the biggest public float in Australia, and it showed the enormous latent demand for stakes in big Australian undertakings.

Those who missed out on the shares were so angry that they

threatened to sue the GIO, their brokers, Australia Post or anyone else they thought could be blamed for depriving them of the chance to make a certain killing. The GIO was issued at $2.40 on 29 June 1992 and opened a month later on the stock exchange at $2.53. By mid-August, however, it had fallen to $2.24 and by the end of that month it had fallen below $2.20 as the market became concerned about the risk of big payouts as a result of Hurricane Andrew. The nation had been fighting over a ticket to lose money, at least in the short term.

The GIO has emerged as a case study of how not to privatise a government enterprise if you want to retain the goodwill of the public and encourage Australians to buy shares in productive enterprises, rather than leaving their money in the bank or spending it upgrading their homes. However, it should be emphasised that the GIO is a good business, even though it operates in the high-risk area of insurance, and it is using its strong base to extend the scope of its operations into financial services. After the float, the GIO picked up Victoria's SIO for an incredibly low price, and this greatly improves its long-term outlook.

Although the GIO Australia float was tipped for more than a year before the actual event, behind the scenes in 1991 the NSW Government debated whether to float the company or sell it to other insurers. When a float was chosen as the best way to proceed, GIO was expected to be an exciting privatisation that might give shareholders a similar return to the Commonwealth Bank float. But the businesses were very different and the NSW Government was more interested in maximising its sale price than promoting investor goodwill at the expense of a low float price.

Perhaps the first indication of danger for potential shareholders came in February 1992, when it was revealed that the regulators' safeguards against over-promotion of floats might not be applied to the GIO. The Government's marketing advisers thought GIO shares could be marketed like soap powder or deodorant, not realising the response such a campaign would elicit, particularly since the issue was to be conducted like a 100-metre sprint: first to the line got the shares.

In the scramble to get shares, few people tried to read the prospectus in detail. Even if they had made the attempt, their chances of gaining an understanding of the company were not good; it was one of the most confusing documents ever presented to Australian investors. Indeed, professional investors are only now coming to grips with its meaning. Now that the issue is over, the GIO's managing director, Bill Jocelyn, is free to speak out. Metaphorically speaking, he says, he would have 'burned' sections of the prospectus and would have conducted the whole issue differently.

Jocelyn knew his company better than many of the advisers, and in the early stages submitted to the NSW Government that the best way to float the GIO was for the Government to underwrite it and offer it to policy-holders first, then the public and finally the institutions. But while he was advocating this system, the GIO was still under threat of being sold to his rivals.

Once his advice had been rejected, Jocelyn took an almost fatalistic approach to the exercise. With the benefit of hindsight, he should have taken a harder stance and been much more active in promoting his views. As it turned out, institutions, brokers' clients, the public and policy-holders were encouraged to compete against each other for a share of the action, and there were fees galore. In all, it cost the GIO more than $27 million to float.

Jocelyn, who did not believe the float should be advertised, expressed his opposition as a member of the privatisation committee. 'I don't like advertising campaigns much', he says. 'I said my piece and then shut up. The advertising was overdone.' In fairness to the NSW Government, they did not believe $1.2 billion could be raised for an insurance float without a strong advertising campaign. They were as surprised as anyone else by the magnitude of the response.

The advertising campaign for the issue, which in Victoria had been preceded by a strong campaign promoting the organisation itself, indicated the company was a bricks-and-mortar investment with a stake in some of Australia's largest companies. In fact, it is a company in a high-risk business subject to wide variations in profit. For example, the company could be hit for as a much as $28 million as part of claims against its reinsurance business because of Hurricane Andrew on the east coast of the United States (although the final loss could be as low as $2 million).

After a month of heavy promotion, the prospectus was issued to those who had applied for it. Prominent on page three was the statement: 'Your application is more likely to be accepted if you apply early'. The prospectus contained an envelope that stated in bold type: 'Please rush this to . . . GIO Australia share offer'. People were, in effect, being bullied into sending their cheques to the company without attempting to read the prospectus. Thirty-two hours after the issue opened, it was closed. Many people in WA and other places never got a prospectus because of delays in the post. Even in the worst days of the mining boom, it is doubtful whether anything was pushed as hard as the GIO. Jocelyn says the system caused competition between GIO customers, brokers' clients and institutions, and 'created a false sense of demand'.

The advertising campaign attracted a huge volume of share buyers, some of whom did not own shares or held only Commonwealth Bank shares. Many made the decision to invest because their friends had done so well in the Commonwealth Bank float. Stockbrokers realised the enormity of the buying power that was being generated by the advertising campaign and the press articles and allowed their clients to be circulated with prospectuses. The brokers received a commission when clients applied for and were allotted shares.

Many brokers' clients borrowed money to buy stock, expecting a quick profit. Institutions did not want to miss out on their share of the easy money and took up more than they wanted on the expectation that public demand would force up the price. Although the prospectus was unintelligible, the fact that the stock offered a dividend yield of 5.8%, including a 14-cent fully-franked payment in November, was a clear attraction.

But there were some warnings. J. B. Were's Craig Drummond, who was rated Australia's top banking analyst in BRW's broking poll last year, said the NAB represented better value. He was immediately criticised by BT's Max Powditch who believed GIO was good value.

There were also some isolated warnings in the daily newspapers, including an article by the *Sydney Morning Herald*'s Max Walsh, pointing out that the GIO was deeply in the high-risk business of reinsurance—the area that had caused Lloyd's of London so much loss. But most of the papers, including the *SMH*, ran items suggesting a good premium was likely.

But what was not realised by the brokers' clients and the institutions that overbought was that the huge demand created by the advertising and public relations campaign would in the main be from people who would not think of ringing a stockbroker to buy GIO shares once their application had been rejected or reduced. So, when the stock listed, the unsatisfied buying demand created by the prospectus was not reflected on the sharemarket. Professionals who were in for a quick profit sold, and the shares fell below the issue price of $2.40 a share.

If Jocelyn's plan had been heeded by the NSW Government, the institutions and brokers' clients would have provided the sharemarket buying power to ensure the issue opened well, but the issue price and the fees would have been much lower. Of course, in fairness to those involved, the All Ordinaries index fell sharply after the prospectus, and that inevitably reduced the attraction of the stock, particularly since the tender process by which the float was organised valued it towards the high end of the market. But the overall fall in the market only partly explains the fall from a realistic expectation of $2.65 a share (a premium of about 25 cents) to a low of $2.24 within six weeks of the prospectus.

Jocelyn says in many ways he is relieved that the advisers' predictions of $2.90 or $3 were wrong, because if the shares had reached that level they would have fallen sharply later, creating a much worse situation. He does not believe the discount will harm the company's goodwill in the longer term.

One of the most informative parts of the prospectus was the description by the GIO's directors on page 17 of where the company's profits came from. Among the points made by directors were:

- The company's general insurance business is divided into two parts: 'short-tail', such as household insurance, where claims are known quickly and profit or loss can be determined reasonably accurately each year; and 'long-tail', such as workers compensation or public liability, where it may be years before the final cost of settling claims is determined and the exact profit or loss known. The GIO sets aside provisions for future claims in its balance sheet and releases part of those provisions to the profit and loss account when final outcomes are clear.
- When 'long-tail' business is run down, if more money has been set aside for claims than proves necessary, so-called 'run-off profits' emerge. These lead to growth in yearly earnings that is really a reflection of past years' activity. Directors have highlighted the sentences describing run-off profits to alert shareholders that they have been significant to the GIO during recent years.
- Insurance companies such as the GIO also make profits by investing the premiums they receive. Accounting standards now require that annual changes in the market value of all assets, including shares and property, be included in the profit-and-loss account, which means there are going to be big variations in insurance company earnings.
- The GIO also makes profits from life insurance, but their distribution is different from general insurance profits because they are controlled by the Life Insurance Act. The group also sought to make money by borrowing and lending to others and charging fees for the management of investment funds.

Unfortunately, after it had set out the company's sources of profit, the prospectus virtually went downhill. The directors boldly set out what they believed to be the profits of the company, claiming that the GIO had earned $109.6 million in 1988–89, $104.7 million in 1989–90, $95 million in 1990–91 and $54 million in the half-year to 31 December 1991, which would lead to a profit of about $105 million for 1991–92.

Directors said they expected after-tax profits for the following three years to match the $100-million average rate achieved in the previous five years. Profit in the 1992–93 year was expected to be lower than 1991–92, but 'an appreciable improvement' was expected in 1993–94. The $105-million forecast profit equalled 21 cents a share, which meant that at $2.40 the price/earnings ratio (the share price divided by earnings a share), was 11.4. Directors expected a stable dividend for two years.

All this was standard, but then came the confusion. On the page following the directors' profit estimates was a much bigger table prepared by the investigating accountants, Coopers & Lybrand and Ernst & Young. Their profit figures bore little relationship to those of the directors. The two firms told shareholders that the GIO had earned profits of only $52.4 million, or 10 cents a share, in 1990–91, instead of the $95 million claimed by the directors. This meant it was floating on a huge price/earnings ratio of 23.

However, instead of the half-yearly profit to 31 December 1991 being $54 million as the directors had claimed, the investigating accountants reckoned it was $69.3 million—$16.9 million more than the full 1990–91 investigating accountants' yearly profit figure. Prospective shareholders were virtually being told to toss a coin as to who to believe. The result was that although directors and accountants could agree that the company had earned somewhere between $540 million and $576 million during the past five-and-a-half years, readers of the prospectus had no clue in which years the profits were earned, or which divisions had earned them. The accountants had followed accounting standards but directors believed they were right. Before the prospectus was issued there were huge debates between the parties. The debates were intensified by the fact that the two firms charged $8 million for their report and the other work they did. The sufferers in the debate were the readers of the prospectus.

Jocelyn is scathing in his criticism of Coopers & Lybrand and Ernst & Young. 'The investigating accountants' report went off the rails. It was an absolute disgrace, a waste of public money. It was one of the more scandalous efforts I have seen in my life in the Public Service.' Jocelyn adds that the GIO will not take the slightest notice of the report in its future communications with its shareholders. 'There have been fifteen ceremonial burnings of the report', he says with some passion. However the accountants also have strong views about the validity of their report.

A painstaking reconciliation of the two versions of the GIO's profit reveals a great deal about its business that shareholders should understand. In defence of the investigating accountants, it seems they looked at the five-and-a-half years of profits and made a hindsight judgement about when they were earned.

The Fee Bonanza

	$m
Investigating accountants	
Coopers & Lybrand	4.26
Ernst & Young	3.71
Sub-total	**7.97**
Actuaries	
Reinsurance—Coopers	0.17
Life insurance—Tillinghast	1.65
General insurance—Trowbridge	1.21
Sub-total	**3.03**
Advice to Government	
BT Australia	1.01
Potter Warburg	0.48
Tillinghast	0.50
Malleson	0.04
Allen Allen & Hemsley	0.59
Sub-total	**2.62**
Underwriters	
County NatWest, Bain, Potter	1.22
Malleson	0.41
Sub-total	**1.63**
GIO advice	
Blake Dawson	1.76
Costs of converting GIO to corporate structure, preparations for privatisation	10.00
Sub-total	**11.76**
Total	**27.01**

The Profitability Gap

	1990 ($m)	1991 ($m)	6 mths to 31/12/91 ($m)
Directors' profit	104.7	95.0	54.0
Accountants' profit	105.4	52.4	69.3

The first area of controversy concerns the directors' moves in 1988 and 1989 to set aside a $50-million special provision for disasters. When the Newcastle earthquake and Sydney hail-damage claims hit the company, they used that provision to cover part of the losses, rather than reduce the profit in the eighteen months to 31 December 1991. The investigating accountants reversed the earlier provisions and reduced the 1990–91 and December 1991 half-year profits by $50 million.

The GIO has substantial investments in property. Some of the property is actually owned by the life insurance bond- and policy-holders, and the balance is held as an investment by the company. In the year to 30 June 1991, the last full year before the float, the directors did not write down the holdings, but put a note in the accounts that they were being reviewed. They subsequently made a write-down that, with other adjustments, came to $48 million in the half-year to December 1991. The investigating accountants transferred that write-down from the December half-year to the 1990–91 year.

The accountants also completely revised the way the GIO allocates its claims, boosting profit in 1989–90 and 1990–91 but reducing it in the 31 December 1991 half-year. There were many factors in these adjustments, but the main one was the so-called run-off profits. In July 1987, the GIO ceased to underwrite workers compensation, following the introduction of WorkCover in NSW. It put the old workers compensation business in a separate basket and began paying out the claims from the money put aside. As time went on, it became clear that there was more in the basket than was required for claims. In all, $260 million was taken out of the workers compensation pool or other claim surpluses to contribute run-off profits, which represented 30% of the total before-tax earnings during the five-and-a-half years covered in the prospectus.

The GIO explains that run-off profits are a regular part of insurance because the company is constantly adjusting the claims provision in the light of events. Nevertheless, the accountants' view was that the GIO used too much of the run-off profits in the half-year to 31 December 1991, and they allocated them to previous years.

Piecing the two stories together, we see that two big problems were about to hit the company in the period leading up to its float. The first was the earthquake and hail damage and the second its property write-down. In effect, it eliminated the earthquake and hail problem with prior provisions and offset the property write-down with a large chunk of run-off profits. The investigating accountants' timing adjustment meant that the 1990–91 profit was slashed but the December half-year received a big boost.

The GIO's shareholders will need to get used to these fluctuations. In the 1992–93 year, profit has been affected by lower interest rates. In the past, lower rates lifted the value of the company's long-term bonds, and a profit was made. Now lower rates are affecting income. In addition, the GIO has $100 million less for income generation because its switch to a public corporation required it to pay deferred taxes to the NSW Government.

A higher profit is expected in 1993–94 because insurance premiums have been raised in most states. The Victorian increase will be most helpful because losses were incurred as the group battled the SIO for market share. It is not easy to negotiate a big acquisition in the midst of a public float, but Jocelyn realised he had to move quickly and acquire the SIO while the Victorian Government, approaching an election, was desperate for cash.

The GIO bought SIO Victoria for about $170 million—the value of its net assets. Moreover, it had the chance to approve the value of the assets and claims it was acquiring, and insisted on property being written down to two-thirds of book value. Because no cash payment was being made for the value of the business (goodwill), the purchase price was funded by selling the SIO's own assets. However, the GIO may need to inject up to $50 million into the SIO to finance future business.

To be able to take a rival out of the market at virtually no cost is an incredible deal. But the best was to come: any redundant staff will be hired or paid out by the hapless Victorian Government. In addition, a commission is payable to the Government on policies sold during the next five years. Theoretically, this is the goodwill payment, but it will only be made when policies are sold. However, no commission is payable if the other part of the Victorian Government's insurance operation, the Transport Accident Commission, moves into the GIO's area. So Jocelyn not only pays his goodwill as he earns it, but opens up a wonderful market and keeps competition out at the same time. Deals like that come once in a lifetime.

The addition of the SIO will also boost the size of the GIO. When the float was conceived, some felt the GIO looked too small to fit the image of the powerful group being portrayed by the public relations machine. It has about $2.5 billion in investments made on behalf of life insurance bond-holders, and those bond-holders receive all the gains and suffer all the losses from any movements in those assets. Because of the structure of the policies, they could be said to be part of the company balance sheet. By including the life insurance bond assets, the GIO's total assets rose from $4.5 billion to $7 billion. Shareholders' funds were not affected because the liability to pay bond-holders offset the value of the assets.

The company plans to drop the life assets and liabilities out of future published accounts; this will make the balance sheet much easier to understand. The life insurance business is reflected in the balance sheet at a value of $108 million (some analysts believe it should be higher); also included is another $140 million, which is the capital required to support the life business.

The GIO's task now is to put the float shemozzle behind it. But it still has a looming controversy to handle: an emerging dispute with a rival, QBE Insurance, over the way insurance company accounts should be presented. Jocelyn has always believed strongly that the assets of insurance companies should be in the books at market value, so it is plain for all to see what has happened. He believes that once this happens, liabilities must be treated similarly. So the GIO sets out its current estimates of claims and then increases them by the expected inflation rate and other factors. It then assumes a 7.5–8% return on the money held to meet those claims and discounts the reserve accordingly.

The accountancy bodies have endorsed Jocelyn's view, and it has become an accounting standard. QBE believes that Jocelyn, and the standard, are wrong. It insists that assets should not be in the books at market value, and investment earnings should be streamed over seven years. It is vigorously opposed to any suggestion that claims should be discounted back by trying to estimate future income returns.

QBE and the NRMA feel so strongly about the matter that they appealed (unsuccessfully) through the Administrative Appeals Tribunal and the Federal Court, to avoid being forced by accounting standards to estimate future returns and value their assets at market value (they believe this would cause directors to breach the law).

Malleson Stephen Jaques' John Atkin says the standard requires any unrealised profits to be taken up in a statement of earnings, even for long-term investments. 'But this conflicts with the case law, which is clear on this point', he says. 'I would urge directors to exercise extreme caution before they take unrealised gains for the profit and loss statement. It is essential directors are satisfied the gains are permanent in character.'

If QBE is forced to comply with the standards and reduce its claims reserve by expected future earnings, it plans to lift its reserve by a similar amount so there is no change to profits.

Increasingly, the sharemarket is going to try to compare QBE and the GIO. The strategies of the companies are very different. In the 1980s QBE's John Cloney sold its interests in managing property and equity trusts and other funds management activities to concentrate on insurance. He picked almost the top of the market.

The GIO is taking the reverse stance, using its insurance base to build a substantial funds management business. It is paying out two-thirds of its expected 1991–92 profit in dividends, and the figure will be even higher this year. Using QBE's basis of profit calculation (which is different from the GIO's), QBE pays out only about one-third of its profits in dividends. The GIO has a much deeper involvement in high-risk reinsurance, although those premiums are now rising.

With hindsight, it seems an issue price of $2.20–2.25 would have given a modest initial profit to subscribers and left a cushion in case of a market fall. Woolworths and Qantas/Australian Airlines must pay the price for that misjudgement. They will need to look long and hard at the GIO float and make sure they do not make the same mistakes. Another similar episode would set Australian public share ownership back a long way.

Where We Are in the World

HOW THE WORLD RATES AUSTRALIA

If Sir Ron Brierley had looked at Australia's balance sheet in his heyday, he would have been excited: here was an enterprise that was asset rich but suffered from poor management. All it needed was reorganisation and new talent.

The Competitiveness Report from 1991's World Economic Forum is a fascinating balance sheet, revealing Australia's strengths and weaknesses in comparison with thirty-two other countries. The forum used published statistical data and interviews with 12 000 executives. The countries were divided into two baskets: members of the OECD (plus Hungary) and ten others surveyed because of their importance to world trade. Among the twenty-three in the OECD basket, Australia's ranking fell from 13 to 16, but that masks remarkable rankings in the detailed categories.

Of the 330 categories, Australia ranks in the top six in fifty-one (15%) of them. These are, mainly categories that tend to emphasise our natural advantages. We are in the bottom five in a similar number of categories. Our poor rankings clearly show that Australia lags behind other countries in management and social structures.

A startling finding is the huge amount of space Australians occupy compared with residents of the other thirty-two countries. The survey shows that in an area/population ratio, Australia has 28 417 square metres of arable land per capita. Canada is next with 17 930 square metres. The US has 7710 square metres, and New Zealand, which is not densely populated, has 1544 square metres. Even allowing for tough country, Australia's biggest resource, arable land, is largely unused.

Australia's labour force has been growing faster than that of any other country in the OECD basket and its population growth ranks highly. However, as the world becomes more crowded, surveys such as this from the World Economic Forum that expose Australia's underutilised arable areas will lead to increasing international debate on the subject.

The forum shows that Australia ranks second in indigenous energy and in self-sufficiency in non-energy raw materials—a remarkable strength. In government investment and telecommunications it is fifth (per capita). Despite the recent rises in executive salaries, Australia pays its chief executives much less than most other countries. Based on buying power, Australian chief executives receive 35% of that paid to chief executives in the US and are among the cheapest in the world, although Japanese chief executives are even less expensive. Since the main job of a chief executive is to manage the workforce, perhaps Australia is getting what it pays for.

The survey confirms Australia's worst fears about labour problems. In 'the extent to which industrial relations are conducive to labour peace', Australia ranks 32nd: only Hungary has a worse industrial relations scene. So much for the accord. We also have the highest employee turnover in the OECD. Only four countries have worse worker motivation and labour absenteeism.

With such a labour problem, Australia needs incentives to invest, and the most effective way to generate money for investment in plant and equipment is through the depreciation provision. But, as the survey grimly sets out, Australia has allowed the mandarins at Treasury to dominate the Cabinet on depreciation. Accordingly, on the 'extent to which amortisation of fixed assets encourages growth' Australia ranks close to last among the thirty-three countries. Clearly, Australia's depreciation rates are not world-competitive. New Zealand's are slightly worse and Hungary is at the bottom. Australia's competitors for capital, including Malaysia, Singapore, Taiwan and Thailand, rank in the top brackets of those using depreciation allowances to attract investment. Australia also ranks badly on interest rate costs.

So, of the three key elements of productive investment—labour, depreciation and interest—Australia ranks at the bottom. Not surprisingly, when local and overseas banks tossed money at Australia in the 1980s, it did not go into productive investment (the sums did not work) but rather to asset speculation.

In internationalisation issues, Australia has some promising figures, particularly in the growth of merchandise and services exports, but it ranks badly in exports of manufactured products and in export flexibility.

Australia has not bothered to maximise its advantages by having efficient rail, roads and ports. Superficially, it is gratifying to know that six of the thirty-three countries have worse port access, until it is considered that three of the six (Austria, Hungary and Switzerland) are land-locked. Ranked lower are Italy, Indonesia and Mexico. New Zealand's reforms have been recognised and it has risen.

Leaving aside a national view, the World Forum's balance sheet will increase long-term pressure on Australia to import people to help the country take advantage of its space and potential. It is not a conclusion that Australians will find appealing, but in the years ahead it will be discussed increasingly by those countries who have surplus people.

Australia's competitiveness: where good, where bad

Rank (out of 23)

Infrastructure

Good

1 arable area
1 coal production
1 imported natural resources
2 total indigenous energy
2 change in net imports of oil
2 self-sufficiency in non-energy raw materials
2 domestic natural resources
3 enterprises' share of energy consumption
4 GDP and energy consumption
4 net imports of oil and oil products
5 crude petroleum production
5 energy imports vs merchandise exports
5 state investment in telecommunications
6 natural gas production

Bad

20 railways
19 roads
19 port access

Government

Good

3 central government total debt
3 agricultural policies
3 price distortion by government subsidies
4 terrorism
4 improper practices

continued

5 central government domestic debt
5 indirect tax revenues
5 equal opportunity
6 government final consumption expenditure
6 total tax revenues
6 total income taxes
6 government subsidies to private, public enterprises
6 free flow of credit
6 expropriation

Bad

22 financial failure
20 effectiveness of fiscal policy
20 values
19 government employment
19 support for government policies

Management

Good

4 remuneration of CEOs
4 change in manufacturing earnings
6 social needs and corporate boards

Bad

23 employee turnover
22 corporate credibility
21 new business generation
21 corporate profits
20 manufacturing unit labour costs
20 labour absenteeism
19 managerial initiative
19 competitive pricing
19 labour-saving technology

People

Good

1 growth of labour force
1 growth of employment
2 population over 65 years
4 population and economic growth
4 population under 15 years
4 urbanisation

Bad

22 industrial relations
21 long-term unemployment

continued

20 worker motivation
20 alcohol and drug abuse

Science and technology

Good

3 change in patents granted to residents
6 private funding of business R & D

Bad

21 total R & D personnel in industry
19 business expenditure on R & D
19 R & D scientists and engineers in industry
19 change in patents granted to non-residents

Finance

Good

3 financial deregulation and service industries

Bad

22 real short-term interest rate
22 risk capital
21 depreciation

Internationalisation

Good

3 export performance
4 growth in the volume of merchandise exports
4 growth in exports of services
4 direct investment flows inward
4 direct investment stocks inward
5 export market diversification
6 direct investment flows abroad

Bad

23 current account balance
23 exports of manufactured products
23 export flexibility
22 trade legislation
22 expatriate work permits
22 international alliances
21 exports of goods and services
21 diversification index for commodity exports
21 national protectionism
20 balance of trade in total services
20 exchange rate index
19 exchange rate stability
19 foreign investment at home

continued

Domestic economic strength

Good

1	gross domestic investment
2	real growth in services
3	real GDP growth
6	total gross domestic investment
	Bad
23	recession
22	expected growth in industry for 1991
21	growth in food production
20	economic flexibility
19	accuracy of official forecast in mid-term
19	growth in production of capital goods

Source: World Competitiveness Report 1991, jointly published by IMD Management School and the World Economic Forum

TRADE DEEDS, NOT WORDS, SAYS JAPANESE GURU

KENICHI OHMAE, the chairman of McKinsey & Company in Japan and the best-known management expert in Asia, is not frightened to express views about Australia that most Japanese keep to themselves. He sees the fall in the Japanese sharemarket and the failure of Gatt to reach its targets as opportunities for Australian enterprises to forge a much wider range of links with Japan, Taiwan and South Korea, but he questions whether Australians have the necessary resolve.

Ohmae, author of the book *Borderless Trading*, says 'The Australian mentality is a very strange mentality. In a way it is ambivalent at best; if you use a not-so-good word, it is schizophrenic'. Australia has made net progress over the past couple of years turning away from a 'nostalgic Oxford-Cambridge mentality' to saying its future is with these Asian countries, he says. But, on the other hand, Australia has not performed the tangible actions that should flow from such a conclusion.

Australia has an 'FOB [free-on-board] mentality' he says. After the commodities go on to the boat, Australians sit back and wait to receive the money in 100 or 120 days. So, although Australian executives now have a commitment to Japan, Korea and Taiwan, when it comes to really 'having a go and living in the countries, there seems to be a big gap'. Very few Australian executives have lived in Japan for longer than two years and many Australian mining houses that have 60% of their sales in Japan do not have Japanese as senior executives.

Ohmae says executives of large Australian companies are very experienced 'in investment, in capacity expansion, cost reduction and logistic systems but when you talk about a $5-million investment to establish a research operation in Japan, they would be very reluctant. But that's where the market is'.

The fall in the Tokyo stockmarket means that Japanese property prices will come down and Japanese companies will be much more affordable and accessible. Australian companies will be able to take a 5% or 10% equity position and forge much closer links with the Japanese market. 'But Australians are sometimes afraid of Japan; they have a realisation that the Japanese market is huge but say those guys could eat us alive', Ohmae says.

An encouraging sign is the recent zinc-smelting joint venture in Japan by MIM which is, Ohmae says, 'a very, very pro-active activity. It is the first major step I have seen in this direction'.

Ohmae says the Taiwanese market is about the same size as the Australian domestic market. 'So I ask Australians: "Are you willing to put the same kind of resources, quality thinking and attention to Taiwan (as you would to your local market), because it is the same size?" And it is virtually left open because there are not many well-managed companies in Taiwan'. Australians are reluctant to go to Taiwan partly because there is no diplomatic recognition. Often they choose China instead.

> But then I query Australians: 'Do you think you can really establish a good, trust-based 100% relationship with China because it, too, is resource-based and may be competing with you? Isn't Taiwan more complementary?' And then they will say 'Yes', but they are so ambivalent about going out and establishing fully fledged relationships with Taiwan.

Ohmae believes that, in the absence of world agreements on trade Japan will have to develop either multilateral or bilateral relationships to safeguard its security of supply.

> We cannot ignore the United States because that is a very important political and trading partner. On the other hand, if you really believe in complementary relationships I would think that Korea, Japan, Taiwan and Australia should sit down and really form a trust-based relationship, similar to the Japan–US security treaty and to what you've got with New Zealand.
>
> The problem of Apec [Asia-Pacific Economic Co-operation group] or Asean [Association of South-East Asian Nations] is that they've got countries with conflicting interests, countries at very different economic develop-

> ment stages and some countries with whom you compete on resources. But if you pick up those three [Korea, Taiwan and Japan], they have so many things that are complementary.
>
> Korea, Taiwan and Japan all have something in common: they are small countries in terms of land mass, do not have very much in resort facilities; they are basically industrial and mountainous. Amenities are secondary to industrial development and professional services are not well developed.

Koreans have begun to come to Australia, and love it, but they prefer a different style of accommodation from the Japanese, and direct flights from Australia to Seoul are limited. 'You say these countries are important but . . . it is just amazing that you haven't shown these things by physical actions; you know that is the problem', Ohmae says.

> Australia has the best medical system in Asia but has never offered it to these people. We need to beg so that Brisbane hospital can be used by some guy [who is critically ill] in Japan. But Australian patients and taxpayers then complain. You have tremendous professional services, ranging from architects and engineers to medical. In addition, I think you could become an education centre, as was the case with the United States.

Although Ohmae acknowledges there are many Asian students already in Australia, he says

> I don't know of many Koreans who are doing this. I don't see why you couldn't establish yourselves as the academic and medical centre for Asia. Australia is the only Asia-Pacific country where the amenities preceded the development.
>
> You can teach us in many ways: in furniture, interior design ideas, bold architectural design. We have been working with an Australian computer software company. Over time they just dominate. They are much smarter, faster . . . they are much better than the Japanese.
>
> Australians have had this tremendous luck with resources and higher standard of living. Now they have to find the means to sustain this. The only way is to globalise and become much more market-oriented and to start offering professional services, because they are very high value-added.

However, Ohmae warns that Japan is very wary of Australia. 'Australians negotiate like cowboys. So while Australia is a natural partner, it is dangerous to depend too much on Australia', he says. The Japanese perspective on resource negotiations is very different from Australia's. Ohmae says Australia had a 60–70% share of the Japanese market in many commodities but when it found Japan did not have any other source of supply, it was tough in negotiations on prices.

> Years ago, when Whitlam was in power, he went to China; that threatened Japan because a communist government was tying up with a socialist government. The Japanese said: 'In the long term this is dangerous, so we have to diversify into Brazil and a few other places'. The rest is history: we have diversified. It's the same with sugar and woodchips. In woodchips, Australia had a 60–70% share of the Japanese import market but negotiated on price for short-term gain. Japan immediately diversified into Chile and then increased the American portion.
>
> I think what happens is that Australians feel exploited . . . so when the first moment arrives to negotiate from power, they just dump everything.

Ohmae says that this forcing up of the price scares the buyer.

> In steel, I think they have learned this lesson. Now Australians have invited Japanese capital, and the supplier-producer-buyer mentality is much more stable. I think there is a trust base between companies like CRA and BHP with the Japanese producers and, amazingly, it is profitable for Australians, too. So after 20 years, they have a full trust-based relationship.

But Ohmae says this good experience is not shared with the community, so other industries are going through the same learning process and journalists and politicians want to talk about the problems. From the Japanese side, one of the problems is property. Ohmae says Australia has never attracted Japan's top property developers nor has it really wooed Japanese investment in manufacturing.

> If foreigners buy a piece of land, they have to start construction within a year. Then, during this construction they have to sell 50% [of condominium units] to foreigners. But the remaining 50% must be sold to Australians. Given the different requirements of layout and all kinds of amenities, it will take a schizophrenic architect to give 50% to Australian and 50% to Japanese. It is much better to say you can't do it, or to say, in this zone or in this area it's OK to do so. The country is big enough.

Against this background Ohmae brings a Japanese view of the multi-function polis.

> I will tell you what is wrong with the multi-function polis. It was a mirage to begin with, it was just a painting in the sky. And then you took it seriously and debated every which direction. It was in Queensland, now [it is] in Adelaide and I wish them good luck, because there is no substance behind it. If you have the energy to debate such trifling issues, I think one thing you should do is to think about establishing your own research facility in Japan. It is much cheaper and much more helpful because there are very strong trends in the market.

Kenichi Ohmae has an unconventional view of the dispute between the US and Japan. The close linking of the Japanese political and bureaucratic systems with special interest groups has not only made the modernisation of Japan more difficult but it also means it is difficult for the Government to change. For example, Japanese who want to open up the rice market really cannot say what they think. But if Americans say it, 'it's OK', Ohmae says. That's why American opposition has been the critical element in combating corrupt Japanese interest groups.

> The US and Japan have lived long enough and often complain about each other. Many of these things are orchestrated. Bureaucrats talk very closely, and Japanese bureaucrats are telling American bureaucrats to say, OK, [on the] next visit trade negotiators should say these things and they will respond. It's all orchestrated.

But the great risk for Japan is that things will get out of hand as the mutual anger between the Americans and the Japanese increases in intensity. Ohmae believes it can be controlled. 'I say that when all the facts come out it will be OK and there are ways to make all these facts come out. I don't think it will get out of hand. I know these bureaucrats, I talk to them all the time. It's all calculated'.

On the effect of the fall in the Nikkei stock index on the Japanese banking system, Ohmae says

> It will 'kaput' the financial system and rightly so. There is no reason why Japanese banks, for example, should have a 60% share of the top 50 banks in the world. Anomalies that existed because of Japanese hyper-inflation on the asset side will be eliminated. We should let these bad guys go, I mean these are extremely bad wheeler-dealers. We have tonnes of them and they ought to go. Many corporations will suffer because of them but the good ones and individuals will remain intact and we are still a hard-working, highest-savings nation. The basic needs for consumption, improvement of lifestyle are there but this is not going to turn around in a few months. It is going to take a few years.
>
> I was the only one who was saying 18,000–17,000 for the Nikkei a year ago because everyone was saying it would bounce back. I was saying this figure because I calculated the net present value of these companies' operations. Now it seems there is a process taking place, calculating the deflated property back into the share price, so it could go down to 15,000, but at that point it's rock bottom because the company's intrinsic value is not lost.
>
> Japan is becoming a normal, more rational, explainable country.

J. P. MORGAN SNIFFS NEW OPPORTUNITIES

THE NEW YORK investment bank J. P. Morgan is exuding confidence. It avoided the big losses that most investment banks experienced when the speculative entrepreneurs of the 1980s failed. Now, irrespective of the way the market moves in the short term, it can see a bright future for investors. Delivering that message to Australia was the president and chief executive officer of J. P. Morgan Investment, New York, David Brigham.

Brigham sees the enormous changes taking place around the world as bringing a much wider range of profitable options for investors in the 1990s. Some of the opportunities will come from the collapse of communism. 'This controlled-experiment economy has been a disastrous failure and capitalism, or business, to a great extent has won', he says.

> I am struck by the number of governments, small and large, particularly some emerging ones, talking about developing their capital markets, which means share flotations, bond flotations, and the free exchange of capital for investment purposes. For many years we had an economic system in the West that was to some extent based upon a military alliance against a common enemy. Many countries were members of that common enemy's economic sphere, and this has failed. Countries are free to pursue natural economic interest more so than in the past.

Brigham believes that the present increased interest in shares may be partly a result of the recognition that free enterprise, or the democratic form of capitalism, is a superior economic system and that there is no longer a perceived military threat. But he is also warning that world growth will be slower with the global restructuring that is taking place. 'Business has to be leaner and more efficient. While that's all well and good, there is pain in the meantime and the growth period coming out of this recession is more prolonged, slower and lower', he says.

Brigham uses the US service sector as an example of what is happening. In the past, the US manufacturing industry went through restructuring during recessions, but the service sector could pass on its costs. However, now it is finding 'tremendous resistance' so it also must restructure (80% of US employment is in services). This situation is happening to businesses all around the world and restructuring is recognised as inevitable, and 'everybody seems to be getting around to it'.

He says: 'I am quite constructive on the three-to-five-year period; I think we are going through a period in which companies are facing the realities of a slower trading environment. They will have to provide more efficiencies in their production, in their management activities, and pay more attention to the bottom line'. Companies are placing greater emphasis on profitability than they have in the past ten years, Brigham says. Internationally, there is more shareholder awareness, and shareholders are more vocal. 'Shareholders are a little bit more enfranchised and I think that's a positive trend.'

Brigham believes that with a small rise in growth, the positive effect of these developments on the bottom line could eventually be quite dramatic. 'The leverage is tremendous. These things have a way of producing incredibly leveraged earnings at some point.'

The Morgan approach to taking advantage of the long-term opportunities created by these developments remains unchanged: to look at a business with a similar perspective to that of the company's management, which must be thinking long term rather than six to twelve months. 'We look at a company's earning power, three years and beyond. Morgan doesn't look at industries as if it is going to invest in this industry or that industry, it looks company by company.' In terms of the Standard & Poor's 500, Morgan is sector neutral. It assesses its investments from the bottom up, placing more importance on the health of individual operations than on the sector. 'We take a longer point of view using a concept called normalised earnings: what a company would earn in a normal sustainable year', Brigham says. Morgan also studies the generation of 'cashflow over long periods of time' because it is 'the cash that pays the bills; a lot of profits could be just accounting'.

But opportunities are arising not only in the sharemarket. Property has always been seen as an inflation hedge, but in Britain, for example, inflation-indexed bonds, guaranteed by the Government, have become a large proportion of institutional investors' assets, replacing property as a traditional inflation hedge.

Another area of opportunity is the so-called hybrid securities—investments that do not come under traditional strict classifications, as do shares and bonds. For example, a Japanese company may issue bonds in Swiss francs with an option to place shares at a fixed price. 'We find that area of the market particularly interesting and we are launching a fund, which we call the multi-market fund', Brigham says. These new securities coincided with a big increase in opportunities in countries from South America to Eastern Europe.

> I think we are going to be faced with a lot of markets to invest in that we wouldn't have thought of investing in five or six years ago. We will have to make some choices about where we commit our resources . . . Do you put your money into Turkey, do you put your money into Argentina, do you put your money into a whole bunch of new places?

Asked whether these new markets in equities, currencies, bonds and privatisations will tend to lower investment prices in established markets, Brigham says: 'I think not—not in the five-year span—because it will not be developing at a pace that would quickly suck money out of your traditional proven currencies that have provided decent returns'.

Many companies in which Western institutions invest also will take advantage of the opportunities. Brigham says Australia will need to compete against other countries which will have rival proposals. But he adds: 'If investors see return opportunities, you will have no trouble raising money. Money seeks return. Money seeks real return and I think it is going to be more the case going forward'.

Brigham says one of the most important new developments will be privatisation and he has some clear guidelines.

> You like to see a management that is concerned with shareholder returns. You don't want to see a half-way house, government-owned . . . with only a foot in the private company—a sort of hotchpotch. You like the privatisation process where the government is turning to the private sector to manage for shareholder returns.

Morgan believes that the best privatisations often occur when the privatised body is exposed to competition that prevents it making monopolistic profits through high charges to consumers.

Brigham believes that research by institutions has declined internationally in favour of broker research. Morgan's strategy is to expand its research around the world in order to approach investment on a longer-term basis.

WATCH EUROPE, SAYS BMW CHIEF

THE WORLD chairman of BMW, Eberhard von Kuenheim, has a prediction that goes against conventional thinking: the next ten years will be the 'decade of Europe', and the development and economic growth there will become more exciting than in the Asia-Pacific region. And so at the Asian summit of the Australian Business Council in 1992, von Kuenheim devoted much of his speech to extolling the advantages of Europe. In separate discussions with BRW he revealed how BMW is working on the next stage of its growth in accordance with his view of world changes.

Von Kuenheim has an amazing record. There is probably no other head of a world company of the size and scope of BMW who has been twenty-three years in the job. There is certainly no motor industry head who can match his record. Von Kuenheim won the top job in BMW in 1970 at the age of 41, and was then the youngest chief executive in a major German industry. At that time, the company had a turnover of DM1.1 billion and an annual production of 150 000 cars. In 1991 production reached 550 000 cars and the group turnover was DM30 billion ($24 billion). He has succeeded by anticipating many of the changes that have taken place in the motor industry, including modern techniques of maintaining links between factories and suppliers.

Von Kuenheim's optimism for Europe in the 1990s stems partly from the conclusions he reaches when he defines the market.

> When we say Europe, we must also include Scandinavia and Eastern European countries such as Poland, Hungary, the Balkans and last, but not least, the European part of the former Soviet Union, the Baltic states and White Russia. If Eastern European countries join the European Community one day, the population involved will then exceed 400 million. But even now the European business zone is about twice the size of the US domestic market and three times as large as the Japanese market.

The excitement and opportunity that the former Soviet states present is particularly illustrated by Russia and by the Ukraine. Von Kuenheim says: 'The Russians have endless resources of land, oil, gas, diamonds, gold and whatever. In the Ukraine there is the best soil for farming. You don't need any artificial fertilisers there—what you plant can almost grow by itself'.

But von Kuenheim emphasises that the question remains whether the people can develop these resources after seventy years of education in communism, being taught not to be creative, not to take initiatives and not to show a high profile. 'To change such a people, that's a problem', he says. 'It's a chance and a risk at the same time.'

In the former East Germany, 16 million people will face the challenge of the changing economics, and large investments will be required. What was once a great power now 'needs a handout from us if its people are not to starve', von Kuenheim says.

> All the Western nations must take up this challenge. To hundreds of millions of people, salvation must come from Central Europe in particular. From Germany's airfields, the biggest aid program since the Marshall Plan after the Second World War has now started. It is a matter of life or death; these people have to survive the winter, and at the very least they need their daily bread. After this, we must change our approach and help people to help themselves.

Much of the success of BMW stems from von Kuenheim's strategy of concentrating the company's production facilities mainly within

Germany itself and within a relatively short distance of each other. But BMW is looking outside Germany as it prepares for growth next century.

Von Kuenheim says that although Germany is at the heart of European development, it is hampered by the high level of its wages, social benefits and taxes. In addition, too many rigid regulations leave the country at a disadvantage against other European centres. Accordingly, German industry is vulnerable to 'greenfields' plants which do not have the initial social costs of looking after long-term workers. Von Kuenheim is head of the Association of European Automotive Manufacturers, which represents 9% of the total manufacturing output of the European Community and almost 34% of total world automotive production. As association head, von Kuenheim is determined to ensure that the European motor industry does not suffer the same fate as US vehicle makers. He has made sure the German Government is aware of disadvantages its motor industry suffers in competing with new Japanese plants. Cars represent a much bigger portion of European GDP than they do in America.

Von Kuenheim says Japan took a long-term view of the US market and sold cars there at low prices to get market share, but he is critical of the way in which the US industry met the challenge. Promising people were no longer attracted to the motor industry, and little was done to save the industry from its troubles. 'The most brilliant young men from Harvard no longer went into the motor industry but went to Wall Street and analysed why the industry in Detroit or Chicago was not as good as it once was.' He believes the motor industry is a more important part of the economy in Europe than it is in the US. Von Kuenheim's description of the US of course also applies to Australia.

CHAPTER 10

Just a Few More Thoughts

STEEL PRICES—A WARNING FOR BHP

SOMETIMES *BRW*'s reports elicit strong responses. For example, we revealed that Palmer Tube Mills has been paying 20–40% less for steel in the US than in Australia. Now Ralph Waters, group general manager (industrial products) of Email, one of BHP's biggest customers, has written to say that although the steel maker's costs are world-competitive, he believes it is overcharging, that its steel operation has been able to stay profitable when so many overseas have not by keeping its margins high—in effect, passing on the problem of low world steel prices to its customers.

Waters says 'Good luck to BHP if it can be managed, but [it is] not much good in the long term if there are no local customers left'. In its defence, BHP might point out that its customers can import steel to compete with its products and Australian steel must pass through our terrible transport system and other infrastructure bottlenecks. BHP Steel chief Ron McNeilly says BHP's prices compare well with Japan's but are higher than those in the US, where a price war has driven almost all steel makers into the red. Meanwhile, BHP has cut its prices marginally, and in some circumstances does give concessions to exporters. It has also undertaken an extensive and successful export drive to maintain profits.

On the other hand, if Australian steel prices were reduced substantially and BHP worked to recoup some of its lost revenue by making deeper cost cuts, we might actually see a net rise in Australian employment. BHP has an agreement with its workers that they cannot be retrenched (although that does not stop them from striking at the drop of a hat), but its customers are shedding thousands of jobs. BHP managing director John Prescott has put his reputation on the line on the basis that he will deliver world-best practices in steel.

In 1992, many businesses will be examining whether it is worthwhile for them to stay in Australia, given the need to export to survive. If Australia's steel, glass and packaging industries charge above world prices, whether because of company policy or infrastructure costs, then more secondary processing will go overseas, further dismantling Australia's industrial base. Ralph Waters' letter is a clear warning to BHP and others of the new debate.

THE TOURISM CHALLENGE

COMING to grips with change may be hard for managers and workers, but it is even harder for politicians. I attended a conference organised by the Inbound Tourism Organisation of Australia, at which the main speaker was the Minister for Tourism, Alan Griffiths. His audience was made up of hotel operators and organisers of a huge variety of tours and attractions. Griffiths, who has been one of the best ministers in the Keating Government, gave a strong speech setting out the enormous potential of Australian tourism, and explaining how the Government was right behind it. It was exciting stuff.

But there are things he does not understand—for example, that people who have put money into tourism, particularly hotels and other enterprises employing large workforces, are bleeding. Returns are not justifying the further investment needed to meet expected demand. Clearly, some operators are doing very well, but many more are suffering because over-capacity and competition from rival suppliers overseas are enabling bulk buyers to push down prices.

Worse still, labour costs are boosted by shift allowances and a host of add-on costs established when tourism was not yet thought of as an internationally competitive industry. In other words, although Australian labour is basically competitive with the rest of the world, the add-ons kill it and make other countries better places to invest, particularly in hotels. Our depreciation allowances don't match our rivals, either.

Obviously, the increases in revenue and the job-creation programs Griffiths outlined cannot take place until those who provide the capital can make money. Looking to the Opposition, John Hewson would do away with shift allowances and payroll tax—moves that would transform the industry, if it could handle the goods and services tax and the absence of a tourist department in Canberra. Tourism operators are clearly frustrated by both political parties.

SINGAPORE JUMPS AHEAD

I WONDER how many members of the Federal Cabinet know that Singapore is targeting every multinational regional head office in Sydney, Melbourne and elsewhere, with the specific aim of enticing them out of Australia and into Singapore? (In fairness, Singapore's main target for this drive is Hong Kong, but we are also swept into the firing line.) It was brought to my attention by a lengthy report entitled *Developing Australia as an International Financial Centre*, produced by the Australian Financial Centre Committee. The real power of the report is in an appendix containing clippings from Singapore newspapers, in which it is plain that companies are being established in Singapore to manage Australians. Singapore is offering enterprises prepared to set up regional headquarters there a tax rate of only 10% on regional income derived by providing management services to other countries (central administration, treasury and research). The tax incentives last for up to ten years.

So the Australian branch can be levied appropriate fees that attract only 10% tax for the headquarters in Singapore. Moreover, offshore banking business, conducted through what are known as 'Asian currency units', also is taxed at 10%.

Singapore is well aware of the enormous advantages in hosting offshore banking and head office activity—the 10% tax revenue is money that would not otherwise be received. More importantly, a whole range of service operators, ranging from lawyers and accountants to engineers and designers, generate income that pays full tax. The spin-offs are greatly expanding the knowledge base of the country.

Trying to persuade Treasury to allow such benefits to flow to Australia seems an impossible task, given the fight it put up to prevent proper depreciation rates. Nevertheless, the committee has set out how Australia should follow Singapore and enjoy the employment skills and government revenue that would follow. It believes that many companies would prefer Australia to Singapore.

The committee suggests 'consideration' be given to extending similar concessions to existing Australian multinational companies. But this is a more complex question because it involves an actual loss of revenue. Singapore appears to have overcome the problem by giving companies regional head office status on a case-by-case basis after considering what each regional head office will bring to the country. Other countries in the region have followed Singapore. If we are to be part of Asia we must do as the Asians do . . .

UNIONS

UNIONS play an important role in the creation and maintenance of unemployment through their rigid rules and pay rates. But despite this, the plan by the ACTU to help the economy move forward makes a lot of sense. There is clearly a strong body of forward thinking in the ACTU which, unfortunately, is not matched by the antics of many of its member unions, who have little concern for the unemployed.

It seems strange, yet it is so logical, for unions to be advocating higher depreciation. But Australia's depreciation rates are way out of line with world standards, adding to the incentive to set up plants overseas.

The ACTU plan of intensifying micro-economic reform in the workplace and insisting on local buying by governments on the condition that suppliers undertake structural reform, would create a most unwieldy process. Nevertheless, it has the germ of an idea that might force world-best practice into a vast number of enterprises and, in particular, whip union extremists and bad managers into line.

At least on the surface the ACTU is starting to understand that part of Australia's employment growth must come in our ability to develop big resource projects, provided they meet world environmental standards.

Another ACTU suggestion, a plan to force superannuation funds into a national development fund, might become necessary if restrictions on trustees become too harsh. My impression is that it is not necessary, or desirable, at this stage. The ACTU does not dare suggest the end to shift penalties, which would be a boon to tourism and travel-related employment, and is probably our main chance of employing less-skilled people.

BANKS—OVERSEAS THE PROBLEM IS SERIOUS

THE FALL on world stockmarkets has underlined the need to take more seriously the problems of banks in Japan and the US. And as we all know, Australian banks also have a version of the US institutions' problem because our banks are taking a tougher line on loan securities held by smaller businesses.

In Japan, the problem has been widely documented, although the game has become more deadly. Japanese banks are allowed to include 45% of unrealised capital gains earned on their investment portfolios as capital. Thus, when the share and property markets were rising, their capital expanded. This extra capital gave them new freedoms, which many used to back highly speculative Japanese entrepreneurs, who are now insolvent.

In the past nine years, the value of the Japanese banks' total assets overseas rosc from $90 billion to $890 billion. Most of this money is linked to property. The Japanese Government will be required to make its number-one priority the preservation of its banking system. At the same time, we should not forget that the Japanese have an extensive network of first-class industrial companies whose operations are not dependent on the banking system. Nevertheless, a recession in Japan is inevitable and will not only affect our exports but also world capital supplies.

The US banking system has its own problems, and these are affecting its recovery. Albert Wojnilower of First Boston Asset Management believes the US recovery in the early 1980s relied on a big rise in entrepreneurial businesses, helped by bank funding. But loans by domestic commercial banks have been shrinking—a decline unprecedented in post-depression times.

Wojnilower argues that there is strong demand in the US for loans, but the local banks and other institutions cannot satisfy it because of a shortage of capital. This is partly a result of the 1988 decision by the world's main central banks to phase in formal credit-risk-based capital requirements on their countries' commercial banks. In addition, the new US banking laws have still more comprehensive requirements.

For most US banks, meeting the higher capital standards has been the principal priority. Inevitably, bank capital has been rendered scarce and expensive, so a reduction of exposure to the private sector has become the preferred, or even the sole, available alternative for many institutions. As a result, potential employers of labour that is being made available by defence-sector cutbacks and other industry rationalisations cannot gain funding, so delaying economic recovery.

Local banking

It is important that the Reserve Bank Governor Bernie Fraser and the chiefs of all of our banks spend some time reflecting on the level of risk involved for their operations as well as Australia in massive foreign currency and interest-rate dealing.

Australian banks, correctly, have been careful to ensure they are not exposed to big swings in the Australian dollar, unless it is part of a deliberate and carefully considered strategy. However, our dollar ranks in the top six traded currencies in the world, and that activity is much larger than the level of our trading in goods and services warrants. A substantial number of the deals, one way or another, involve the world banking community and, more often than not, include an Australian bank. So, in the Reserve Bank Bulletin, 1990–91 normal overseas-trade-related transactions by banks totalled about $120 billion—a level you would expect.

But, in addition, the banks' foreign-exchange, interest-rate and other market-related contracts totalled an incredible $1412 billion in 1989–90, $1597 billion in 1990–91 and in the first nine months of 1992 had risen to $1824 billion. This shows just how extensive Australian bank involvement is in these markets. All the banks have highly-skilled teams who are clearly making strong contributions to profit while developing an important industry for Australia.

These days billions roll off the tongue as millions once did. But just to put that figure of $1824 billion into perspective, it is about four-and-a-half times Australia's gross domestic product (admittedly, GDP is calculated on a net basis) and five times the total local assets of Australian banks quoted in the Reserve Bank Bulletin.

To be fair, the Reserve Bank calculates that the actual amount of liability risk involved in the deals is about $100 billion—a substantial sum, but well below the gross value of the transactions. This calculation takes into account only the deals in which there is a paper loss. The Australian banks would only get into trouble on these deals if one of the parties could not fulfil its obligations in a loss-making transaction and the Australian bank was forced to act in its stead. International banks are often on the other side, so big world banks would need to fail before there would be big losses.

I am not in any way suggesting that a world banking crisis is nigh, but the fall in Japan's sharemarket, clearly putting pressure on its banking sector, adds to the impact on thc total banking scene of the world CBD property glut. Australians need to understand that the banking community is locked into the world much more closely than you might expect from simply looking at normal trading. We are at risk in the same way as London, New York and Tokyo are, but our banking community and industrial infrastructures are much smaller. Bernie Fraser needs to watch the Nikkei more closely than most.

ENVIRONMENT

RECENTLY I spent some time with a parent of a graduating chemical engineer who is having great difficulty finding work. It is likely that the engineer and his colleagues will have to go overseas, where there are shortages of skills. That may not be a bad thing, because they will learn proper labour and management practices and will not return to our country until we have mastered them too. In addition, if our executive remuneration is not taxed on a world-competitive basis, the incentive to come home will be even less. Australia is, in effect, spending a fortune developing skills that other countries profit from. We will not get the benefit until our governments learn the value of capital formation and end impositions such as the payroll tax, until our unions understand international work practices, and until our chief executives stop making excuses for their lack of efficiency.

Paul Keating's most effective weapon for reducing unemployment is to reverse the Hawke Government's policy against new resource projects—and it will not cost him a cent. In this context, it is staggering to discover that Ros Kelly, the minister responsible for the environment and one of Keating's main supporters, heads an office that has not yet realised there is a link between extreme environmentalism and unemployment. Discussions and the formation of a consultative process suggested for a while that the Environment Department was beginning to understand that much could be achieved by co-operating with industry.

One series of consultations on ecologically sustainable development involved a concept known as biodiversity, which essentially involves conserving ecosystems. While the consultations were in progress the department was running its own parallel committee, which included a large number of green scientists. The departmental committee operated without industry input, although a lone farmer representative was recruited. Industry did not realise that this committee was the one with real clout, and was lulled into a belief that the department had turned over a new leaf.

A leaked draft from the department, dated late 1991, is a shocker. It indicates consideration of measures that would require an enormous increase in reports for almost every new land-based development program. The industry people have become aware that the report foreshadows the arrival of a new range of weapons with the power to stop or delay development and keep unemployment high. Admittedly, the report may yet be refined, but the fact that the public servants did not use the established industry consultative process shows that they have their own agenda.

Jobs in danger

It is very hard for people in Canberra to understand what is happening beyond the borders of the ACT. For example, policies that won votes in the last election are now increasingly seen as a way to make the dole queues longer. So we have the bizarre situation in which the Prime

Minister and the Treasurer will have policies aimed at reducing unemployment, while another section of the bureaucracy (the Environment Department) has worked on a scheme that could have bound us to an international convention that industry experts believe would eliminate Australia's steel and aluminium industries, among many others. As it happens the danger was averted.

In the 1992 environment summit in Brazil, Australia tried to lead the world into cutting carbon-fuel emissions. The Opec nations, like Australia, are big fossil fuel exporters, but they understood the implications of such a policy. And so they requested special consideration, as fossil-fuel-dependent countries, in the event that the Australian-backed plan should be adopted. We did not request help but rather naively reckoned the carbon emission targets could be achieved at no significant cost.

The Americans say we need to be absolutely certain just how serious the greenhouse problem is before plunging the world into depression through draconian carbon measures. In fairness, I should point out that many people genuinely believe that global warming is a much greater threat than any employment problem Australia or any other nation may face. As a community, we need to be sure they are right. Clearly, the Americans are not sure and played a big role in bringing economic sanity to the summit.

Before the 1990 federal election, Paul Keating helped roll the then Environment Minister, Graham Richardson, when he urged Cabinet to impose emissions limits. But after the election, according to an October 1990 report by the *Age*'s Canberra correspondent Michelle Grattan, Keating changed his mind, taking the view that the problem was potentially so big that measures should be taken immediately. In turn, he delivered a win to the new Environment Minister, Ros Kelly, who was under pressure at the time. Kelly has been a great Keating supporter. However, in the October 1990 Cabinet decision she and Keating were opposed by John Dawkins, John Button, Alan Griffiths, John Kerin, Peter Cook and Ralph Willis. Griffiths and Dawkins were 'vehement', Grattan reported at the time.

Of course, at that time the Government did not realise how deep the recession would become. In my view, Australia should be helping the US to hasten scientific investigation of the greenhouse effect. If we are so serious in our concern about emissions that we are prepared to sacrifice the job prospects of so many Australians, then perhaps it is time to consider alternatives, including much more research into the cleaner burning of fossil fuels and storage of nuclear waste, as well as the use of hydropower and wind and solar energy.

RETAILING—BIG LEAGUE POISED

LARGE retailers in prime sites who have innovative merchandising policies can greatly increase their turnover and profits in better economic times. That's the clear message of Paul Simons in forecasting a 50% rise in Woolworths' turnover during the next four years. If he can do that then there is potential for Peter Wilkinson and Brian Beattie to do even better at Coles because they start from a lower base. That's exactly what Coles Myer's new chairman, Solomon Lew, has in mind. Smaller shops will need to watch out because those sorts of growth rates from the majors will only be achieved with a rise in market share.

GOLD

THERE WAS an irony in the gold price falling just as white South Africans voted to proceed with apartheid reform. South Africa in the early 1980s accounted for half the world's gold output but now provides about 35%. The US, Australia and Canada are increasing their share of the balance. South African mines are labour-intensive and wages have been increasing faster than the inflation rate, possibly because of social pressures.

Accordingly, South African mines are becoming comparatively expensive and, on a straight economics basis, massive closures are likely. But whether the Government can stand the fallout likely to follow mass sackings of black miners remains to be seen. It might choose to copy the Soviets and push gold on to the market irrespective of the price, to raise money and employ people.

Australia has several smaller mines that are likely to close after their forward contracts have expired if the price stays down. But most of our major mines are viable. The operation that will be watched most closely is the GMK Homestead big pit at Kalgoorlie, where there is still a clear margin between the cash costs and the market price but where there is also large debt, currently well covered by forward sales contracts.

The only way out of the overall South African problem is to increase the wealth of the nation and that means going out and challenging our iron ore and coal markets. Later in the decade, to get out of its problems, Eastern Europe will need to be active in the rural sector and Russia in minerals. So both our commodities markets could be under a lot of pressure. That's why it is important now to be making sure we have our base markets as protected as possible.

PROPERTY—TIME TO TAKE STOCK

EVERY BANKER, superannuation trustee and funds manager with investments in commercial property has had to come to terms with reality: Sydney CBD property, Australia's leading market, has fallen more than 50% from the peak it reached between late 1989 and early 1990. Most other Australian non-retail commercial property markets will have had greater falls. Many retail properties have performed well, but others have been hit hard while the whole property industry was adversely affected by the delay in property valuers coming to grips with what happened.

For a long time it was difficult to get most valuers to come to terms with the change in the market. With notable exceptions, valuers simply could not comprehend a fall of this magnitude. Late in 1991 Aust-Wide and its trustee took the view that their only hope of survival depended on unit-holders knowing exactly what the properties were worth, not what they might be worth if the market rose. As it turned out the problems of Aust-Wide were much deeper and could not be solved by simply facing up to the value of property.

Sydney's Grosvenor Square, in which some of its trusts have a stake, in 1991 was revalued downwards by 37% from the peak, and 1 O'Connell Street by about 40%. The O'Connell Street valuation was conducted by Colliers and Richard Ellis after a briefing from the trustee, Permanent Trustee Co Ltd. Clearly, all parties realised they could be liable if the charade of the three previous years continued. It could be argued that at the height of the market Aust-Wide erred on the side of optimism, although that view would be hotly disputed by the previous valuers, the trustee and the managers.

During 1990 and 1991 *BRW* called for reform of valuations, because it was clear the valuers had not understood the magnitude of the asset fall. There was hope of reform in 1990 when the president of the New South Wales Institute of Valuers, Garry Rothwell, advocated valuers put forward a range of values based on differing parameters. The trustees commissioning the valuation adopted the one that corresponded to their current reading of market uncertainties and variables. But the industry never took up the challenge.

Despite these incidents many valuers kept their heads firmly in the sand even though a most crucial area of their work was the property units of superannuation funds, which are bought and sold every day. These deals are effectively property transactions, so it was vital they be done at the correct price. Some life offices had valuers on staff to do the basic valuations, which are checked by outsiders.

Nevertheless, during 1990 and 1991 there remained unease about property valuation and some life office boards realised they must ensure this system was working to reflect the true value of properties, given that daily transactions were taking place. Failure by directors to carry out their task could make them liable personally—they may already be in trouble if they have not cut values substantially.

Finally, late in 1991 a section of the valuation industry led by Roy Woodhouse of Baillieu Knight Frank reckoned it was time to face reality. Woodhouse brought together a powerful taskforce which included accountants Coopers & Lybrand, law firms Minter Ellison and Arthur Robinson & Hedderwicks, the ANZ and National Australia banks, life offices National Mutual and CML, investment banker CS First Boston and the government insurance groups SGIC of South Australia and the Victorian TAC. The taskforce thankfully developed some commonsense solutions by taking the 1990 BRW-Rothwell theme a step further, advocating that property valuers be required to prepare a market and an investment valuation for all properties.

The old practice of valuers was to try to produce one valuation that takes into account all relevant circumstances, including a willing seller and buyer, and a reasonable negotiation period during which values remain static. The taskforce pointed out that a market value of a property can be different from its investment value, particularly in either a slump or a boom. By publishing a real current market value and an assessment of investment value, a valuer can highlight diverging trends.

The taskforce also advocated getting more data on property industry material, such as proposed property developments, extensions and refits; an end to the 'imprudent' practice of letting the borrower engage or control a valuer; and to require directors to engage independent valuers to report market and investment valuations each year.

The profession was initially shocked but eventually agreed with the taskforce and actually went one further advocating valuers should make valuations at market. All those who had campaigned for so long cried 'hallelujah'.

In the June and September 1992 quarters big city property fell further yet. If anything, the 'real value' of income-producing property had risen in that period reflecting lower interest rates. What we were seeing is valuers catching up with the market. Many superannuation trustees now believe they should not invest in property. That sentiment was wise when inflated values were used to calculate property unit prices, but after valuations come into line with reality, trustees should be taking another look.

If you are holding units in superannuation property trusts that have not gone down substantially, be very suspicious and ask the funds manager for a full explanation. But once the values have been adjusted by the required margin, remember that property in Australia is a basic security that is now the subject of a price correction.

Accountants like valuers

The fall in the property market approximately equates the slump in the sharemarket crash of 1987. Property usually falls about nine months after a share crash but this time the slump was delayed, partly because of the actions of Paul Keating in his days as Treasurer. You will remember that just before the sharemarket crash Keating had put the brakes on the economy. He then released them and the delay fuelled the boom in property.

But in the end, the two markets fell by about the same amount. The All Ordinaries index has recovered some of the lost ground, but five years later in October 1992 it still had a way to go, even though top companies were mostly selling at levels above 1987. Just as property falls after a share crash, so it rises . . .

The property market adjustment may prove even more difficult than that following the sharemarket crash because of the huge overhang of unsold property. Banks have many problem loans with a property backing; life offices' statutory funds will need close examination; surpluses in superannuation funds with large property investments need to be watched; and the book values of balance sheets have required adjustment. In many ways the accountancy profession in 1992 is like the valuers of 1989. They do not realise the change in asset values. Accountants still call property a 'tangible asset' when in fact it is 'intangible'. Commercial bricks and mortar have no value unless a business can use the premises. Conversely accountants think the value of a business is an 'intangible asset' and want to write it off. The value of a business is easily determined by reference to profits and cashflow and is an asset with a rising value if the business is going well and a declining asset value if times are tough. I am not suggesting that such a radical change is required but the whole basis of accounting standards needs to be reviewed in the light of the rise in the importance of goodwill in asset value. A large number of accountants know their standard selling organisations are wrong but are powerless to bring change—especially as accounting standards effectively have the force of laws. Nevertheless a 'Roy Woodhouse' may still emerge among the accountants.

PROFITS

The case for uniformity

And on the subject of accounting, in today's world, commercial success normally starts with discovering customers' needs and serving them in the most efficient way. So manufacturing or service companies that may have been production-oriented in the past have either cottoned on to this concept or are finding themselves in danger of going out of business. However, it is much harder for industry boards and organisations to come to grips with this change in our society.

An illustration of this comes from an unusual quarter: the Accounting Standards Review Board. The customer, in this case the securities industry, had come to the board asking for help on calculating earnings per share. The board passed on the request to the Australian Accounting Research Foundation in accordance with normal practice, and the foundation began working on the problem. The industry is plagued by many different methods of calculating earnings per share, and it wanted standardisation.

Uniformity is important because the relationship of earnings per share to share prices, the price/earnings ratio, is a key factor in determining values. There are only two factors in earnings per share: profit and the number of shares. But when it came time to deciding the number of shares to be used in the calculation, almost every analyst had a different method in complex cases.

The research foundation, led by Angus Thomson, did a wonderful job working with the securities industry to determine a uniform formula that made sense, although obviously not everyone would agree with it. In particular, the foundation devised a formula for determining whether to count as 'shares' options or convertible notes that give holders the opportunity to take up shares at some time in the future.

The formula works on the basis that if a 'theoretical conversion' of such options or notes reduces profits per share for existing shareholders, then it is worthwhile to swap them for stock. But if it increases existing shareholders' returns, then conversion is not going to be worthwhile. The formula showed some lateral thinking and is an advance on the simple comparisons between exercise or conversion prices and current sharemarket prices.

Then the foundation came to the second part of the sum, the actual profit to be used. Most analysts use net trading profits before abnormals in calculating earnings per share. Public share investors must do the same thing if they are to follow the market. The sharemarket, therefore, does not want trading profits confused with the abnormal or extraordinary items, which most analysts take into account in assessing companies' assets and overall standing. Accountants can argue about the merits of this practice but, rightly or wrongly, that is what customers want.

While the Accounting Research Foundation developed an understanding of the situation, the profession's standards board did not heed the customers' requirement. So, in its standard on draft earnings per share it has demanded that companies use the earnings that include abnormal items in their calculation. The board was following its own beliefs as to what constituted profit. What it should have done was to follow the example of many other countries and ask for two earnings-per-share calculations: one before abnormals and one after.

A dismayed customer, the Securities Institute of Australia president, Max Powditch, has called on his organisation's members to write to the standards board and urge it to get this right. CRA's accounts released in 1992 provide a good example of the chaos the draft standard would cause, if adopted. The company included in its abnormal items a write-down of mines and a superannuation surplus. After those calculations, it was in the red to the tune of about $34 million. Under the draft standards, it would have no earnings per share. But its share price rose after the announcement because its net trading profit was $377 million before equity accounting and $350 million after counting its equity-accounted loss in non-subsidiaries.

Either way, the overall result was better than the market expected. (Most security analysts would prefer to use the $350-million equity-accounted profit, but this also has been excluded in the draft standard.) In fairness, the Accounting Standards Review Board is in fact becoming increasingly aware of its customers' needs and I believe that, with the help of Powditch and many letters, it will see the light. If it does not, small shareholders will be at a great disadvantage because they may not have the ability to make the analysts' adjustments and so will not understand why the market has moved, as it did in the case of CRA.

Helping investors

A useful way of assessing companies in profit-reporting season is to look at the relationship of EBIT (earnings before interest and tax) to sales. Managing directors who have been doing their job should have reduced costs substantially during 1990–92, to adjust to current levels of demand. It would be of great help to the market if directors indicated to shareholders in the preliminary profit statement whether significant progress was expected in the ratio of EBIT to sales in the 1992–93 year and, if relevant, 1993–94.

Where EBIT-to-sales ratios improve, the next step for investors to determine is whether the managing director has achieved a permanent reduction in costs (that is, if sales rise, will costs remain low or will they increase in line with volume). Given that the recovery in Australia looks likely to be restrained, the management of EBIT to sales is going to become increasingly important.

DIRECTORS

THE AUSTRALIAN Securities Commission will remember March 1992 as a good month, given the media coverage of the writs the commission issued against Compass directors. In the process the ASC has effectively told every professional director in Australia to steer clear of any new start-up company or any trading corporation that is at all risky. The challenge of starting a new airline attracted the former head of BHP's steel division, David Rice, and former CRA and MIM finance director John Carden to the board. If they were to lose to the ASC in the courts, their retirement savings would be put at risk. At the same time they have to decide how much of their retirement savings to pledge towards the legal costs of the court case—they have no big company to stand behind them.

And it may not have helped them to have abandoned ship as the losses mounted. Leigh Brown, a partner in Minter Ellison, resigned from the Compass board on 28 August, more than three months before the collapse, but was still charged. Further, officers of the company who were not directors were also charged, making it risky being involved as an executive or even perhaps a consultant to a new enterprise.

What Compass did was to devise a way to provide air travel for Australians at a fraction of the cost of conventional carriers. They under-estimated the capital costs of such an exercise and the price war that would follow. More particularly, they did not respond to the miscalculations early enough, which indicates management control may have been defective. There is no doubt the directors can be blamed for that lack of response, especially as their market share could have attracted equity supporters had the board actively sought partners.

Compass was building up a store of goodwill that was only to be dissipated when the financial weakness of the business crippled the operation. The size of that goodwill was illustrated by the success of the liquidator in selling the brand and the buyer, Southern Airlines being able to restart the airline. What the courts will have to decide is whether the value of the goodwill during the months leading up to the crash made the company solvent.

CEOs

As the role of Australian chief executives changes, more of them are going to find it difficult to cope, thus putting even more responsibility on boards to evaluate whether they have the right person in the top job. Let me give you two examples of CEOs facing challenges that would not have occurred in the late eighties.

A number of young executives on a Monash University/David Syme Faculty of Business study tour discovered their companies' operational practices had fallen well behind those of enterprises visited in Singapore and Japan. A traditional reaction by a chief executive would be to 'get rid of the trouble-maker' as fast as possible. But a modern CEO might ask the young executive to show him where to go in order to share the same experience, thus enabling the CEO to check the conclusion. Not too many Australian CEOs could handle that.

The modernisation of a company can really only come from the top down, so boards need to think seriously about appointing chief executives with first-hand experience of the management techniques that have been developed in the most advanced Asian countries.

At the Business Council's Asian summit, Australian enterprises were shown many reasons why it makes sense to expand in Asia, in spite of the management skills developed by our rivals. But the whole process will not work unless the CEO is deeply involved and has the skills to spearhead the exercise, including developing relationships in the region. Similarly, only executives who are enthusiastic about the project are worth sending.

Some Australian companies have gone to Asia mainly to defend domestic markets rather than to participate in growth. Despite the success stories, overall, Australian companies have not been enthusiastic about Asia. Many do not differentiate between the various countries and want to sell products designed for Australia rather than determining the needs of the country they are targeting. Nevertheless we are seeing in Australia enormous growth in manufacturers, particularly medium-sized operators, who regard overseas markets, especially Asia, as equally important as local ones. Many find exports even more important.

MANUFACTURING—FACING UP TO THE TRUTH

THE AUSTRALIAN Manufacturing Council's set of advertisements tells Australians the truth about our debt problems, falling living standards, the need for efficient manufacturing (including more plants to upgrade our raw materials), the lessons from Japan and Taiwan, the need to harness entrepreneurial skills, and many other aspects of the changes required to turn Australia into an internationally-based society.

What makes the advertisements so remarkable is the composition of the council. On the one hand it includes people such as BHP's John Prescott, ICI's Michael Deeley, SA Brewing's Ross Wilson, Du Pont's Dick Warburton, Amcor's Don Macfarlane, Siemens' Klaus Lahr, South Pacific Tyres' Rod Chadwick and Kambrook's Frank Bannigan. But there is also a wide range of union officials led by metals and engineering's George Campbell, the vehicle builders' Wayne Blair, ACTU's Bill Mansfield and the clothing workers' Anna Booth. Each of the executives knows that the ultimate survival of local manufacturing, let alone expansion, depends on a whole new approach to work practices by both middle management and unions, plus a different attitude by governments, which have given a low priority to development and employment generation.

As the two sides discussed these problems as part of the advertising series, the union officials would have comprehended the enormous changes required by their organisations and management if Australia was to have any hope of attracting, against world competition, the investment necessary to revitalise manufacturing.

PRODUCTIVITY

MCINTOSH & CO LTD's David Lansley and Cathy Stern have discovered remarkable differences between companies. It is always possible that Australia will go into a sharp upswing, but if our recovery is modest, the big share price gains in the next two or three years will be made mostly by companies that have achieved substantial productivity improvements. Accordingly, much more research is likely in this area as brokers and institutions evaluate managing directors' labour management policies as the key element in their overall strategies.

Through its survey, McIntosh discovered that some of the recent workforce productivity improvements have occurred as companies rationalised their expansion moves of the 1980s. In some ways, companies were correcting their previous mistakes. Nevertheless, there were big differences within the various sectors. In building products, for example, in 1990–91 James Hardie achieved a 25% rise on its 1988–89 productivity. Pioneer International's gain was 12.6%, while CSR recorded a rise of 8.4% and Boral only 0.4%.

Although James Hardie had the ability to restructure parts of its business following acquisitions in the late 1980s, its achievement is remarkable and a great credit to the talents of its leaders, David Say and John Reid. At the other end of the scale, Boral says it has always attempted to run a leaner ship than its competitors, thus reducing the need—and its ability—to make substantial permanent workforce reductions.

Boral adjusted shifts, stock levels and hours to maximise its flexibility in the face of weaker demand. But it has substantial excess capacity, and also cut staff in the 1991–92 financial year.

In manufacturing, the textile, clothing and footwear and transport-equipment sectors were the worst performers; chemicals and petroleum were the best. Overall, however, manufacturing companies performed much better than those in the services sector, probably because they had to compete with imports.

In retailing, Woolworths improved by 6.5% in the two years to 1990–91. Coles Myer (4.4%) and Brashs (4%) were further behind. However, Brashs achieved a very big rise in capacity. Retail suppliers, such as Pacific Dunlop (13%), Email (11.6%), SA Brewing (8%), Arnotts (7.9%) and Amcor (8.5%), have run rings around their customers. Retailers had been expected to reap significant benefits from technological change.

The survey shows that the banks' management also has been slow. The National Australia Bank and the ANZ were not able to improve their productivity by more than 5%. However, there has been more work in the sector in the 1992–93 year.

The McIntosh researchers found that very few of the big companies were preparing to make enterprise agreements with their workforces. Many were still thinking about the fact that wage rises would be small in the 1992–93; their wage strategies revolve around conditions in their industries, rather than their own situations.

The researchers believe that in general Australian managers have a lot to learn and, in the area of work-practice reform, are performing below the standards that will be required of them. Instead of using this valuable time to begin direct negotiations with their workforces, most have restricted direct negotiations to 'greenfield' sites; Pacific Dunlop's Southern Tyre operation is a good example.

Usually, such negotiations take about a year. Of the companies surveyed, only Arnotts is singled out as having a clear program, although Woolworths, SA Brewing and Brashs appear to be making some progress.

The boards of all Australian companies need to evaluate whether their managements are able to handle direct wage negotiations to gain substantial productivity improvements, usually associated with additional investment. Stockbrokers and institutions are at least realising that management's ability to negotiate with staff should be an important criterion in selecting an investment.

A LEAKY BOAT

THE DRAFT prospectus issued by Kerry Packer's Consolidated Press magazine group highlights a crazy game of cat and mouse that occurs every time a big new float hits the market. The designers of the Securities Act tried to differentiate between professional investors and the public. In summary, the professionals can receive an offer of securities and/or sub-underwriting without a full prospectus. However, they are not allowed to pass the documents on to anyone else, including the media. The company itself is not allowed to make announcements that detail its issue to the public without a prospectus being lodged. The media are allowed to record details of these unofficial offerings, providing they do not produce reports that induce members of the public to buy shares.

What happens, of course, is that institutions and others who receive the draft documents leak them to their friends in the media. The securities industry watchdogs can never seem to discover who is passing the information along, even though in some cases some very selective lines are being peddled. The watchdogs could pull the reporters into court and demand that they reveal their sources, but journalists have a code of ethics that forbids them from doing this. Wisely, the Australian Securities Commission's chairman, Tony Hartnell, does not want to fill the jails with journalists or leading institutional managers.

There is no way that Australia's richest man could have floated his magazine empire without the media knowing about it: the Securities Act's aim of dividing access to information was always going to be a nonsense. The sooner this rule is abolished, the more respect people will have for the law. It should be possible to design rules that enable the public to know when draft prospectuses are in the system.

THE CIS CONNECTION

AUSTRALIANS should not race off to what used to be the Soviet Union to try to do business. However, Australia has been trading with Russia and its allied states for a long time and some of our connections go very deep. And we do have advantages for future trading that mitigate at least some of the distance problems.

A group of Russians came to Melbourne in October 1991 to study our property titles system. One of the problems facing Russia is that freehold titles, if they exist, date back to the turn of the century. A new system needs to be devised, probably based on leaseholds.

AWARDS

Student of the year

One of the jobs I enjoy most each year is being one of the judges for the *BRW*-AMP Business Student of the Year Award in association with the AIESEC student organisation. On the panel, you get a real feel for the thinking of our better business students.

In 1992, the quality of those coming forward was remarkable, and they were thinking much more deeply about the future—both their own and that of the nation. Our winner, David Tonuri from the ANU, not only has an outstanding academic record and a clear view of the future, but also brought together a group of people to tackle the practices in his university's student union, practices that are repeated on campuses around Australia. The cost to the students was slashed.

My congratulations go not only to Tonuri, but also to all our entrants. They showed that Australia has some wonderful people coming forward.

Scientific excellence

As we begin to measure our young people, our managers, workers and equipment by overseas standards, it is important to recognise that a group of people has been measuring their achievements in international terms for generations.

The Clunies Ross National Science and Technology Award which started in 1991 (and where I am also a judge) is designed to acknowledge the contribution of scientists who not only devise new technology, but implement it. Often those developments require a personal effort because they are not backed by international corporations. My congratulations to Ern Dawes, John Gladstones, Graeme Jameson,

Michael Rickard, Donald Metcalf, Ralph Sarich and Paul Trainor, who were the first winners.

There are a number of other awards that tell us about emerging trends in our population.

A small business plan

It is fashionable to attack teachers, but the National Schools Small Business Plan Competition is an example of how they are helping both their students and the country as a whole. The competition is organised by the Australasian Commercial and Economic Teachers' Association and is helping our young people prepare for the environment they are likely to encounter when they go into business for themselves. Congratulations to 1991 winners Scott Oates of Canberra and Emma Clements of Western Australia.

Women and the future

One of the most important new business trends in Australia is the rise of women operating their own businesses. Many small-business organisations are noting this pattern around the country. This trend is likely to accelerate rapidly. For the most part, women have tended to survive the crash better because they had not borrowed heavily.

The Young Achiever of the Year awards go to Year 11 students who actually set up and operate businesses. In 1991 there were sixteen finalists and only three were boys. The four chosen to go overseas were all girls. Given that the small-business sector must provide our employment growth, this is a most significant trend. Women will be the driving force behind our prosperity in the decade ahead.